The FRANK ZAPPA Companion

The FRANK ZAPPA *Companion*

Four
Decades of
Commentary

*Edited and
introduced by*
**RICHARD
KOSTELANETZ**

Assistant Editor
JOHN ROCCO

SCHIRMER BOOKS
An Imprint of
Simon & Schuster Macmillan
New York

Prentice Hall International
London Mexico City New Delhi Singapore Sydney
Toronto

Copyright © 1997 by Schirmer Books

Schirmer Books
An Imprint of Simon & Schuster Macmillan
1633 Broadway
New York, NY 10019

Library of Congress Catalog Card Number: 96–41352

Printed in the United States of America

Printing number
1 2 3 4 5 6 7 8 9 10

Library of Congress Cataloging-in-Publication Data

The Frank Zappa companion : four decades of commentary / edited by Richard
    Kostelanetz ; assistant editor, John Rocco.
            p. cm.
        Includes bibliographical references (p.) and index.
        ISBN 0-02-864628-2 (alk. paper)
        1. Zappa, Frank—Criticism and interpretation. 2. Music and society. I.
Kostelanetz, Richard. II. Rocco, John (John M.)
ML410.Z285F7   1997
782.42166'092—dc20   96-41352
                                                                   CIP
                                                                   MN

This paper meets the requirements of ANSI/MOSP 739.48-1992 {Permanence of Paper}.

Contents

Dying is the privilege of the weary. The present day composers refuse to die. They have realized the necessity of banding together and fighting for the right of the individual to secure a fair and free presentation of his work.

—MANIFESTO OF THE INTERNATIONAL COMPOSERS'
GUILD BY EDGARD VARÈSE, JULY 1921

Introduction

"No Commercial Potential" was a favorite ironic epithet for Frank Zappa, who made arts history, as well as a small fortune, from ugly music played by people who on appearance alone could never get past anyone's front door. The theme of his early performances was dressing down, not only sartorially but musically and linguistically. His main group, The Mothers of Invention, wore unkempt-looking clothes, long unruly hair, and oddly trimmed beards. Their music explored abrasive dissonance at the end of an era dominated by harmonious, seductive ballads. Their lyrics were often obscene. Who in 1960 could have predicted that someone would succeed in making ugliness, if not freakiness, the epitome of hip in the late 1960s?

It was commonly assumed at the time that Zappa must have been, like other visible freaks, involved with mind-changing drugs, which were likewise regarded as hip. In truth, it seems, he wasn't. One incident, perhaps apocryphal, has an admirer giving him a bag of brown flakes; Zappa's colleagues had to tell him that the gift bag contained hashish. The hidden truth was that any definition of hip at the time had as much to do with outward disfunctioning (e.g., dressing down) as inner tripping.

His musical style depended from the beginning upon the mixing of high with low—upon switching between, say, modernist classical music and pop with blithe ease and rapidity (and often parodying them both as well). Though Zappa was forever crediting Igor Stravinsky and Edgard Varèse as his musical mentors, his real precursor in this stylistic respect was the American composer Charles Ives (1874–1954), who at the beginning of the century mixed snatches of Beethoven's Fifth Symphony with neighborhood tunes. This esthetic principle of mixing high and low, which would have been unacceptable a decade before, became more common after the 1960s, at a time when Ives's once-neglected music became better known as well. This principle persists in the music of John Zorn (b. 1953), among many other younger musicians.

A radical from his professional beginnings to his premature end (on December 4, 1993, at the age of 52), Zappa won the respect of some, but not all, of his colleagues in both pop and highbrow composition. Indeed, his popular music had as many enemies as fans, but because of the loyalty of the latter he survived. Admirers of his extended "serious" compositions included the French musical mogul Pierre Boulez. Zappa was once invited to give the keynote address to the American Society of University Composers; the 1995 meeting of the American Musicological Society included an extended paper on Zappa's work. My own opinion (as someone who has written more about classical music than pop) is that the best of his music appeared before 1973, as many of his later concerts and records disintegrated into extended vamping jams.

Though Zappa was often a vulgar pop musician, he could be courageously critical of pop music vulgarity, at times functioning as an acerbic critic of the music business and eventually of world politics. It was not for nothing that his dissonant records were particularly treasured by Eastern European dissidents. Having influenced the man who became president of a new Czechoslovakia, he thought about running for the American presidency, and might have done so, had he not been hit with terminal cancer.

He was present in some form or another for a quarter-century, if not as a performer, then as a record producer, sometimes as a cultural commentator. In contrast to other pop stars, he did not lapse into silence or absence; he did not, for instance, let putatively savvy managers ration the release of long-awaited albums. Indeed, in a courageous twist, he took several bootleg recordings of his own music, improved them technically, and released them under his own label. Nobody else involved in rock music, very much a business for the short-lived, could generate such rich and continuous cultural resonance.

Printed on the cover to his first album, *Freak Out* (1966), is an extraordinary list of "These People Have Contributed Materially in Many Ways to Make Our Music What It Is. Please Do Not Hold It Against Them." With 162 names, this list reflects Zappa's precocious intelligence, polyartistic literacy, intellectual integrity, and various ambitions. Among the names are the writers James Joyce, Lawrence Ferlinghetti, Bram Stoker, and Theodore Sturgeon; the highbrow composers Arnold Schoenberg [by then dead for fifteen years], Edgar [sic] Varèse, Igor Stravinsky, Leo Ornstein, Alois Haba, Charles Ives, Anton Webern, Pierre

Boulez, Karlheinz Stockhausen, Roger Huntington Sessions, Vincent Persichetti, Mauricio Kagel; the music historian John Tasker Howard; the blues singers Howling Wolf, Muddy Waters, Buddy Guy, Little Walter, and Willie Mae Thornton; the record producers Tom Wilson and Phil Spector; the jazz improvisers Cecil Taylor, Roland Kirk, Eric Dolphy, and Charles Mingus; the Beatles' manager Brian Epstein [but not the Beatles]; the off-shore disk jockey Wolfman Jack; the perverse painters Salvador Dali and Yves Tinguy; the pop singers Joan Baez, Bob Dylan, and Tiny Tim; the sexologist Eberhard Kronhausen; the earlier rock singers Elvis Presley and Johnny Otis; the Italian-American martyrs Sacco and Vanzetti; the comedian Lenny Bruce; the oversized actors Sonny Tufts and John Wayne, all of whom indicate not only that Zappa knew what he was doing professionally but that he could identify the sources of his learning. Though Zappa could be an ironist, all of these acknowledgments were apparently serious (even Wayne and Tufts, whom I take to represent strong performers who could stand out from any group). Though Zappa's formal education ended at a local junior college, I finished college and then graduate school. Nonetheless, as a self-conscious intellectual born in the same year as Zappa (1940), I would have included many of the same names on my short list at the time.

Even at a time when record albums (not to mention performing groups) began to have outrageous names, Zappa should still be credited with some of the most inventive coinages, beginning with the name of his group, but also including *Freak Out, Absolutely Free, The Grand Wazoo, One Size Fits All, Joe's Garage, Baby Snakes, Jazz from Hell, Freaks & Motherfu*%!!@#, 'Tis the Season to Be Jelly, Piquantique, Electric Aunt Jemima, Our Man in Nirvana, The Yellow Shark,* etc. If inventive titling isn't a measure of literary talent, I don't know what is.

It seems curious in retrospect that a man who apparently had no loyal friends outside his family, who surrounded himself with paid retainers, who terminated most of his professional relationships with firings and lawsuits, should still have an audience. Unlike most culture heroes who create the impression, however artificial, of someone you'd like beside you, he was someone that most of us would sooner watch than know (or want to know). It is common to attribute his continuing success to appeal to different audiences, some appreciative of his musical inventions, others of his obscenity.

My sense is that his advanced pop has continuously attracted sophisticated teenagers who, even as they move beyond him, retain an affection for his work. Immediately after his death, the Columbia University radio station, WKCR, presented a marathon of his work, its regular disk jockeys for jazz and avant-garde music speaking knowledgeably about his work. Many announcers at many other university radio stations elsewhere must have done likewise in December 1993. In this respect of influencing bright youth who grow up, he reminds me of the writer-philosopher Ayn Rand; and just as her eccentric work has survived her passing, so will his.

What should not be forgotten is the fact that Zappa lived dangerously, doing professionally what had not been done before and others would not do after him, at a time and in a country where such adventurousness was possible, even as he was continually warning that such possibility should never be taken for granted. For all the continuing admiration of his example, there has been no one like him since.

Acknowledgments

Essential gratitude goes to Richard Carlin for commissioning yet another book from me and to his colleagues at Schirmer Books for shepherding this volume into print. The pieces are reprinted as they appeared, except for an added comma here or there. I thought of writing a biographical introduction, rather than this collection of notes; but since William Ruhlmann did the former so well, I'd rather than duplicate or, worse, steal from him. I'm grateful to the critic Allen Kozinn for generously sharing his Zappa clippings, even though nothing of his appears in this book, to John Rocco for his knowledgeable assistance, and to Anson John Pope for proofreading.

Abso
Free

His L
Times

ZAPPA, FRANK: ENTRY FROM *BAKER'S BIOGRAPHICAL DICTIONARY OF MUSIC* (1992)

Nicolas Slonimsky (1894–1995) was not only the foremost musical lexicographer of his time; he was also a friend and sometime stage colleague of Frank Zappa's. This entry was written after the two met and reflects Slonimsky's bemused vision of Zappa and his work.

Zappa, Frank (F. Vincent), seeded American rock artist; b. Baltimore, Dec. 21, 1940, of Italian descent (Zappa means "hoe" in Italian). The family moved to California. From his school days he played guitar and organized groups with weird names such as The Omens and Captain Glasspack and His Magic Mufflers. In 1960 he composed the soundtrack for the film *The World's Greatest Sinner*, and in 1963 he wrote another soundtrack, *Run Home Slow*. In 1965 he joined the rhythm-and-blues band The Soul Giants; he soon took it under his own aegis and thought up for it the surrealist logo *The Mothers of Invention*. His recording of it, and another album, *Freak Out!*, became underground hits; along with *We're Only in It for the Money* and *Cruising with Ruben and The Jets*, these works constituted the earliest "concept" albums, touching every nerve in a gradually decivilized California life-style—rebellious, anarchistic, incomprehensible, and yet tantalizing. The band became a mixed-media celebration of total artistic, political, and social opposition to the Establishment, the ingredients of their final album, *Mothermania*. Moving farther afield, Zappa produced a video-movie, *200 Motels,* glorifying itinerant sex activities. He became a cult figure, and as such suffered the penalty of violent adulation. Playing in London in 1971, he was painfully injured when a besotted fan pushed him off the stage. Similar assaults forced Zappa to hire an athletic bodyguard for protection. In 1982 his planned appearance in Palermo, Sicily, the birthplace of his parents, had to be cancelled because the mob rioted in anticipation of the event. He deliberately confronted the most cherished social and emotional sentiments by putting on such songs as *Broken Hearts Are for Assholes,* and his release *Jewish Princess* offended, mistakenly, the sensitivity of American Jews. His production *Joe's Garage* contained Zappa's favorite scatological materials, and he went on analyzing and ridiculing urinary functions in such numbers as *Why Does It Hurt When I Pee.* He managed to upset the members of his own faith in the number titled *Catholic Girls.* His *Hot Rats,* a jazz-rock release, included the famous *Willie the Pimp,* and exploited the natural revulsion to unclean animals. In 1980 he produced the film *Baby Snakes,* which shocked even the most impervious senses. He declared in an interview that classical music is only "for old ladies and faggots." But he astounded the musical community when he proclaimed his total adoration of the music of Edgard Varèse and gave a lecture on Varèse in N.Y. Somehow, without formal study, he managed to absorb the essence of Varèse's difficult music. This process led Zappa to produce truly astonishing full orch. scores reveling in artful dissonant counterpoint, *Bob in Dacron and Sad Jane* and *Mo' 'n Herb's Vacation,* and the cataclysmic *Penis Dimension* for chorus, soloists, and orch., with a text so anatomically precise that it could not be performed for any English-speaking audience.

An accounting of Zappa's scatological and sexological proclivities stands in remarkable contrast to his unimpeachable private life and total abstention from alcohol and narcotic drugs. An unexpected reflection of Zappa's own popularity was the emergence of his adolescent daughter, curiously named Moon Unit, as a voice-over speaker on his hit *Valley Girls,* in which she used the vocabulary of growing womanhood of the San Fernando Valley near Los Angeles, with such locutions as "Grody to the Max" (repellent) and "Barfs Me Out" (disgusting). His son, Dweezil Zappa, is also a musician; his 1st album, *Havin' a Bad Day,* was modestly successful. In 1985 Zappa became an outspoken opponent of the activities of the PMRC (Parents Music Resource Center), an organization comprised largely of wives of U.S. Senators who accused the recording industry of exposing the youth of America to "sex, violence, and the glorification of drugs and alcohol." Their demands to the RIAA (Recording

Industry Association of America) included the labeling of record albums to indicate lyric content. Zappa voiced his opinions in no uncertain terms, first in an open letter published in *Cashbox,* and then in one direct to President Reagan; finally, on Sept. 19, 1985, he appeared at the 1st of a series of highly publicized hearings involving the Senate Commerce, Technology and Transportation Committee, the PMRC, and the RIAA, where he delivered a statement to Congress which began "The PMRC proposal is an ill-conceived piece of nonsense which fails to deliver any real benefits to children, infringes the civil liberties of people who are not children and promises to keep the courts busy for years, dealing with the interpretational and enforcemental problems inherent in the proposal's design." Audio excerpts from these hearings can be heard, in original and Synclavier-manipulated forms, on his album *Zappa Meets The Mothers of Prevention.* Other recent recordings which make extensive use of the Synclavier include *Francesco Zappa* and *Jazz From Hell.* With P. Occhiogrosso, he publ. an unrestrained autobiographical vol., *The Real Frank Zappa Book* (N.Y., London, Toronto, Sydney, and Tokyo, 1988), rich in undeleted scatological expletives.

WILLIAM RUHLMANN

FRANK ZAPPA: THE PRESENT DAY COMPOSER (1994; REVISED 1996)

The longest artistic biography so far is William Ruhlmann's, which initially appeared in the magazine *Goldmine,* published for record collectors. Its author is an independent music writer living in New York.

"Information is not knowledge, knowledge is not wisdom, wisdom is not truth, truth is not beauty, beauty is not love, love is not music. Music is the best."

—*Frank Zappa*

It may be that just about everything has been said about the '60s by now. In the '70s, they were canonized; in the '80s, they were demonized; in the '90s, by which time more than half of the population was born in the '60s or later, they're ancient history.

But whether you loved the '60s, hated the '60s, or haven't thought much about them, they certainly represented—and continue to represent—

a climate of aberration. Unexpected things happened, unexpected people emerged, unexpected ideas were countenanced. It was, depending on your point of view, a window of opportunity or a gateway to hell. In either case, it has now closed.

Before the '60s, it would have been hard to imagine a creative artist who mixed an interest in doo-wop, suburban culture, contemporary classical music, withering satire and explicit humor getting a hearing from a major American record label, much less gaining access to the kind of distribution system necessary to sell his wares to a large audience.

"One of the good things that happened in the '60s," wrote Frank Zappa, "was that at least some music of an *unusual* or *experimental nature* got recorded and released." Today, it is again hard to imagine that happening.

It was hard enough to conceive of it in the fall of 1965, when MGM Records' new A&R man Tom Wilson saw Zappa's group, the Mothers, at the Whisky A-Go-Go in Los Angeles and decided to sign it to the newly activated rock division of MGM's Verve Records subsidiary. Frank Zappa always maintained that Wilson had made a snap decision, mistakenly thinking of the Mothers as a conventional white blues band and only discovering how strange their songs were after they'd been signed and he had them in a recording studio.

This is an exaggeration at the very least. Wilson was one of the more extraordinary record men of the era. After graduating from Harvard in economics in 1954 and spending a period working with avant-garde jazz figures like Cecil Taylor and John Coltrane in the late '50s and early '60s, Wilson had become a staff producer at Columbia Records and taken over Bob Dylan's recordings from John Hammond, an unusual assignment for an African-American with a jazz background, but one he handled well, especially when, in early 1965, Dylan decided to go electric.

It was Wilson who put together the band that played on *Bringing It All Back Home*, the album that gave birth to folk-rock. It was Wilson who introduced his friend Al Kooper to the Blues Project. (Kooper, who says he owes his career to Wilson, notes that, if anything, the Mothers were far less accomplished and adventurous musicians in 1965 than Wilson was.) And it was Wilson who took a forgotten track off a failed folkie album from 1964, overdubbed a rhythm section, and produced Simon and Garfunkel's "The Sound Of Silence" in the gold-selling, #1 form we know it today.

That was one of Wilson's final acts before he left Columbia for MGM in the second half of 1965. At that time, MGM had a problem. It was well-established in country music, jazz (through Verve, a label it had purchased in 1960), and folk (through a deal with Folkways), but its top pop seller, Connie Francis, had cooled off, and though it had picked up American rights to a couple of British Invasion groups—notably the Animals and Herman's Hermits—it didn't have a foothold in the emerging American rock scene of 1965. Wilson, obviously, was strong in exactly that area, which is doubtless why label head Jerry Schoenbaum lured him away from Columbia. Wilson's task was to build a new rock-oriented roster on Verve, and the way to do that was to sign emerging bands that seemed to fit into the style of the time.

Wilson brought the Blues Project with him from Columbia. (He also nearly brought Bob Dylan, who came close to moving to MGM in 1966.) In New York, Verve signed the Velvet Underground, a band with the current guitar-rock sound, an unusual, literate lyrical style, and, in Lou Reed, a singer whose voice was just as flat as Bob Dylan's. It didn't hurt that they had the arty imprimatur of Andy Warhol.

The music that the Mothers were playing at the Whisky, whatever Zappa may have said about it later and however it was subsequently marketed, also fit the pattern. Much of it was catchy guitar-based rock, and it had provocative, unusual lyrics. From the beginning, Zappa would describe the group as "ugly" and "repugnant," but this was the same tactic Andrew Loog Oldham had used successfully with the Rolling Stones the year before. The Mothers weren't signed in spite of what they were, they were signed because of what they were.

"I started . . . at a time in the business when, if you were doing something odd, you could get in and get a contract—not a lucrative contract, but you could at least get a contract of some sort to make a record," Zappa told *Guitar Player* magazine in 1992. "And you could build an audience based on whatever the acceptance would be in that odd thing that you did. Today it would be impossible for anybody to get a contract and do what I did."

Even, it seems, Zappa himself, as he added, "If I were to go out and try to get a record contract today, as a new artist, I couldn't get one." But if it's no wonder that Tom Wilson quickly decided to sign a band as weird as the Mothers to Verve in 1965, the wonder is that the times had become so weird that the Mothers could become a logical prospect for a major label whose intent, after all, was to sell singles to pre-teenagers. In the fall of 1965, though, those pre-teens had taken to buying such songs as "Like A Rolling Stone," "Eve of Destruction" and "The Sound of Silence," and the Mothers' "Trouble Every Day" is very much of a piece with those hits.

Of course, Frank Zappa was no folk-rock wannabe and the Mothers were not the Turtles. (They would be eventually, but that's getting ahead of the story.) If it's reasonable to say that Zappa found his opportune moment in 1965, a moment that hadn't occurred before and wouldn't have again, it's also reasonable to suggest that a composer/musician of Zappa's talent, intelligence, and persistence would have found some outlet, even if he had not gained the opportunity he did to reach a mass audience in 1965.

For one thing, Zappa was no ordinary young rock 'n' roll musician in 1965. When he signed to Verve, he was almost 25 years old, and he had been playing professionally in bands in the greater Los Angeles area for a decade. Not only could he read music (a rarity among rock musicians), but he had studied music theory and composition, was familiar with some of the most advanced "serious" music of the day, and had been composing a variety of works since his teens. He had also run his own recording studio. He had been married; he had appeared on national television; and he had spent a short stint in jail. He was, in fact, on probation as he stood on the stage of the Whisky.

It has never been entirely clear at what point the band that became known as the Mothers also became, in essence, Zappa's backup unit rather than a group of equals, formerly known as the Soul Giants, that Zappa had joined, replacing another guitarist. Maybe the change came with the new name, adopted on Mother's Day, probably in 1965. But likely, the formal business organization of the Mothers, with Zappa the bandleader and the rest on salary, came after the Verve signing.

Jim Guercio, a friend of and sometime bass player with the Mothers, remembers the band's manager, Herb Cohen, coming around the studio with contracts to be signed while the first album was being made. Guercio refused to sign, and left the group soon after, though he notes that his departure also came about because, while he shared Zappa's desire to integrate classical composers like Erik Satie and Edgard Varèse into pop music (and would do so when he began producing Blood, Sweat and Tears and Chicago later on), he was less interested in propagating Zappa's bathroom humor to teenage America along with it.

Of course, there was always more to the comic aspects of Zappa's approach than that. There was, to begin with, an absurdist tradition he found both in the classical musicians he admired and in artists such as Salvador Dali. Even for his instrumentals, Zappa would choose colorful juxtapositions of words—"Bogus Pomp," "Watermelon In Easter Hay," etc.—suggestive of the '50s beat poetry of Allen Ginsberg, Gregory Corso, and others.

Perhaps one of Zappa's primary influences in this regard was comedian Lenny Bruce, for whom the Mothers opened at the Fillmore Auditorium in San Francisco in 1966, and whose questioning of authority, especially with regard to sexual taboos, was explicitly echoed in the Mothers' music—the censored "Don't come in me" section of *We're Only In It For The Money* echoes Bruce's "To Is A Preposition, Come Is A Verb" routine, which also was censored. (Zappa's own explanation of his song titles was simpler, of course. "Well, you have to call them something," he said in 1993, "so why not call them something amusing?")

But for all the specific artistic antecedents to Zappa's approach, it's also notable what he was not. He may have played "Louie, Louie" in a hundred bars around L.A., but Zappa had little affection for the music or the culture of teen America, circa 1965. His hair was long, longer in fact than most, but his basic look—the mustache and the imperial, or, as he called it, the "Ghengis" (that little tuft of hair below the mouth), a tribute to R&B bandleader Johnny Otis—had been in place since high school. He did not take drugs, and he despised the emerging community that San Francisco columnist Herb Caen would dub "the hippies."

Of course, in 1965, especially if you had long hair and played the guitar, it was easy for most people to miss the distinction. But Zappa was always a workaholic, even in the sunshine daydream days of the mid-'60s, and though he traveled in the world of sex, drugs, and rock 'n' roll, he doesn't seem to have indulged. (Even in his domestic habits, Zappa seems to have been unconventionally conventional. After breaking up with his first wife, he had a steady girlfriend, Pamela Zarubica, who appears on the Mothers album *Uncle Meat* as Suzy Creamcheese, and through whom he met Gail Sloatman, his second wife, to whom he was married from 1967 on.)

In a way, the hippie demeanor served to cloak Zappa's real strangeness. Unique among musicians of his generation, Zappa wanted to forge a career as a composer who took into consideration both the classical tradition that had advanced to the experimental styles of Stravinsky, Cage, and others, and the vernacular tradition of popular music including rock 'n' roll and R&B.

And he intended to do that in a commercial form—to make a living. It was not incidental that Zappa printed a modified quote from Edgard Varèse, "The present-day composer refuses to die!" on the sleeve of the Mothers' first album, *Freak Out!* From the beginning, and throughout his life, Zappa's intention was to pursue the career of "the present-day composer," and in the 1960s, adopting the guise of a rock 'n' roll musician was one—albeit an unusual—way to do that.

This is not to say simply that Zappa was a classical composer masquerading as a rock guitarist to get the money to be able to write and perform his serious work. Clearly, he put much of his effort into advancing rock guitar playing as well, and he was obsessed by rock culture even as he despised it. Zappa led rock bands for more than 20 years, and most of the recordings he released during his lifetime consisted of rock-oriented music played onstage by those bands.

True, in the last decade of his life, he mostly abandoned stage work and group recording (he mounted only one concert tour between 1984 and his death) and concentrated on composing and recording his compositions on the elaborate synthesizer computer the Synclavier. But even then he was constructing retrospective albums out of the band recordings of earlier years, a project he had announced several times earlier in his career before it finally rolled out in the form of the six volumes of double-CDs called *You Can't Do That On Stage Anymore*.

Still, Zappa cannot be understood in the conventional terms of a rock music career. Though he began working with a standard record company contract, he was circumventing it as early as a year after signing it, and he eventually gained the rights to almost all his recordings and established his own company to release his works. In doing so, he followed no standard marketing practice. He was remarkably prolific, and in a time when most established popular recording artists carefully spaced out their record releases, he thought nothing of issuing several multi-disc albums almost simultaneously, especially after he gained complete control of his work. In 1981 and again in 1984, for example, he released *seven* LPs' worth of new material in a single year.

He was able to do this successfully because he had established a broad cult audience, including, especially in later years, a fanatical European following, that hung on every note he played. Like those of other prominent rock musicians, his concerts were heavily bootlegged, and in the 1990s he turned the tables on the bootleggers by releasing their products himself in boxed sets and individual discs. The result is a massive amount of recorded material that only begins to hint at what else there is. For while Zappa was releasing reams of vintage recordings in the '80s and '90s, most of his new work remained in the Synclavier. It will only be in coming years that we will get to hear it, so that Zappa's ultimate position in the world of music remains to be determined. But let's review what we know so far.

Frank Vincent Zappa was born on December 21, 1940, in Baltimore, Maryland. Zappa was the first son born to an immigrant Italian father from Sicily and a first-generation Italian-American mother. There would be three more children: Zappa's brothers Carl and Bobby and his sister Candy. Zappa's father had come to the U.S. as a child. He attended the University of North Carolina at Chapel Hill, paying his way by working as a barber, the occupation of his father. He also, as his son would later write, "played guitar in some sort of 'strolling crooner' trio."

After college, Zappa, Sr., initially taught history at Loyola University, then became a meteorologist and metallurgist, and held a variety of jobs in different locations. During World War II, he worked at the Edgewood Arsenal in Edgewood, Maryland. But his son's frail health—the young Frank suffered from asthma and related sinus problems—caused him to take a job in Florida, though the family eventually moved back to the Baltimore area.

The Zappas were Catholic, and there was some attempt to put Zappa into parochial school, but it was shortlived. "When the penguin came after me with a ruler," Zappa said of a nun, "I was out of there." Nevertheless, he continued to attend church until he was 18. "Then suddenly the lightbulb went on over my head," he said. "All the mindless morbidity and discipline was pretty sick—bleeding this, painful that and no meat on Friday. What is this shit?"

In the winter of 1950–51, around the time Zappa turned 10, his family moved to Monterey, California, where his father had taken a job teaching metallurgy at the Naval Post-Graduate School. In 1953, the family moved south on the peninsula to Pacific Grove, where Zappa, now 12, attended a summer school studying drums, his first musical instrument.

Later in 1953, the family moved to Pomona, where Zappa's father got a job with Convair; in 1954, they were in El Cajon, where the elder Zappa worked on the Atlas guided missile system. That's at least six moves by the time Zappa turned 13, and it isn't hard to see a pattern familiar to Army brats and other children frequently uprooted from their social situations and forced to encounter new neighborhoods and new schools. As an adult, Zappa would evince extreme independence and a tendency to disdain social conventions and even social ties (in his autobiography, he claimed to have no friends, only employees, though he seems to have enjoyed family life and, even before the onset of his fatal illness, was an extreme homebody). You don't have to be a psychoanalyst to see the root of those characteristics in a pre-adolescent continually subjected to changing circumstances.

Zappa first came in contact with Edgard Varèse around this time, when he read an article in *Look* magazine about record seller Sam Goody, whose talents as a salesman were touted by noting his ability to sell a record of *Ionisation,* which featured various percussion instruments and sirens. Drummer Zappa was intrigued, and he managed to find a copy of the record. In addition to his interest in Varèse, Zappa began to become interested in popular music as R&B started to invade the pop charts and be called rock 'n' roll. Zappa collected R&B and blues records. "It was records, not TV, which I didn't watch, that brainwashed me," Zappa wrote in *Evergreen* magazine in 1970. "I'd listen to them over and over again. The ones I couldn't buy, I'd steal, and the ones I couldn't steal I'd borrow, but I'd get them somehow. I had about 600 records—45s—at one time, and I swear I knew the title, group and label of every one."

Zappa also continued his interest in drums and joined his first band, the Ramblers, in 1955. At 14, he played his first professional gig at the Uptown Hall in San Diego; the Ramblers made $7 for the whole group.

By the time of Zappa's sophomore year in high school, his family had moved yet again, this time to Lancaster in the Antelope Valley north of Los Angeles, where his father worked at Edwards Air Force Base and Zappa attended Antelope Valley Joint Union High School. For his 15th birthday in 1955, his parents allowed him to place a long-distance phone call to Edgard Varèse. But when Zappa called, Varèse's wife explained that the composer was in Brussels at the moment. When he returned, however, Zappa did get to speak to him on the phone, though they never met in person.

Around this time, Zappa bought his second LP, Stravinsky's *The Rite of Spring.* "I listened to those albums [the Varèse and the Stravinsky] for about two years before I owned any others," he said in 1970. "And I liked them equally as well as rhythm and blues, so my whole background is just those elements."

Zappa organized his second group, an eight-piece, integrated R&B unit called the Blackouts, at Antelope Valley High School. Jim "Motorhead" Sherwood (his nickname deriving from his love for cars) was not an official member of the group, but Zappa got to know the future Mothers member at this time. Another new friend was classmate Don Van Vliet, who shared Zappa's interest in R&B records. Though Zappa remembered being a marginal student, he formed relationships with several teachers, notably Don Cerveris, his English teacher, through whom he would later get to write a film score, and his music teacher, Mr. Ballard, who let him conduct the school orchestra and even had it play some of his first compositions. By his senior year, Zappa had abandoned the idea of being a drummer and commandeered his brother Bobby's guitar, which he took to quickly. "In four weeks," he said in 1968, "I was playing shitty teenage leads."

Zappa graduated from high school on June 13, 1958. He then enrolled at Antelope Valley Junior College, but didn't stay long. When, in the spring of 1959, the Zappa family moved yet again, this time to Claremont, Zappa did not go with them. Instead, he moved into an apartment in the Echo Park section of Los Angeles. Don Cerveris, no longer teaching, had written a screenplay for a Western called *Run Home Slow,* and Zappa was engaged to write the score, but the project was postponed due to a lack of financing. In 1992, when he released a piece called "The Little March," recorded by the Mothers in 1969 and taken from themes based on the score, Zappa noted, "The plot had something to do with a bad ranch lady, a nymphomaniac cowgirl, and a hunch-back handy-man named Kirby who eventually winds up pooching the nympho in a barn, next to the rotting carcass of the family donkey."

Zappa was forced to move back in with his parents, and he enrolled at Chaffee Junior College in Ontario, California, where he studied harmony and composition. This second college sojourn lasted only a little longer than the first, into the fall semester of 1959, but Zappa's attendance is chiefly notable for his first romantic attachment. It was at Chaffee that he met Kay Sherman, whom he married, apparently in late 1959.

The couple moved into a house in Ontario, with the new Mrs. Zappa working as a secretary in a bank and her husband taking a variety of jobs including silk-screening, copywriting, window dressing, and selling *Collier's Encyclopedia* door to door. He also worked as a musician, forming the shortlived Boogie Men, and then playing with Joe Perrino and the Mellotones at Tommy Sandi's Club Sahara in San Bernardino. It was experiences like these that would inspire his sarcastic views of the entertainment business, and he found the work so unappealing that he seems to have given up music entirely for a time.

In June 1961, Zappa was hired to provide the score for another low-budget movie, *The World's Greatest Sinner,* written, directed, and produced by the character actor Timothy Carey (known for playing villainous roles in such films as *East of Eden, The Killing,* and *Paths of Glory*). The score was recorded in November and December, using an eight-piece rock 'n' roll group, a 20-piece orchestra, and a 55-piece orchestra. The movie opened in April 1962. Zappa was never paid, but he later developed the movie's theme as "Holiday in Berlin" on the *Burnt Weeny Sandwich* album.

It was also around this time—in 1962 or '63—that the first public performance of Zappa's classical music took place, at Mount St. Mary's College. "Mount St. Mary's was the first time I had a concert of my music," Zappa explained in 1992. "As with most of the other concerts of my music, I had to pay for it . . . That was a bargain, though, because it was only $300. It was a student orchestra. There were probably 50 people in the audience and—for some strange reason—KPFK taped it, and I got a copy . . . There was one thing called 'Opus 5,' and there were aleatoric compositions that involved a certain amount of improvisation, and there were some written sections that you actually had to play. Some of the things were graphic, and there was a tape of some electronic music that was being played in the background with orchestra, and I had some 8mm films that were being projected."

Through a friend, guitarist Ronnie Williams, Zappa met Paul Buff, the owner of the low-budget Pal Recording Studio in Cucamonga, near Ontario, in 1962. Buff had designed a unique five-track tape recorder and, with the help of Zappa, Williams, and others, he turned out a series of singles either leased to small labels or issued on his own Vigah! Records label.

About this time, Zappa met Ray Collins, who would become the lead singer of the Mothers. "I was drinking in a bar, the Sportsman, in Pomona," Collins recalled. "Frank and his friends were playing. There wasn't even a stage. I figured that any band that played 'Work With Me, Annie' was all right. They either asked me to sing with them, or I simply became too drunk and wandered up there and asked to sing with them. In any event, Frank and I got together. I told him about an idea I had for a song. 'How's your bird?' was an expression Steve Allen used to do on his TV show. One day, Frank called me up and said, 'I wrote it. Let's record it.' So, we did."

Not long after, Zappa appeared on Allen's show, playing a "bicycle concerto." "It's very funny," Zappa told the local Ontario newspaper, "You play a bicycle by plucking the spokes and blowing through the handlebars." He got on the show, he said in 1992, by just calling them up and saying, "I play the bicycle . . . They were booking all kinds of goofy things on there," he said.

Zappa had continued playing out as well, forming a band called the Soots that featured his high school friend Don Van Vliet on lead vocals. Zappa nicknamed Van Vliet "Captain Beefheart." The band was short-lived, though it made some demos that Dot Records passed on. Zappa next formed a trio he called the Muthers or the Mothers; they didn't last long either.

In late 1963, Zappa came into some money ($2,000 in fact), because

Run Home Slow, the movie he had worked on several years before, had finally found financing. Zappa bought a new guitar and took over Paul Buff's mounting debts in return for control of the recording studio, which, as of August 1, 1964, was renamed Studio Z. He also used some of the money to pay for a divorce from his wife and moved into Studio Z to live. He was joined by his friend Motorhead Sherwood and a couple of girls, one of them 18-year-old Lorraine Belcher.

Studio Z had a storefront with signs reading, "Record your band" and "$13.50 per hour." It also doubled as a film studio, and Zappa was planning a movie called *Captain Beefheart vs. The Grunt People.* One day in the fall of 1964, a plainclothes policeman came into the studio and asked Zappa to make a stag film for him. Zappa, with Belcher's help, made a suggestive audio tape instead, and he found himself under arrest for conspiracy to commit pornography. The tape, he later wrote, was "nowhere near as bizarre as the vocal noises eventually released on side four of the *Freak Out!* album." Nevertheless, he was convicted, apparently of a reduced charge, sentenced to six months in jail with all but 10 days suspended, and put on probation for three years. He was now ineligible for the draft, no small matter in the emerging Vietnam War era.

The bust, along with a street-widening plan, put an end to Studio Z. "I was looking for something to get into," Zappa said, "and I received a call from Ray [Collins], who had been working with a group called the Soul Giants in a local bar in Pomona called the Broadside. He had just had a fight with the guitar player, and he was out, and they were looking for a replacement, so I went down there, and I joined the band."

In addition to Collins, the singer, the Soul Giants consisted of saxophone player Dave Coronado, bass player Roy Estrada, and drummer Jimmy Carl Black. Their repertoire contained the standard bar band fare of the time—"Louie, Louie," "In The Midnight Hour," etc. Zappa convinced them to start playing his original songs, or, as he put it in 1970, "I talked them into getting weird." That, of course, required them to adopt a weird name, and they did: Captain Glasspack and the Magic Mufflers. (Zappa was not, however, able to convince all the band members; Coronado quit and went back to his job at a bowling alley.)

Playing original material is not the way to make it on the bar circuit, and the group struggled. "We'd play something weird, and we'd get fired," Zappa recalled in 1968. "I'd say hang on and we'd move to another go-go bar—the Red Flame in Pomona, the Shack in Fontana, the Tom Cat in Torrance . . . Eventually, we went back to the Broadside in Pomona and we called ourselves the Mothers. It just happened by sheer accident to be Mother's Day, although we weren't aware of it at the time. When you are nearly starving to death, you don't keep track of holidays."

The Mothers moved into Los Angeles to try their luck in the city's club scene. They also tried other band members: folk guitarist Alice Stuart; Henry Vestine, later of Canned Heat; Jim Guercio; Van Dyke Parks; Dr. John; and others. With a band to play his material and the inspiration of the burgeoning L.A. scene, Zappa began to write a series of songs, "Who Are the Brain Police?," "Oh, No, I Don't Believe It," "Hungry Freaks," "Bow-Tie Daddy," and others, inspired by what he saw around him. He also drew on his suburban upbringing.

The band acquired a manager in Mark Cheka, introduced to Zappa by Don Cerveris. Cheka, in turn, brought in Herb Cohen, who eventually took over the Mothers' management alone. Cohen, then in his early 30s, was a club owner (the Purple Onion and others) who had handled various folk artists as well as comedian Lenny Bruce, a hero of Zappa's. He was well-placed to help get the Mothers on the club circuit in Los Angeles, and he did, almost immediately. They played the Action, the Whisky, and the Trip in the late summer and early fall of 1965. Cohen, who knew Tom Wilson, got him to see the Mothers at the Whisky, which led to their record contract. While the Mothers were at the Trip, Zappa met 18-year-old Pamela Zarubica, with whom he was soon living.

Freak Out!, the first album by the Mothers of Invention (the group's name was lengthened at the insistence of Verve Records executives), was recorded at TTG Studios in Los Angeles between November 1965 and January 1966, with a final session in March. By now, the group had expanded to a quintet with the addition of second guitarist Elliott Ingber, who, according to the LP's extensive liner notes, had just gotten out of the army, which perhaps explained his short haircut. (Also featured on the album was the voice of "Suzy Creamcheese," played on this recording by Jeannie Vassoir.)

Zappa and Wilson quickly used up their recording budget, as Zappa tried to put all of his interests, including the influence of Varèse's *musique concrète* on the record. The result was too much material for a single disc, though double albums were unheard of in 1966. The problem was solved in the way it would be solved by others in the future: Zappa agreed to take a cut in the song-publishing rate to compensate Verve for the expense of releasing two LPs for the price of one.

The result, with a kind of negative Technicolor cover, hit record stores in July 1966. There had never been anything quite like it. Zappa's satiric lyrics were beyond anything else being written at the time, and the album as a whole, with its many local references and its extensive commentary on the inside of the fold-out jacket, suggested a whole world listeners around the country had never encountered before. It was also one they didn't necessarily understand. Later, when Zappa would begin to attack the hippies, there would be some confusion as to how he could do that after having celebrated "freaks" on this album and on its follow-up, *Absolutely Free*.

"The origins of hippies as per San Francisco flower power Haight Ashbury is quite a different evolution from the L.A. freak movement of which I was a part," Zappa explained to one interviewer. "There was just a difference in the concept of it. I was never a hippie. I never bought the flower power ethic . . . Most of the people in the L.A. freak scene around 1965 were getting their costumes together, dancing a lot. The real freaks weren't using any drugs at all."

"Whereas in L.A. you had people freaking out; that is, making their own clothes, dressing however they wanted to dress, wearing their hair out; that is, being as weird as they wanted to be in public and everybody going in separate directions—I got to San Francisco and found everybody dressed up in 1890s garb, all pretty specific codified dress," Zappa elaborated to another interviewer. "It was like an extension of high school, where one type of shoe is the 'in' shoe, belt-in-the-back peggers, or something like that. It was in the same sort of vein, but it was the costume of the 1890s. It was cute, but it wasn't as evolved as what was going on in L.A. In San Francisco they had a 'more rustic than thou' approach." From the outside, of course, the distinction between "hippies" and "freaks" was a little hard to see.

Freak Out! was received enthusiastically by what "underground" press there was, but, lacking anything remotely resembling a hit single, did not sell much beyond L.A. initially. Even "Any Way the Wind Blows," which Zappa noted had been included for its accessibility, didn't sound much like what was on the radio at the time. Oddly, for one as far-seeing as Zappa, when he sat down to write pop music, he wrote late '50s, early '60s, doowop-derived pop, not the pop-rock of 1966.

Although the album did not, at first, sell well enough to get in the charts, it served as a calling card for the group. As Verve recording artists, they had already been able to get dates outside of the L.A. area, playing in Hawaii and Texas in the late winter of 1966, then in the spring touring through San Francisco, Washington, D.C., Detroit, and Dallas. On June 24 and 25, they opened for Lenny Bruce at the Fillmore Auditorium. (Bruce died on August 3.) When the Mothers returned from one of the

Texas trips, Zappa was met at the airport by Pamela Zarubica, who brought with her Gail Sloatman, a friend she had met at the Whisky. Sloatman (born January 1, 1945) was the daughter of a scientist who worked for the U.S. Navy, a background similar to Zappa's. Soon after, Zarubica took off for Europe, and Sloatman moved in with Zappa.

By this time, Zappa had expanded the Mothers' lineup further with the addition of a second drummer, Billy Mundi, keyboard player Don Preston, and reed player Bunk Gardner (while Elliott Ingber had left to join the Fraternity of Man), to make the Mothers a far more versatile seven-piece ensemble.

In November, the Mothers went back into TTG to cut their second album, *Absolutely Free*. Unlike the first album, with its freewheeling and expensive recording sessions, *Absolutely Free* was cut fast and cheap, in four double (i.e., six-hour) sessions. By Thanksgiving Day, the Mothers were in New York City appearing at the Balloon Farm on St. Marks Place, a residency they would maintain through New Year's Day, 1967. The resulting media coverage, including a review in *The New York Times,* may have helped sales of the six-month-old *Freak Out!,* which finally entered *Billboard* magazine's Top LPs at #139. It would never get any higher than #130 on the 150-position chart, but it would be on the chart for a total of 23 weeks.

Though the Mothers of Invention were exclusive Verve Records recording artists, Zappa was signed to the label only as a performer, and he was approached by Nik Venet of Capitol Records to make an album as a composer/conductor. In January, he wrote an orchestral work called *Lumpy Gravy,* which was recorded in February at Apostolic Studio in New York. (Parts of the album were also recorded at Capitol Records Studio in L.A. in December 1966 and back at Apostolic in the fall of 1967.) Verve then protested, and the album was held up. The Mothers' next record release, in April, was a non-LP single, "Why Don't You Do Me Right?"/"Big Leg Emma," which did not chart.

The Mothers had now moved to New York to live, and on Easter weekend they began a residence at the Garrick Theater on Bleecker Street. On May 24, they opened what was billed as an Off-Broadway show, *Absolutely Freeee* (also called *Pigs & Repugnant*). Basically a Mothers concert performance, it also included various theatrical elements, such as a cord running from the light booth over the audience down which various objects were run, and other improvisatory and audience-participation pieces (or, as Zappa put it, "enforced recreation") at various times. *Absolutely Freeee* ran through the summer of 1967, closing on September 5.

The Mothers' second album, *Absolutely Free,* was released by Verve on May 26. With only a single disc to fill, Zappa combined the traditional song structures and more experimental forms he had separated on the two LPs of *Freak Out!*, creating, for example, the medley of tunes on the first side including "The Duke of Prunes" and "Call Any Vegetable." While still satiric, the lyrics tended toward the humorous and absurdist, a timely tenor given that the album was released one week before *Sgt. Pepper's Lonely Hearts Club Band.* Not that anyone would confuse the more light-hearted Beatles with Frank Zappa and the Mothers, especially on songs like "Brown Shoes Don't Make It," when they sang, "Quit school. Why fake it?/ Brown shoes don't make it."

In August, the Mothers began recording their third album at Mayfair Studios in New York. By this time, Zappa's old friend Jim "Motorhead" Sherwood had officially joined the group on saxophone, and Ian Underwood had also been added on wind instruments, bringing the band up to a nonet. In this form, they finished most of the album and the Garrick Theater residence in September, took off for a short American tour, and then embarked on their first European tour, playing the Royal Albert Hall in London on September 23.

Just prior to the tour, Zappa married Gail Sloatman, who was nine months pregnant with their first child, a daughter they would name Moon Unit. They would have three more children, two sons, Dweezil and Ahmet, and a second daughter, Diva. "People make a lot of fuss about my kids having such supposedly 'strange names,'" Zappa wrote, "but the fact is that no matter what first names I might have given them, it's *the last name* that is going to get them in trouble."

It seems to have been on this U.K. trip that Zappa posed sitting on a toilet for a photograph later published in the British underground paper *International Times.* Turned into a poster with a caption reading *"Phi Zappa Krappa"* and extensively bootlegged, the photograph became an icon of the '60s.

Zappa's original intention for the third album was that it be "an oratorio thing" (as he told Frank Kofsky in *Jazz And Pop* magazine), combining Mothers music with spoken word segments by Lenny Bruce. The album was to be called *Our Man in Nirvana* and was originally scheduled for release in September. In the wake of *Sgt. Pepper* and its followup single, "All You Need Is Love," however, Zappa conceived a savage parody of the Beatles and reorganized the album into its final form, minus Lenny Bruce, which he called *We're Only In It for the Money.*

The album was released by Verve in January 1968. It got early notice for its cover. With the help of artist Cal Schenkel, who would draw and design many later covers, Zappa had put together a parody of the inside and outside jackets of *Sgt. Pepper*, though the album initially was issued with the inner photo of the Mothers on the outside and the elaborate recreation of *Sgt. Pepper*'s front cover on the inside. As the Beatles had, Zappa filled the photograph with images of people, monsters, and other objects he knew. The word *Mothers* was spelled out in watermelons, tomatoes, and carrots. Zappa had wanted a bust of Edgard Varèse, but they couldn't find one so they used Beethoven.

The cover suggested the contents, as Zappa unsparingly satirized the new hippie culture. "I'm really just a phony/But forgive me 'cause I'm stoned," sings the narrator of "Who Needs the Peace Corps?" and that pretty much summed up Zappa's disdain. The album ended with "The Chrome Plated Megaphone of Destiny," an instrumental piece inspired by Franz Kafka's short story "In the Penal Colony."

Rolling Stone magazine, which began publishing in the fall of 1967, got its first chance to review a Mothers album with *We're Only In It for the Money*, and in its April 6, 1968, issue, Barret Hansen [later known as Dr. Demento] raved, opening his notice, "Frank Zappa is a supreme genius of American music today. To lay it on the line," Hansen went on, "the Mothers' new album is the most advanced work to be heard in rock today. Whether it is the *best* is a moot point—how would you compare it with, for instance, Otis Redding? But Zappa's ingenuity in conception of form, in innovations of recording techniques, and in the integration of vastly differing types of music, beggars all competitors. His rhythms and harmonies are truly sublime, and his lyrics contain the most brilliant satire in the whole pop world." *We're Only In It for the Money* peaked at #30 on the *Billboard* chart, and stayed in the charts 19 weeks, making it the most successful Mothers or Zappa album until the appearance of *Over-Nite Sensation* in 1973.

Though released through Verve, *Money* bore the logo for Bizarre Productions on its cover. According to Zappa, this was because Verve had accidentally failed to pick up the Mothers' option. (Standard contracts at the time were five-year deals actually signed for one year with four options—to be picked up or not by the company.) Zappa and Cohen then negotiated a deal with Verve to release Mothers' records through their own production company. Later in the year, Bizarre and its sister record label Straight would begin to release albums distributed by Reprise, the subsidiary of Warner Bros. Records.

The Mothers, meanwhile, spent the month of January recording at

Apostolic Studios, returned to England in February, then played various dates around the U.S. By this time, they had added a 10th band member, percussionist Art Tripp. On February 14, they announced that they had begun work on two films, *Uncle Meat,* a "surrealistic documentary on the group," and a monster movie to be made in Japan. In March and April they were at Sunset Studios in L.A. working on an *Uncle Meat* record album. On March 11, America's teenagers were treated to an appearance by Frank Zappa on *The Monkees* TV show. Zappa would also have a cameo in the Monkees' movie, *Head,* which opened in November.

The conflict over *Lumpy Gravy* was resolved in early 1968, when Verve agreed to acquire the album from Capitol. It was released in March with a credit describing Zappa as the conductor of the Abnuceals Emuukha Electric Symphony Orchestra and Chorus.

Perhaps the Mothers' most surprising gig of the period was their appearance on April 12 at the annual awards dinner of the National Academy of Recording Arts and Sciences, dispenser of the Grammy Awards. "NARAS was tired of getting flak for being out of step with the times," writes Henry Schipper, in *Broken Record: The Inside Story Of The Grammy Awards* (Birch Lane Press, 1992). "The organization's New York board thought that . . . the Mothers . . . might bring some credibility to the awards. . . ." Instead, Zappa denounced NARAS as "a load of pompous hokum," and, says Schipper, "the performance was a kind of karmic nightmare for NARAS," in which the Mothers, "dressed in freak clothes," performed a "twisted version" of "Satin Doll" while dismembering baby dolls and offering arms and legs to the audience. Zappa and the Grammys didn't hook up again for quite a few years after that.

In June, Zappa moved back to L.A., living in "The Log Cabin," a house originally owned by cowboy actor Tom Mix in Laurel Canyon that had become a commune and was now turned into the Mothers' headquarters. The Mothers, minus Billy Mundi, who quit to join Rhinosaurus, continued to tour throughout 1968, returning to Europe in September and October. On October 28, they played at the Royal Festival Hall in London and were accompanied by 14 members of the BBC orchestra, who assisted in a theatrical skit that preceded the concert proper. It was a precursor to *200 Motels.*

In November, Verve released the third Zappa or Mothers album of the year, which was not the promised *Uncle Meat* but instead *Cruising With Ruben & The Jets,* an album of material in the early '60s pop style of the Studio Pal singles of 1962–64. In fact, a few of the compositions dated from that era. "Is this the Mothers of Invention recording under a different name in a last ditch attempt to get their cruddy music on the radio?" asked the cartoon figure of Zappa on the album's cover. Inside, Zappa explained the surprising release: "We made it because we really like this kind of music. . . ." The album was not greeted positively by fans.

"I naively thought that if there was some venue for nonstandard material, the material would find a market," Zappa said in 1993. "But it failed because it was independent and had independent distribution. We lost our butt on that one. So the only way you can really do an independent label is to distribute through a major that has some clout to collect from the retailers."

The Mothers continued to tour over the winter of 1968–69. Early in the year, Zappa bought a large house off Mulholland Drive in the Santa Monica Mountains overlooking Laurel Canyon, where he would live for the rest of his life, gradually turning it into a recording facility as well as a home.

Verve's experiment with rock 'n' roll had not proved to be an overwhelming success, and at the same time the MGM Records label was going through financial difficulties that would result in a sale of the company. The release of Cruising With Ruben & The Jets completed Zappa and the Mothers' five-record contract, and they did not re-sign with Verve. Instead, Zappa turned to his Bizarre deal with Reprise for future releases. He was obliged, however, to construct a "greatest hits" album for Verve, and Mothermania/The Best Of The Mothers, an 11-track compilation drawn from Freak Out!, Absolutely Free, and We're Only In It for the Money, was released on Verve in March. Subsequently, Verve would release other Mothers' compilations without Zappa's involvement.

The Mothers toured in the early part of 1969 as a 10-piece, with the addition of new second guitarist Lowell George. Zappa also took on the role of guest lecturer at various colleges, starting with a talk given at the New School for Social Research in New York City on February 21 prior to an appearance by the Mothers at the Fillmore East. His talk was billed "Pigs, Ponies And Rock & Roll," and he earned an honorarium of $1,500. Zappa would later lecture at UCLA, Villanova, and the University of South Carolina.

April marked the releases of the first two Straight Records albums, including Trout Mask Replica by Captain Beefheart and His Magic Band, produced by Frank Zappa. Also released was Uncle Meat, the first Mothers album issued on Bizarre Records. It was a double album containing "most of the music from the Mothers' movie of the same name which we haven't got enough money to finish yet," according to a note on the cover.

"*Uncle Meat* is sort of the missing link between the early albums which were basically song-type things . . . into what we're doing now, which is a lot more serious music, if you want to use that expression," Zappa explained at the time, "and very little of it is vocal music, you see." Some of it was vocal music that, in songs like "Sleeping in a Jar," was similar to the material on *We're Only In It for the Money.* Some came from live performances, Zappa's first mixing of live and studio material. And, as he said, much of it was exploratory instrumental music, notably the "King Kong" suite that took up all of the fourth side. "This soundtrack-without-a-movie is a consummate piece of work," wrote reviewer Alec Dubro in the May 31 issue of *Rolling Stone.* What Dubro, in the San Francisco spirit of his magazine, liked most was that the album consti-tuted "a very unflattering and absolutely unretouched photograph of that hostile and incomprehensible environment known as Los Angeles."

As the closest thing to a followup to *We're Only In It for the Money* after the side excursions of *Lumpy Gravy* and *Cruising With Ruben & The Jets, Uncle Meat* was more of a commercial hit. The Mothers played in Canada in May, then went to Europe in May and June. They played the Denver Pop Festival in late June, then were back in L.A. in early July, where Zappa began producing an album for a "groupie group" he had organized called the GTO's. In August, Zappa began recording a new solo album, *Hot Rats,* and the Mothers played dates in New York and L.A. They toured Canada for a week from August 10 to 17. On August 20, Zappa announced that he was disbanding the Mothers of Invention since he simply couldn't afford to keep the band going. "I was paying everybody in the band a weekly salary of $200," Zappa wrote, ". . . at that point I was $10,000 in the red."

Zappa continued recording *Hot Rats* through September. The LP was released on October 10. Largely an instrumental album, *Hot Rats* featured such compositions as "Peaches En Regalia" and "Son of Mr. Green Genes," as well as "Willie the Pimp," which had a vocal by Captain Beefheart. Zappa played a generous amount of guitar on the album. It has become one of his most celebrated recordings, and it began to establish him both as a virtuoso musician and composer beyond his satirical efforts with the Mothers. "This recording brings together a set of mostly little-known talents that whale the tar out of every other informal 'jam' album released in rock and roll for the past two years," wrote Lester Bangs in *Rolling Stone.* "If *Hot Rats* is any indication of where Zappa is headed on his own, we are in for some fiendish rides indeed."

Meanwhile, Zappa had gone back to work on the *Uncle Meat* film, though none of it would be released for many years. On December 6–7, he appeared at the Shrine Exposition Hall in L.A., and the same month came a new Mothers album, *Burnt Weeny Sandwich,* though these events did not indicate the band's reformation.

Bookended by songs that might have appeared on *Cruising with Ruben & The Jets, Burnt Weeny Sandwich* was a largely instrumental album with a lot of solo piano work by Ian Underwood. As noted, some of its music derived from Zappa's early film soundtrack, *The World's Greatest Sinner.* It was the first archival album of unreleased material Zappa had assembled, and thus represented the beginning of the releases of vintage recordings that would become a major part of his catalog, the evidence of a prolific composer whose work schedule was never fully accommodated by the release schedules of record companies. In fact, the album originally was intended as a sampler for a 12-LP set called *The History & Collected Improvisations Of The Mothers Of Invention.* Zappa never could come to an agreement with Reprise to release this massive collection; finally, in the 1980s, he released the 12-CD *You Can't Do That On Stage Anymore* series.

In January 1970, World Pacific Records released *King Kong: Jean-Luc Ponty Plays The Music Of Frank Zappa,* an album featuring Zappa as player and arranger and also featuring Mothers past and future George Duke, Art Tripp, and Ian Underwood. Zappa continued to work on the *Uncle Meat* movie in the spring of 1970, until money again ran out. He also played selected dates as Frank Zappa and the Mothers of Invention with a lineup that included Ray Collins, George Duke, Aynsley Dunbar, Billy Mundi, and Jeff Simmons. Zappa had been invited by Los Angeles Philharmonic conductor Zubin Mehta to present a work for the orchestra's "Contempo 70" contemporary music festival, and used the commission to write and rehearse *200 Motels,* a piece for a rock group and an orchestra on the familiar theme of "life on the road."

"During the [Mothers of Invention's] first five years, I had carried with me, on the road, masses of manuscript paper, and, whenever there was an opportunity, scribbled stuff on it," Zappa wrote. "This material eventually became the score for *200 Motels (Based On An Estimate Of The Number Of Gigs We Played In The First Five Years—40 Jobs Per Year?).*" *200 Motels* was performed at the Pauley Pavilion on the campus of UCLA on May 15 with the L.A. Philharmonic and a pickup Zappa/Mothers lineup including Simmons, Dunbar, Underwood, Collins, and Mundi, along with Don Preston and Motorhead Sherwood. Movements one, three, and four of what Zappa described as a two-and-a-half-hour work he had been writing for three years were heard at the show.

The immediate impact of the performance was the organizing of a new edition of the Mothers. Howard Kaylan and Mark Volman, the two lead singers from the recently defunct Turtles, approached Zappa backstage after the show and expressed interest in working with him. By June, they were onstage at the Fillmore East, along with Simmons, Duke, Dunbar, and Underwood, in a new, seven-member Mothers.

In August, Bizarre released *Weasels Ripped My Flesh,* an album of Mothers' live and studio material recorded between 1967 and 1970. It consisted largely of what Zappa called "group improvisation—not just accompaniment with solos, but where the group was conducted into a spontaneous piece of music." "This random collection of editing room snippets recorded at Mothers' concerts over the last few years finds the group peerless in the field of amalgamating satire, musical adventuresomeness, and flash. This could be because they're the only ones attempting it, but no matter," wrote Bill Reed in *Rolling Stone,* concluding, "At the very least this must be one of the most impressive collections of outtakes ever."

It was followed only two months later by Zappa's solo album, *Chunga's Revenge.* Unlike *Hot Rats, Chunga's Revenge* was actually a group effort for the most part, featuring the new Mothers performing some of the *200 Motels* material. Probably for contractual reasons, Kaylan and Volman were called "The Phosphorescent Leech and Eddie," a billing they later shortened to Flo and Eddie for their duo albums. The introduction of the two singers brought a new vocal focus to the Mothers, reversing the trend toward instrumental music that had begun with *Uncle Meat.*

The new Mothers continued to tour extensively, staying in the U.S. into November and then going to Europe for dates in the U.K., Sweden, Denmark, Germany, Holland, Austria, Germany, France, and Belgium. Meanwhile, Zappa's increasing reputation as a musician was confirmed by his being named Pop Musician of the Year in the December issue of the jazz magazine *Down Beat.*

In January 1971, the Mothers went to a London film studio where they made a movie version of *200 Motels.* It was shot on videotape (to be blown up to 35-millimeter film stock), using a cast that also included Ringo Starr, Keith Moon, Theodore Bikel (another of Herb Cohen's old clients from his club days), and the Royal Philharmonic Orchestra. Zappa got United Artists to back the film to the tune of $630,000. A concert with the Royal Philharmonic had been planned at the Royal Albert Hall, essentially as a legal gimmick to save money—according to the British musicians' union, if you rehearse an orchestra but do not play a concert (i.e., if you make a film or a record), you must pay recording rates for the rehearsal time. Zappa had to submit a libretto for *200 Motels,* and upon seeing it, Albert Hall manager Marion Herrod cancelled the performance on grounds of obscenity, thus forcing Zappa to pay the orchestra at the higher rate. He sued the Royal Albert Hall.

Overdubs for the *200 Motels* score were recorded back in California in April and May, and then the Mothers embarked on another tour. By this point, another ex-Turtle, Jim Pons, was the bass player, and Don Preston had rejoined on keyboards, replacing George Duke. A third keyboardist, Bob Harris, made the Mothers an eight-member group for the U.S. dates. The Mothers played two nights at the Fillmore East June 5 and 6, just before it closed its doors. On the second night, they recorded a live album, again performing much of the *200 Motels* material, and were joined by John Lennon and Yoko Ono, who jammed with them, marking Lennon's first stage appearance in almost two years.

Fillmore East—June 1971 was rushed out, looking like a white-cover bootleg album, in August. It marked the beginning of two new trends in Zappa/Mothers albums—greater commercial success and critical opprobrium. Zappa's satiric attitude might have seemed provocative and witty in 1967, but in 1971, rock critic Robert Christgau listened to Kaylan and Volman's comic depictions of rock-star excess and pronounced the result "sexist adolescent drivel." Adolescents buy records, however, and *Fillmore East* was Zappa's best chart showing since *We're Only In It for the Money.* The band recorded what would be another live album back at the Pauley Pavilion on August 7.

200 Motels opened in movie theaters in four cities in October (it opened "wide" in January 1972), the same month that United Artists Records released a double soundtrack album. The band, meanwhile, hit the road again in October, and was in Europe by November. It proved to be Zappa's most disastrous tour. In the beginning of December in Montreux, the Casino, where the Mothers were playing, caught fire while the band was onstage. The hall burned down, and though no one was killed, the Mothers lost all their equipment. (The incident inspired Deep Purple to write "Smoke on the Water.")

The band voted not to cancel the tour completely (overruling Zappa), but it did cut a week's worth of gigs and went on directly to London, where it was scheduled to play two dates, two shows per night, December 10 and 11, at the Rainbow. During the encore of the first show of the first night, 24-year-old manual laborer Trevor Charles Howell climbed onstage and pushed Zappa into the orchestra pit. Zappa broke a leg and an ankle, damaged his spine, and fractured his skull. His larynx was crushed, which would lower his speaking (and singing) voice by a third of an octave. Howell was arrested and appeared in court on December 30, where he pled guilty to malicious intent to commit bodily harm and said, "I did it because my girlfriend said she loved Frank." He was sent to jail for a year.

Zappa was out of commission almost as long. He spent nine months in a wheelchair and another three wearing a surgical brace. The Mothers, of course, disbanded. Zappa, forced to stay home, put together a new solo album and produced an LP by a doo-wop group called Ruben and the Jets that included Motorhead Sherwood, which was released in 1993. He also worked on a science-fiction stage musical called *Hunchentoot*. It has never been staged, although songs from it later turned up on the *Sleep Dirt* album.

The next Mothers release, in April 1972, was *Just Another Band From L.A.*, the live show recorded in August 1971 at the Pauley Pavilion, featuring an extended piece of musical comedy called "Billy the Mountain" that took up all of the first side.

On June 12, John Lennon and Yoko Ono released their double album *Sometime In New York City,* which featured an excerpt from their appearance with the Mothers at the Fillmore East the year before. The result displeased Zappa. "During our time onstage, a number of pieces were improvised, but a number of pieces that were played were absolutely written compositions that had already been on other albums—namely, a song of mine called 'King Kong,'" Zappa told writer Kurt Loder in an interview in *Rolling Stone* in February 1988. "The deal I made with John and Yoko was that we were both to have access to the tapes and could deploy them any way we wanted. They got a duplicate copy of the master, and they mixed it their way. I had a copy of the master, and I was gonna mix it and put it out as part of the Mothers album. They put out this record that took 'King Kong'—which obviously has a tune, and a rhythm, and chord changes—and they called it 'Jam Rag,' and accredited the writing and publishing to themselves . . . I can't imagine that album really sold a lot; anyway, it's the principle of the thing, you know?" Zappa would later issue his own version of the same material.

July 5 marked the release of the Frank Zappa solo album *Waka/Jawaka,* a four-song, mostly instrumental LP that continued the jazz-rock tendencies of *Hot Rats*. It featured extensive horn work, especially by trumpeter Sal Marquez. In the summer of 1972, Zappa assembled a big band for the recording of the next Mothers album and selected live dates. The ensemble debuted on September 10 at the Hollywood Bowl as a 19-piece featuring six horns, five woodwinds, a cellist, and a rhythm section including piano, guitar, bass, drums, and two percussionists, plus Zappa on guitar and vocals. The group played a few European and American dates in September, but was too large an organization to keep going, and for shows from October through the end of the year, Zappa pared it down to a 10-piece.

The Grand Wazoo, featuring music by the big band, billed as the Mothers, was released in December. Full of jazz improvisation, especially by Marquez, the album frequently sounded more like a Miles Davis album of the same period than one by the Mothers. It was one of Zappa's more ambitious musical undertakings, but it was nevertheless one of his poorest sellers and the first of his 15 new albums released since 1966 not to make the charts. It would be many years before Zappa made a record as far from the pop-rock mainstream.

Disbanding the 10-piece "Wazoo" orchestra, Zappa organized a new, more rock-oriented nine-piece Mothers band to launch a world tour at the start of 1973. It featured such familiar faces as Jean-Luc Ponty, George Duke, and Ian Underwood, and it hit the road in February and played around the U.S. through May. There was an Australian tour in June and July, and the band spent August and September in Europe.

The first album by this edition of the Mothers, *Over-Nite Sensation,* was released in September by a new Zappa label, DiscReet, still distributed by Warner/Reprise. For the first time, Zappa dominated the album with his new, baritone-bass vocals on a set of comic pop-rock songs with absurd ("Camarillo Brillo," "Montana"), sexual ("Dirty Love," "Dinah-Moe Humm"), and anti-commercial ("I'm the Slime") themes. The result was a sales breakthrough—*Over-Nite Sensation* hit #32, Zappa's best showing in more than five years, and stayed in the charts almost a year. In three years, it went gold.

Zappa and the Mothers toured the U.S. and Canada from October to December, concluding with a six-night stand at the Roxy club in Hollywood, during which they recorded material for a live album. Zappa stayed in L.A. in January and February 1974, doing some recording that would later turn up on the *Bongo Fury* album in 1975. March 1974 saw the release of Zappa's next solo album, *Apostrophe ('),* though, once again, the distinction between Mothers albums and Zappa solo albums had become difficult to follow. *Apostrophe (')* was in every sense a followup to *Over-Nite Sensation,* containing more of Zappa's comic vocal numbers, such as the anti-guru "Cosmik Debris," "Stink Foot," and "Don't Eat the Yellow Snow." And it was even more successful, soaring to #10 by June and, in two years, becoming Zappa's first gold album.

The band continued to tour extensively, playing around the U.S. from February to August, then going to Europe in September. It was around this time that "Don't Eat the Yellow Snow" began to earn radio play. As Zappa explained to *Musician* magazine in 1986, "It was an accident. A disc jockey in Pittsburgh on a station that had a policy of playing novelty records of the '60s received the album in the mail, listened to 'Yellow Snow,' which was 10 minutes long, and said 'My god, it's modern-day novelty record,' cut it down to three minutes and transferred it to tape. Cut it down, put it on cart, put it on the station which was part of a chain. It instantly goes into the Top 20, it's picked up on all the stations on the chain." When Zappa, on tour in Europe, heard about it, he had DiscReet create an edited version of "Yellow Snow" to match the radio version and release it as a single. The result was the first Frank Zappa & the Mothers singles chart entry, as "Snow" reached #86 on the Hot 100.

The double live album *Roxy & Elsewhere* was released on September 10. Presenting Zappa as a funny, sharp-tongued master of ceremonies, and mixing his caustic humor with increasingly complicated musical structures, it was a model of the kind of shows and albums Zappa would be doing over the next decade. By now, Zappa had lost the critics completely: Christgau described *Roxy* as "the usual eccentric clichés, replete with meters and voicings and key changes that are easy to forget." But Zappa had also attracted a new, loyal following, especially in Europe, where people weren't as bothered by his strange lyrics. The European tour ran to the end of October, followed by Halloween shows at the Felt Forum in New York and American dates into December.

In April 1975, Zappa's suit against the Royal Albert Hall for cancelling the performance of *200 Motels* back in 1971 finally went to trial in England. Zappa lost the suit. As he paraphrased the judge's ruling: "[1] The material was *not* obscene, [2] the Albert Hall had, in fact, breached its contract, but [3] as the Albert Hall is a *Royal* institution, it would be improper for an American musician to prevail in a case like this, so— Yankee, go home."

The Mothers toured the U.S. in April and May, having added Captain Beefheart as a vocalist and new drummer Terry Bozzio. Material for *Bongo Fury* was recorded during the tour, but the next Zappa/Mothers album was *One Size Fits All*, released on June 25. By now, Zappa had taken to extensively mixing live and studio tracks on the same songs, such that, for example, as he noted on the album jacket, "the basic tracks for 'Inca Roads' and 'Florentine Pogen' were recorded live at KCET TV Los Angeles during the production of our TV special [*A Token Of My Extreme*, December 1974]. The guitar solo in 'Inca Roads' was recorded live during our 1974 concert in Helsinki, Finland [September 22, 1974]." From here on out, Zappa albums would contain material mixed and matched this way, especially when the *You Can't Do That Onstage Anymore* series started.

One Size Fits All had more of a musical focus than its immediate predecessors, and Zappa even turned some of the lead singing over to George Duke. "It has some story type songs, but it's pretty much rock 'n' roll oriented," was the way Zappa put it. Peaking at #26, it became the fourth straight Zappa and/or Mothers album to reach the Top 50.

On September 17 and 18, Zappa conducted a 37-piece orchestra at Royce Hall, UCLA, playing his symphonic compositions, and recorded the shows. The material eventually would turn up on an album called *Orchestral Favorites*.

Zappa and the Mothers, now a five-piece consisting of Zappa, Napoleon Murphy Brock on sax, Andre Lewis on keyboards, a returning Roy Estrada on bass, and Terry Bozzio on drums, launched another extensive tour in late September. *Bongo Fury*, the live album featuring Captain Beefheart, was released October 2. The North American leg of the tour ran through the end of the year, with a short December trip to Yugoslavia. There was a Far East tour in January and February, and European dates during February and March.

The 1975–76 tour was the last on which the band was billed as the Mothers. From this point on, albums and shows would be credited to Zappa. When Zappa returned from the tour, he split from his long-time manager Herb Cohen, with whom he had worked for more than a decade, and sued him. To the surprise of many, Zappa produced an album for Grand Funk, the much-maligned heavy metal group. *Good Singin', Good Playin'* was released in August and proved to be the band's last charting studio album.

In October 1976, Zappa reached an out-of-court settlement of a suit he had launched in August 1975 against Verve Records for $2 million in unpaid royalties. He was to be paid $100,000, and the masters for the five Zappa/Mothers albums on Verve—*Freak Out!, Absolutely Free, We're Only In It For The Money, Lumpy Gravy,* and *Cruising With Ruben & The Jets*—were turned over to him. He discovered that the tapes had deteriorated in storage. For the moment, the albums remained out of print.

Zappa returned to touring in October, again with a quintet that retained drummer Bozzio but otherwise featured bassist Patrick O'Hearn, violinist/keyboardist Eddie Jobson (formerly of Roxy Music), and guitarist/singer Ray White. (White, along with Ike Willis, who joined later, freed Zappa up from having to sing lead vocals, something he wrote that he did only from necessity until he found "professional-sounding singers" who would sing his lyrics.) As usual, his record releases were one band behind: *Zoot Allures,* released on Warner Bros. October 29 (DiscReet was a victim of Zappa's suit against Cohen), featured the band from the 1975–76 tour and was a hard-rock effort with a lot of Zappa guitar work. "Disco Boy," released as a single, bubbled under the Hot 100 in March and April 1977.

The tour brought Zappa back to New York's Felt Forum for what were becoming his annual Halloween shows, and he recorded them for an upcoming live album that would be called *Zappa in New York.* He was back in New York to play "Saturday Night Live" on December 11, and the band played at the Palladium on 14th Street from the 26th to the 29th, again recording for the *Zappa in New York* LP. For these shows, the group was augmented by horn and reed players, including Michael and Randy Brecker.

The band toured Europe in January and February 1977, after which Zappa was unusually silent, perhaps because of his ongoing legal difficulties with Herb Cohen and escalating problems with Warners. Once again, a multi-record retrospective album was planned for release, this time a four-record set called *Läther* that was to be the first release on Zappa Records, and even got as far as a catalog number before being cancelled due to objections by Warners. Zappa was so incensed he went on Pasadena radio station KROQ and played the entire three-and-a-half-hour album after instructing listeners to tape it. But that was as close to release as it came. Zappa's only new appearance on record in 1977 was his guitar work on the track "Petroleum" on Robert Charlebois's Canadian RCA album *Swing Charlebois Swing.*

Zappa went back on tour in September with a backup band featuring second guitarist Adrian Belew, keyboard players Tommy Mars and Peter Wolf (the future producer of Starship and others, not the J. Geils Band frontman), Patrick O'Hearn on bass, Terry Bozzio on drums, and Ed Mann on percussion. The tour ran through the East Coast and the Upper Midwest up to the end of October, with the usual New York Halloween shows at the Palladium (which were filmed), then picked up in the West in November and December, and on to Europe in January and February 1978.

On March 3, *Zappa in New York* was finally released. Another victim of Zappa's troubles with Cohen and Warners, the album had been held up for a year since being recorded on the Fall 1976 tour. Now released on the otherwise moribund DiscReet as a two LP set, it looked as though it had been stretched onto the two discs: The first side ran less than 11 minutes, for example. The reason was that Warners had insisted on cutting out the nearly 11-minute "Punky's Whips," which referred to Punky Meadows of the heavy metal band Angel. Warners was afraid Meadows would sue. Even without "Punky's Whips," *Zappa In New York,* which consisted of mostly new material, demonstrated that Zappa was even more interested in the perverse than ever. One song was called "Titties & Beer" and another "The Illinois Enema Bandit," and there was an instrumental called "I Promise Not to Come in Your Mouth." The instrumentals were as complicated as ever, notably "Black Page," a showcase for Bozzio.

In a settlement with Warner Bros. Records, the label was allowed to issue three albums of material originally intended for the *Läther* set. The first, *Studio Tan,* was released on September 15; the second, *Sleep Dirt,* was released January 19, 1979. Both consisted of band material recorded between 1974 and 1976. The third album, *Orchestral Favorites,* was released May 4, 1979, and contained the material from the September 1975 orchestra concert at UCLA. Zappa would later reacquire this material and issue it himself. He also gained possession of his Warner Bros. catalog in the settlement. This was not the end of his record company problems, but in the future Zappa would control his material.

He had gone back on the road in Europe from July to September 1978. During this period, Belew and O'Hearn left the band, and singer Ike Willis, who would be heard on much of Zappa's late '70s and early '80s records, had joined. The tour moved to the U.S. from September to December with a lineup consisting of Mars, Wolf, Mann, Denny Walley on guitar and vocals, Arthur Barrow on bass and vocals, and Vinnie Colaiuta on drums. Zappa went to Europe at the start of 1979, where he produced the album *Touch Me There* for violinist L. Shankar (released in September), then launched an extensive European tour that ran into April, followed by a short trip to Japan.

On March 3, 1979, Zappa Records released *Sheik Yerbouti,* Frank Zappa's 26th album (not counting the Verve/MGM compilations). It was a double-LP employing Zappa's usual complement of challenging music and scornful lyrics, beginning with a parody of Peter Frampton's "I'm in You" called, "I Have Been in You," "Broken Hearts Are for Assholes," "Bobby Brown" (a concert favorite about a young man's encounter with a dominatrix), and "Jewish Princess." The Anti-Defamation League of B'nai B'rith filed a protest about the last song with the FCC, asking it to ban the song from radio play (as if that were necessary). Zappa denied he was anti-Semitic, said the song was a satire, and threatened to sue. The album turned out to be one of Zappa's better domestic sellers; "Dancin' Fool," released as a single, hit #45. The LP also earned Zappa his first Grammy nomination, for Best Rock Vocal Performance, Male. He lost to Bob Dylan and "Gotta Serve Somebody."

The world tour that closed in April 1979 brought Zappa's extensive roadwork of the second half of the 1970s to a close. He laid off his band and went to work on a rock opera, *Joe's Garage.* "It was originally a group of songs that had nothing to do with each other," Zappa told John Stix in *Guitar* magazine in May 1986. "One weekend I decided that I would write continuity to it and make an opera out of it. By golly, I did it, and the storyline makes sense, the songs are good, and the album is well-produced."

Joe's Garage was released in two parts. *Joe's Garage, Act I* came out on September 17. With Zappa whispering in a sinister voice, as "the Central Scrutinizer," it told a tale of science fiction paranoia about a time when music was illegal, though most of the content followed the career of a guitarist named Joe in the music business. In case anyone thought Zappa was cowed by the B'nai B'rith, it included "Catholic Girls," which was just as caustic as "Jewish Princess," not to mention "Why Does It Hurt When I Pee?" *Joe's Garage, Acts II & III,* a two-LP set completing the story, appeared on November 19.

On December 21, his 39th birthday, Zappa's second feature film, *Baby Snakes,* opened at the Victoria Theater in Times Square. The nearly three-hour film, which combined live footage from the Palladium Halloween show of 1977 with elaborate clay-figure animation by Bruce Bickford, ran 24 hours a day with its soundtrack played through a rock 'n' roll P.A. system brought in for the occasion.

Zappa began the 1980s with a new world tour. The new Zappa band was a six-piece, with Zappa, Ike Willis and Ray White on guitars and vocals, Tommy Mars on keyboards, Arthur Barrow on bass, and David Logeman on drums. It ran through the U.S. from February to May, then went to Europe from May through July. Zappa spent the rest of July and August at home, where he had finished building his own studio, "The Utility Muffin Research Kitchen," working on his next album, *You Are What You Is.* He then went back on tour in the U.S. for the rest of the year, replacing Logeman with Vinnie Colaiuta and adding keyboard player Bob Harris and guitarist Steve Vai.

Zappa would not have an album release for all of 1980, but he did have one single ready, "I Don't Wanna Get Drafted," which bubbled under the Hot 100 for six weeks in May and June. Zappa did not tour in the first half of 1981, but on April 1, he hosted "A Tribute to Edgard Varèse" by the Orchestra for Our Time, conducted by Joel Thome at the Palladium in New York and attended by Varèse's widow, Louise.

On May 11, Zappa released five new LPs' worth of music. Issued by mail order were three albums of guitar solos culled from live performances in 1979 and 1980: *Shut Up 'N Play Yer Guitar, Shut Up 'N Play Yer Guitar Some More,* and *The Return of the Son of Shut Up 'N Play Yer Guitar.* And to retail, Zappa released a new double live album, *Tinsel Town Rebellion.* The albums were released on Zappa's new imprint, Barking Pumpkin Records. As usual, the recordings mixed basic tracks recorded at one show with solos recorded at another. On *Tinsel Town,* Zappa included several older songs, such as "I Ain't Got No Heart" and "Brown Shoes Don't Make It."

The studio album, *You Are What You Is,* another double, followed in September. Zappa particularly had it in for society's notions of appearance and fashion on this record, with songs such as "Beauty Knows No Pain" and "Charlie's Enormous Mouth." In addition to the current band, the album featured Motorhead Sherwood and Jimmy Carl Black, as well as Zappa's children Ahmet and Moon on vocals. A video of the title song, which featured a lookalike of President Ronald Reagan sitting in an electric chair, was not shown on newly launched MTV.

Zappa went back on tour in September, playing on the West Coast, through the Southwest and the South before heading into the Northeast, then through the Midwest and back out to the Coast in a counterclockwise trip around the country that ran into December. The Halloween show at the Palladium in New York was broadcast on MTV and on the Westwood One radio network.

Zappa stayed off the road, working in his home studio, in the first few months of 1982. In May, he released a single-disc LP, *Ship Arriving Too Late to Save A Drowning Witch,* the album that contained "Valley Girl," a monologue by Moon Zappa filled with local slang that became a novelty hit. "[The song] started off at the end of an overdub session, just me on guitar and Chad Wackerman on drums," Zappa told interviewer Philip Bashe. "The tape sat around for months while I did a tour. Then I sat down and wrote some lyrics, and the tape sat around again. One day at a vocal session, I got out the track and had the guys in the band sing this chorale thing I'd written, so now we had guitar, drums, and chorale background. A few days later, I woke up Moon in the middle of the night and had her come down and do a monologue. She did five separate ones, all of which I ping-ponged together to make the one version that's on the record. Finally, the bass was added last."

The song "was a hit from the minute it went on the radio," Zappa told interviewer Josef Woodard. "They played it on KROQ [Los Angeles], the phones exploded. Next thing you know, they had an acetate. It wasn't even released. It was something that people wanted to hear. The worst thing about that record is the fact that nobody really listened to it. They listened to the slang in there, it has a reasonably good beat, a couple of nice chords in it, but it's a monologue record. People didn't even listen to what the song was saying. The whole coverage of the song barely mention[ed] what the song was really saying, that these people are really airheads."

"Valley Girl" became Zappa's highest charting single ever. It reached #32, and the album hit #23, staying in the charts 22 weeks. Zappa earned his second Grammy nomination (along with Moon) for "Valley Girl," for Best Rock Performance By A Duo Or Group With Vocal. They lost to "Eye of the Tiger," by Survivor.

The U.S. tour of 1981 had been relatively poorly attended, but Zappa encountered different problems when he launched a European tour in May 1982. At many locations, crowds were rowdy, and shows were sometimes curtailed or cancelled. Zappa was popular in Europe, able to play large outdoor venues, but he had begun to attract a typical young rock 'n' roll audience that had come to party as well as listen. The tour ran through July, ending at what Zappa referred to as "the infamous Palermo riot concert," during which the crowd—and the band—were tear-gassed.

"The '82 band could play beautifully when it wanted to," Zappa would write in the liner notes to *You Can't Do That On Stage Anymore, Vol. 5*, which contained an entire CD of performances from the 1982 European tour. "It is unfortunate that the audiences of the time didn't understand that we had no intention of posing as targets for their assorted 'love offerings' cast onto the stage. . . ."

Zappa traveled to England in January 1983 for performances and recordings with the London Symphony Orchestra. There were several days of rehearsals, a performance at the Barbican Centre on January 11, and then three days of recording sessions at Twickenham Film Studios on January 12–14. "Thanks to songs like 'Dinah-Moe Humm,' 'Titties & Beer' and 'Don't Eat The Yellow Snow,'" Zappa wrote in his autobiography, "I managed to accumulate enough cash to bribe a group of drones to grind its way through pieces like 'Mo 'N Herb's Vacation,' 'Bob In Dacron' and 'Bogus Pomp' . . . in performances which came off like high-class 'demos' of what actually resides in the scores." On February 9, Zappa conducted *Ionisation* at an Edgard Varèse memorial concert at the San Francisco War Memorial Opera House in commemoration of the 100th anniversary of the composer's birth.

Zappa's 36th album, *The Man from Utopia,* was released in March. The cover, a painting of a Zappa-like figure raving onstage, designed by illustrator Tanino Liberatore, referred to the July 6, 1982, concert in Milan, a mosquito-infested outdoor show attended by 50,000 fans. Following the success of *Ship Arriving Too Late,* the album was a sales disappointment. The same month, Barking Pumpkin released the sound-track to *Baby Snakes* as a picture disc LP.

On June 9, Zappa released the first results of the London Symphony Orchestra sessions, *Zappa Vol. 1,* containing four pieces, including the three-part "Mo 'N Herb's Vacation." Zappa did not tour during 1983, and in fact would undertake only two more tours in the last decade of his life. Instead, he stayed at home, acquiring digital recording equipment as well as successive generations of the Synclavier synthesizer computer to write and record his works on.

On January 9, 1984, in Paris, conductor Pierre Boulez premiered Zappa's "The Perfect Stranger," which had been commissioned for his Ensemble InterContemporain. Boulez recorded the work, which was then combined with Zappa's Synclavier work and released as *Boulez Conducts Zappa—The Perfect Stranger.* The album entered the classical chart in September, peaking at #7, and staying in the chart nearly a year. Zappa received his third Grammy nomination for the piece "The Perfect Stranger," for Best New Classical Composition. He lost to Samuel Barber's *Antony and Cleopatra.* "Since releasing the LSO album," Zappa wrote in 1989, "I have turned down at least 15 commissions from chamber music groups of varying sizes from all over the world who offered me *cash* to write a piece of music." Zappa explained that he didn't have the time and the musicians usually were underrehearsed and unenthusiastic about play-ing new—and complicated—music. He cited the Boulez experience as an example.

Zappa planned his first concert tour in two years for the summer, fall, and winter of 1984, and he seems to have finished up a number of record-ing projects before going out. In its April issue, *Hustler* magazine printed a photo spread depicting a fantasy Broadway show called *Thing-Fish* by Zappa. On April 4, Zappa gave the keynote address at the annual con-vention of the American Society of University Composers (ASUC). After noting that he was not a member of their organization, that they weren't going to like what he had to say, and that he talked dirty, Zappa addressed what he called "the most baffling aspect of the industrial-American-relevance question," which he said was, "Why do people continue to compose music, and even pretend to teach others how to do it, when they already know the answer? Nobody gives a fuck."

He then explained that the tastes of those who commission and sponsor composed music are ruled by a hypothetical teenager with a short attention span, whom he called Debbie, and that, for various reasons, the music of dead people has an advantage in the marketplace over the music of living people. His conclusion: "It's all over, folks. Get smart—take out a real estate license."

On May 20, as part of the "Speaking of Music" series at the Exploratorium Museum in San Francisco, Zappa played his Synclavier versions of the compositions of the 18th century Italian composer Francesco Zappa, a possible ancestor. The following month, Zappa attended performances by the Berkeley Symphony Orchestra of some of his orchestral works. Kent Nagano conducted the orchestra in the world premiere of "Sinister Footwear" and the U.S. premieres of "Mo 'N Herb's Vacation," "Bob In Dacron," and "Sad Jane," plus the large orchestra version of "Pedro's Dowry" on June 15 and 16 at the Zellerbach Auditorium in Berkeley, with staging by the San Francisco Miniature Theater, featuring dancers and large puppets.

Tour rehearsals began on May 21. In an interview conducted around this time and published in *Digital Audio* magazine, Zappa explained that his reason for touring was his dissatisfaction with his experiences in the classical world. He cited an incident at the ASUC convention, at which a harpist who was completely inadequate to play his pieces and those of others nevertheless had to be used because of her tenure, according to union rules. "For these reasons, I have said, 'Okay, that's it. I've been doing this seriously for two years now. I stopped touring two years ago and spent the last two years in Modern Music Land—and I'm leaving,'" Zappa said. "I'm going back on the road."

The 20th Anniversary World Tour was launched on July 17 with the first of six nights at the Palace Theater in Hollywood. Zappa played his way east through July and August, then did various dates in the East and Midwest through early September, moving on to Europe on September 7. He played through Europe until mid-October, then returned to the U.S. through December, ending just before Christmas back in Los Angeles.

The fall saw a flurry of new releases. On October 18, Zappa released *Them Or Us,* a double album of songs. There was also a self-published book called *Them Or Us*. Written in the form of a screenplay, it weaved together the stories of "Billy The Mountain," "Greggary Peccary," *Joe's Garage*, and the upcoming *Thing-Fish*, among other things.

Thing-Fish, a triple album, followed on November 21. It has mistakenly been called an intended Broadway show. Actually, it is a savage fantasy *about* a Broadway show, in which Ike Willis, in an Amos 'n' Andy accent, assaults members of the "audience." As with *Joe's Garage*, the songs were not necessarily written with the album in mind; in fact, many were older songs recycled for this project. (Zappa also reportedly prepared a second "Broadway show," *The Works*, which has not appeared so far.)

Also on November 21 came the *Francesco Zappa* album, "his first digital recording in over 200 years." "He was a composer who flourished between 1766 and 1788," Zappa explained. "Nobody knows when he was born or when he died. He was a cello player from Milan and wrote mostly string trios. I found out about his music and located a bunch of it in the Berkeley Library and the Library of Congress. My assistant loaded it into the Synclavier and now we have a whole album of synthesized performances . . . It's kind of happy, Italian-sounding music. It's nice, and real melodic. It's interesting, too; he does a few strange things harmonically that seem to be slightly ahead of his time—a few little weird things. Basically, it's typical of music of that period except it doesn't sound typical when it comes out of the Synclavier."

If putting out six LPs in five weeks wasn't enough, Zappa followed on April 19, 1985, by releasing a seven-LP boxed set, *The Old Masters, Box One*. Marketed by mail order, the box contained the five Verve albums Zappa had regained rights to in 1976, plus a "Mystery Disc" containing unreleased material from the '60s. Finding the master tapes in poor condition, Zappa had remixed the albums, and he had rerecorded the rhythm tracks for *We're Only In It For The Money* and *Cruising With Ruben & The Jets* to bring the albums' sonic quality up to 1980s' standards. The results were controversial for older fans, though Zappa, in a 1989 interview with *Goldmine* dismissed those who had a reverence for the past as "fetishists" and said he was trying to meet the expectations of younger fans who would be turned off by the inferior sound of the original '60s tapes. The controversy, however, did not go away, and toward the end of his life, Zappa restored the albums to their original form.

In the summer of 1985, Zappa involved himself in the growing censorship debates in the music industry, sparked by the Parents Music Resource Center (PMRC), a group led by the wives of several prominent Washington, D.C., politicians that attempted to counter what it saw as pornography in popular music. Given their matrimonial influence, the founders of the PMRC were able to inspire a Congressional hearing, by the Senate Commerce, Technology and Transportation Committee (several members of the committee had wives in the PMRC), on September 19, at which Zappa spoke, ridiculing the PMRC's concerns. Zappa also gave extensive interviews to the press on the subject and sent out press packages. On February 14, 1986, he again testified against censorship before the State Senate Judiciary Committee of his home state, Maryland, which was considering a new pornography statute to include records.

In October 1985, Barking Pumpkin released *Frank Zappa Meets The Mothers Of Prevention,* which contained excerpts from the Congressional hearing mixed with music. For the European version, Zappa eliminated the hearing material and added other tracks. The album hit #153 in *Billboard,* Zappa's first pop chart listing in three years, and his last.

January 1986 saw the release in Europe of *Does Humor Belong In Music?,* a live album culled from the 1984 tour that apparently came out without Zappa's permission and subsequently was withdrawn. (It finally saw U.S. release in 1995.) A companion home video released in the U.S. did not suffer similar disapproval, however.

Also in January 1986, Zappa entered into a contract with Rykodisc, the pioneering compact disc label, to reissue his catalog on CD and, finally, to release his series of archival albums, now titled *You Can't Do That On Stage Anymore.* The reissue program, as agreed to by Zappa and Rykodisc, was non-chronological and, as it turned out, incomplete, with batches of miscellaneous albums coming out at intervals over the next several years.

On November 15 came a new instrumental album of music recorded on the Synclavier, *Jazz From Hell.* Meanwhile, in 1987, Zappa continued to refurbish his old catalog. In June, in connection with *Guitar World* magazine, Barking Pumpkin released the cassette-only *The Guitar World According To Frank Zappa,* containing guitar solos, some of which were slated for the next album of Zappa guitar playing. On September 17, Barking Pumpkin released *Zappa, Vol. 2* by the London Symphony Orchestra, completing release of the January 1983 sessions.

Zappa's other archival project of 1987 was the founding of a video division, dubbed Honker, which would release a series of home videos. Honker's first two releases, the sampler *Video From Hell* and the three-hour, two-tape *Baby Snakes,* appeared on October 28. (*The True Story Of 200 Motels* and *Uncle Meat* would be issued on January 3, 1989.) Also planned, according to an article in *Billboard* were *Bunny, Bunny, Bunny,* a "really bizarre, punk Ionesco-type play made by Moon Unit Zappa and two of her friends," and *An American Dissident,* "a collection of my most obnoxious interviews and documentary stuff." They have not appeared.

As 1988 began, Zappa was gearing up for his first concert tour in four years. Apparently, the impetus for touring was a proposed reunion with Howard Kaylan and Mark Volman. "The idea first came from Flo and Eddie," Zappa told *Boston Rock* magazine in 1988. "Volman called and said we should go on the road again because we had a lot of fun. I spent $5,000 and rented a rehearsal hall, then Flo and Eddie decided they didn't want to do it. That didn't work out, but we just kept rehearsing. I added the horn section and we did this."

The rehearsals of Zappa's new 11-piece band (containing five horns) took place in January 1988 and the "Broadway The Hard Way" Tour opened in Albany, New York, on February 2, 1988. Zappa was taking a highly political approach this time, having voter registration booths set up in the lobbies of the halls and performing songs criticizing former President Richard Nixon and disgraced evangelists Jim Bakker and Jimmy Swaggert, as well as evangelist-turned-presidential-candidate Pat Robertson. The tour played on the East Coast through April, then moved to Europe and concluded in Italy in June.

Meanwhile, Zappa had once again been nominated by the Grammys. The *Jazz From Hell* album was up for Best Rock Instrumental Performance (Orchestra, Group, Or Soloist), and the "Jazz From Hell" track was up for Best Instrumental Composition. The week before the awards, Zappa discussed his feelings about the Grammys with *The Cleveland Plain Dealer.* "My nomination must have been an accident," he said. "Either that or a lot of people have a perverse sense of humor. I'm convinced that nobody ever heard [it]. I have no ambiguous feelings about the Grammys at all. I know they're fake. I find it difficult to believe that Whitney Houston is the answer to all of America's music needs." On March 2, Zappa won the award for Best Rock Instrumental Performance, but lost the award for Best Instrumental Composition; Zappa did not attend the Grammy ceremony.

Zappa had another 10 weeks of dates in the U.S. scheduled, but dissension within the group led him to cut the tour short. In his *Goldmine* interview, Zappa noted that it simply wasn't economic for him to tour anymore, given the enormous overhead necessary to maintaining a band, equipment, and a road crew. He said he had lost $400,000 on the tour, but that he was pleased with the live recordings he had been able to make.

Rykodisc released *You Can't Do That on Stage Anymore, Vol. 1* on

May 16. It contained material recorded between February 13, 1969, and August 26, 1984, and featured many different lineups of the Mothers and Zappa's bands. Clearly, Zappa's ideas about an archival set of albums had evolved over the years from the multi-LP set he had conceived of as early as 1969. Necessarily, that set would have been dominated by the work of the Mothers, circa 1965–69. Now, Zappa went out of his way in his liner notes to denigrate that lineup. "Great care has been taken throughout to ensure the best audio quality, however early selections of historical interest performed by the original Mothers of Invention, though not exactly 'hi-fi,' have been included for the amusement of those fetishists who still believe the only 'good' material was performed by that particular group," Zappa wrote in the album's liner notes. "Hopefully, comparisons to recordings by the later ensembles will put an end to that peculiar misconception." One can only speculate that Zappa's antipathy toward the '60s band was related to their reorganization as the Grandmothers; he had been trading insults with them in interviews since they got back together.

Just as controversial, if not more so, was Zappa's organization of the material. *"THIS COLLECTION IS NOT CHRONOLOGICAL,"* the notes announced in bold face capital letters. "The performance of any band from any year can be (and often is) edited to the performance of any other band from any other year, sometimes in the middle of a song." The collection, though, did have a certain internal logic, as Zappa explained in *Goldmine* in 1989, noting that he was attempting to simulate a given concert set on each individual disc, with introductions at the beginning and a sign-off at the end. In between, a kind of ideal show would be created, containing unique moments and the best performances of individual compositions.

It's also worth noting that while the launching of the series began a dizzying run of record releases for an artist who had already established himself as one of the most prolific in rock, at least he was trying to address the interests of his hard-core fans. By the 1980s, certain performers—the Grateful Dead being the most prominent example—had attracted unusually large core audiences who wanted to hear every note their favorites played and, unsatisfied by conventional touring and recording schedules, traveled from city to city, tape recorders in hand.

The performers were relatively slow to come to terms with this potentially advantageous situation. The Dead began to allow people to tape their shows, for example, while others sought to clamp down on bootlegging. With the *You Can't Do That on Stage* series and other archival releases of the coming years, Zappa was aiming not at a general audience but at his dedicated following. One of his criteria for using tracks on the series was, "Will it give 'Conceptual Continuity Clues' to the hard-core maniacs with a complete record collection?" Audacious as the series may have seemed to a casual music fan, it was in fact targeted to those most likely to buy Zappa's records. Many of those people were guitar fans. On May 23, Rykodisc released *Guitar*, a 32-track double CD followup to *Shut Up 'N Play Yer Guitar*, earning Zappa his sixth Grammy nomination, for Best Rock Instrumental Performance. He lost to Carlos Santana's album, *Blues For Salvador*.

You Can't Do That on Stage Anymore, Vol. 2 was released October 1. It was taken entirely from a concert given in Helsinki, Finland, on September 22, 1974. Also in October 1988, Barking Pumpkin released an LP version of *Broadway The Hard Way*, an album chronicling the newly written songs from the 1988 tour; the longer CD version came in 1989. (Amazingly, the album was nominated for a Grammy as Best Musical Cast Album, presumably because of its title, which says something about the dire state of Broadway cast albums and even more about the incompetence of the Grammy nominating process.) It was only the beginning of the material Zappa would cull from the 1988 tour.

In the spring of 1989, Poseidon Press published *The Real Frank Zappa Book*, Zappa's autobiography, written with Peter Occhiogrosso. *You Can't Do That on Stage, Vol. 3*, released November 13, 1989, was devoted mainly to the 1984 tour, beginning with its closing show on December 23, when 15-year-old Dweezil Zappa joined his father onstage for the first time, though there are performances on it dating back to 1973.

Zappa took on the unusual role of international business consultant in 1989, beginning when he traveled to Moscow to negotiate licensing of his recordings, and expanding to include other activities. In January 1990, he was back in Moscow representing the Financial News Network (now CNBC), talking about an international business television channel. He stopped off in Czechoslovakia on his way home and met with President Václav Havel, a Zappa fan, and ended up being asked to represent Czech business interests in the U.S., though the American State Department, under Secretary of State James Baker, seems to have been aghast at the prospect. Zappa nevertheless set up a business consulting firm called Why Not?

Though it was not revealed immediately, Zappa's business and other activities were curtailed in the spring of 1990 by the sudden onset of illness. He suffered an intestinal blockage that put him in the hospital, where it was discovered that he had prostate cancer, which had gone undetected for as much as a decade. Now, it was inoperable. The only possible treatment was with radiation. No public announcement was made about Zappa's condition for a year and a half, though rumors began to spread.

As far as the public was concerned, Zappa seemed more interested in non-music business activities in 1990–91 than in his musical career. And there was also politics: In a radio interview on April 15, 1991, Zappa discussed the possibility of his running for president and seemed serious, though such plans faded with the continuance of his illness.

Meanwhile, Zappa fans were reminded of his musical career by a series of record releases in the spring of 1991. In March, Barking Pumpkin released two double CDs culled from the 1988 tour: *The Best Band You Never Heard In Your Life* and *Make A Jazz Noise Here*. The first album contained "big-band arrangements of concert favorites and obscure album cuts, along with deranged versions of cover tunes and a few premiere recordings," wrote Zappa in the liner notes. The selections included "Ring Of Fire," "I Left My Heart in San Francisco," "Purple Haze," "Sunshine of Your Love," "When Irish Eyes Are Smiling," and "Stairway to Heaven" (with the horn section recreating Jimmy Page's original guitar solo), among other covers. *Make A Jazz Noise Here,* on the other hand, emphasized the band's technical prowess, containing such challenging Zappa pieces as "The Black Page" and "King Kong," as well as excerpts of the work of Stravinsky and Bartók. In June 1991, Zappa traveled to Prague, where he appeared with Michael Kocab and his band Prague Select at a concert to celebrate the departure of the last Soviet troops from Czechoslovakia.

Another vintage recording series from an unexpected source was unveiled on July 7, 1991, when Rhino Records' Foo-Eee! label released *Beat The Boots!,* a boxed set of eight Zappa bootleg albums on LP and cassette—*'Tis The Season To Be Jelly, The Ark, Freaks And Other Mother Fu*$@%!, Piquantique, Unmitigated Audacity, Saarbrucken 1978, Anyway The Wind Blows,* and *As An Am*. The albums, which were simply remastered versions of existing bootlegs, otherwise untouched, were also released as separate CDs. Critics noted that the sound quality was surprisingly good.

In the summer, Zappa was contacted by Andreas Molich-Zebhauser, manager of the Ensemble Modern, a German classical group, who wanted to commission him to write some pieces for the group's 1992 Frankfurt Festival. For once, this was not to cost Zappa anything. He agreed, and members of the ensemble flew to Los Angeles to work with him.

A series of tribute concerts under the banner "Zappa's Universe" were planned for November 1991 at the Ritz in New York with Zappa to be present, but when he was unable to travel, his children formally announced that he was suffering from cancer. The concerts went on without him and a video and CD resulted in the fall of 1993, though there was a legal dispute with Zappa about the video.

Rhino issued *Beat The Boots! #2*, containing more remastered Zappa bootlegs on June 16, 1992. This time the boxed version came in CDs, cassettes, and LPs, and the box also contained a scrapbook of Zappa memorabilia and a beret.

Vol. 5 of the *On Stage* series was released on July 10, 1992. Whereas previous volumes of the series had deliberately de-emphasized the '60s era Mothers of Invention, *Vol. 5* presented an entire disc of their work, 1965–69. In his notes, Zappa repeated his line about including '60s material for "the amusement of those collectors who still believe that the only 'good' material was performed by those early line-ups," but he no longer suggested that anybody's mind was going to be changed by the archive series. (All of the second disc was given over to the '82 European tour.)

If you wanted, you could buy both *Volumes 5* and 6 together in a wooden box built to contain all six volumes, but you couldn't buy *Vol. 6* separately until it was released on October 30. The first disc of *Vol. 6* was, Zappa wrote, "a collection of songs dealing generally with the topic of sex (safe and otherwise)."

By the time of the Ensemble Modern's Frankfurt Festival in September 1992, the collection of new and old Zappa compositions to be performed had acquired a name, *The Yellow Shark*, based on a sculpture of a marlin done by Zappa fan Mark Beam that Andreas Molich-Zebhauser had noticed in Zappa's basement. Zappa planned to attend all eight concerts and conduct some of the pieces, but he was able to go only to the first and third shows, before ill health forced him to return home on September 22. The first three shows were recorded for release as an album.

In October, Barking Pumpkin released *Playground Psychotics*, a double CD from the 1971 Flo and Eddie edition of the Mothers that contained Zappa's mix of the performance with John Lennon and Yoko Ono from the Fillmore East.

In February 1993, Zappa organized a "soiree" recording session that featured two Tuvan throat singers (guests of Matt Groening), Johnny "Guitar" Watson, the Chieftains, and L. Shankar. The event was filmed by Nigel Leigh of the BBC and footage was included at the end of a biographical documentary about Zappa shown on the BBC2's *Late Show* in

Great Britain in March 1993 and on the A&E cable network in the U.S. in August 1994.

In April 1993, Barking Pumpkin released *Ahead Of Their Time,* taken from a concert the Mothers of Invention played on October 28, 1968, at the Royal Festival Hall in London with members of the BBC Symphony Orchestra and featuring a theatrical prologue that anticipated *200 Motels.*

In July, Zappa recorded a tribute album to his early hero, *The Rage And The Fury: The Music Of Edgard Varèse.* The recording sessions were filmed for video release. Neither the album nor the video has yet appeared. The final Zappa-related album to be released during his lifetime was the Ensemble Modern's *The Yellow Shark.* It was produced by Zappa, and with this group, it seemed that, near the end of his life, he finally had found a classical music ensemble willing and able to play his music well.

On December 6, 1993, Zappa's family issued a statement that read, "Composer Frank Zappa left for his final tour just before 6:00 PM on Saturday, December 4, 1993, and was buried Sunday, December 5, 1993, during a private ceremony attended by the family. He was with his wife Gail and four children, Moon, Dweezil, Ahmet, and Diva, at home in Los Angeles at the time of his death."

On October 31, 1994, Barking Pumpkin released to mail-order the two-CD *Civilization: Phaze III,* Zappa's first posthumously released recording. Zappa was talking about this album as early as his *Goldmine* interview in October 1988. In the spring of 1992, he told *Guitar Player,* "I finally finished disc one of the *Civilization: Phaze III* album, which is something I've been promising for years and years. Most likely, it's going to be a double CD. But the thing that's unique about the album is, it combines the people inside the piano that were on *Lumpy Gravy* except that on *Lumpy Gravy* there was just this smidgen of what was actually recorded with them. I've had these tapes since 1967 and have extensively edited all this semi-random conversation together into little scenes that form the bridges between the Synclavier pieces that are the bulk of the album. And it's pretty astonishing."

Matt Groening, in a eulogy to Zappa published in *The New Yorker* on December 20, 1993, described one of the tracks from *Civilization: Phaze III,* "N-Light," which he said he had heard the previous spring. He wrote that it was "a 23-minute Synclavier masterpiece . . . a powerhouse of Zappaesque musical ideas, thrown off one after the other in a relentless, complex rush, which sounds at times like several robot orchestras gone berserk, yet always conveys a sense of overall compositional control." The album also contained the tracks "Dio Fa" ("God Lies") and "Beat The Reaper."

In the 1992 *Guitar Player* interview, Zappa also cited a second volume of recordings from *The Yellow Shark* concerts and an album called *The Lost Episodes* ("all the unreleased studio recordings, volume one"), along with *Phaze III*, as the projects that were "on the drawing board." And he noted that he had in the neighborhood of 500 unreleased works stored on the Synclavier.

In its October 29, 1994, issue, *Billboard* under a headline reading, "Ryko Acquires Entire Zappa Catalog," reported that Rykodisc had purchased Frank Zappa's record catalog from Gail Zappa and the Zappa Family Trust. *Billboard* did not report the purchase price, but did note that Rykodisc had had to undergo a $44 million corporate restructuring in order to finance the purchase. The catalog included "several unreleased titles," the article reported, and the first new Zappa releases would appear in 1995. These would include separate releases of albums that had been issued as twofers in the initial Rykodisc CD releases, notably a reissue of *We're Only In It For The Money,* based on a newly discovered two-track master (and thus not using the rerecorded version from the '80s), *The Lost Episodes,* and a compilation album called *Have I Offended Anyone?* whose contents, Gail Zappa said, would be "pretty much what [the title] implies." Classical compositions were not covered under the purchase.

Gail Zappa left no doubt that the sale accorded with Zappa's wishes. "He said, 'I want you out of this business. I want you to relax and have a good time . . .' I very much appreciate that he was so forceful about establishing how he wanted it sold," she told Wheeler.

Rykodisc launched a new reissue campaign in the spring of 1995. "These should be the final, definitive versions of each title," company president Don Rose told *Ice*. All the releases had been remastered yet again under Zappa's supervision before his death. Following the initial six releases, Rykodisc followed with 47 additional releases in May, comprising the entire Zappa catalog from *Freak Out!* to *The Yellow Shark* (with the exception of the *200 Motels* soundtrack). On August 22, having apparently dropped the *Have I Offended Anyone?* compilation idea, Rykodisc released *Strictly Commercial (The Best Of Frank Zappa),* a 19-track "hits" collection including such well-known Zappa tracks as "Valley Girl" and "Don't Eat the Yellow Snow." *The Lost Episodes,* however, stayed in the picture, scheduled for a February 27, 1996, release.

It is much too early to try to assess Zappa's ultimate position in 20th century music. His contemporary position during his life was highly volatile. In the 1960s, he was seen as a part of the rock 'n' roll culture. Even if his lyrics disdained that culture, he clearly was fascinated by it and he used it to market himself. From the early 1970s to the early '80s, he wrote challenging rock-based music with lyrics many critics felt were less satirical than silly, and he earned a dedicated concert audience that appreciated the tone, if not the actual wit, as well as the guitar solos.

In the last decade of his life, he devoted much time to his more "serious" compositions and was taken increasingly seriously by people in classical music. He worked to preserve an archive of his performing years that was as extensive as it was eccentric. And he branched out into other areas—business and politics. He might have been able to achieve a great deal in many different areas if he hadn't become ill at the age of 49 and died at 52.

No doubt he would have written more music. The tragedy of Zappa's relatively early death is that, after a lifetime of making compromises in order to be able to do as much as possible of the work he wanted to do, he finally had arranged things so that he could spend most of his time on his work. At the same time, that work was being increasingly recognized by people other than his teenage rock 'n' roll fans. His death cuts the work short and also, to an extent, interrupts the progress of his reputation. There is always a lull when an artist dies, and his stature must start to be re-established afresh after a few years.

It's hard to say how Zappa will fare among the guardians of culture in academia and arts institutions in the future. One scholarly work, Ben Watson's *Zappa: The Negative Dialectics Of Poodle Play,* was published by St. Martin's Press in the U.S. in January 1995. In the course of nearly 600 pages, Watson attempts to place Zappa within a complicated academic context with references to philosophy, musicology (especially the theories of social philosopher Theodor Adorno), literature, and psychology, among other disciplines. When he sent Zappa a chapter comparing *Apostrophe (')* to *King Lear,* Watson earned an invitation to L.A. just weeks before Zappa's death, though it's not clear from the subsequent article he published in *Mojo* magazine in March 1994 whether Zappa was impressed by his theories or only amused.

Certainly, throughout Zappa's work and throughout his comments about it, there are repeating lyric images and pieces of music placed with a degree of deliberation. As early as 1971, Zappa was asserting the "conceptual continuity" of his work, and when he began to edit a guitar solo from one song onto a rhythm track from another, he referred to it as "xenochronicity." Zappa always possessed a typical American streak of anti-intellectualism—he would talk about being a poor student and insist that he hated to read. But given half a chance in an interview, he was capable of launching into the most esoteric theorizing. (He was, hands down, the smartest musician the author has ever interviewed.)

For example, one aspect of the "conceptual continuity" Zappa claimed for his work was that he clearly approached it with a view toward eviscerating time. He not only crowed to journalists about the unusual and changing time signatures of his songs, but in *You Can't Do That on Stage Anymore,* he leapt at the chance to intercut his recordings from one era with those of another.

"It's all about random sequencing," he said in his *Goldmine* interview.

At the end of his 1992 *Guitar Player* interview, Zappa was asked by Matt Groening to talk about his ideas of time, and he repeated much of what he had written on the subject in *Them Or Us (The Book).* "Well, I think that everything is happening all the time, and the only reason why we think of time linearly is because we are conditioned to do it," he said. "That's because the human idea of stuff is: it has a beginning and it has an end. I don't think that's necessarily true . . . What something is depends more on when it is than anything else. You can't define something accurately until you understand when it is."

Co-interviewer Don Menn asked, "Then what are the limits to our being able to understand what the whole purpose of any of our lives is?"

"Well, why do you have to?" asked Zappa. "I think that *when* is a very important thing, but 'what the fuck' is also a very important thing to ask. Just keep asking, 'What the fuck?' I mean, why the fuck bother? See what I mean? The important thing is, deal with the when. When will open a lot of shit for you. 'What the fuck' really makes it easier to deal with it when you understand the when."

Menn told Zappa he sounded very mystical. "Why?" asked Zappa. "Well," Menn replied, "not just that question so much as the idea that time is a Moebius vortex——" and Zappa interrupted, "No, the shape of the universe is a Moebius vortex. I believe that. Time is a spherical constant. Now imagine a Moebius vortex inside a spherical constant, and you've got my cosmology. But when is very important."

By his own definition, Zappa finally has been freed from the artificial constraints of time, and his work can be considered as a whole rather than in sequence. Nevertheless, how seriously such discussions will be taken in the future remains to be seen. (To use a bit of "conceptual continuity," one can't help recalling Suzy Creamcheese's quoting of Elmer Valentine, the owner of the Whisky A-Go-Go, in *Uncle Meat.* He said, she reported, that Zappa "really had a lot of talent, but he didn't see how anyone could ever make it that insisted on saying 'fuck' onstage.") Ben Watson claims that, if Zappa weren't a rock musician, his work would be as extensively studied as James Joyce's *Finnegans Wake,* and certainly the Zappa fanzines *Society Pages* and *T'Mershi Duween* do sometimes read like arcane doctoral dissertations.

It is just as unclear to what extent Zappa's music may invade the repertoires of symphony orchestras, if at all. Happily, unlike older composers, Zappa's works are available now in his own recordings—a significant part of his life's work is out and can be assessed for what he tried to do.

In describing the concept behind the *You Can't Do That on Stage Anymore* series, Zappa said he was deliberately putting one piece of music, one set of sounds, one key, one time signature, up against another. "I want to find out what happens if you do this," he explained in *Goldmine.* "Sometimes it works, sometimes it doesn't, but at least, if you want to find out what happens if you put this kind of a chord with that kind of note or this kind of a rhythm with that kind of a rhythm, or these kinds of words in a certain kind of a setting, the evidence is there. It's almost like a textbook of odd techniques and things that would be useful for a musician or a composer to learn."

When he was first becoming interested in music, Zappa had read H. A. Clarke's composition textbook *Counterpoint: Strict And Free* far enough to find a warning against using certain note successions. He immediately played those successions, liked them, and discarded the book. For the rest of his life, he continued to try the things people said you couldn't do, and contemporary music and culture is all the richer for it.

● ● ●

The following people made material contributions to the writing of this article over the last 25 years, whether they realize it or not, and the author thanks them: Jane Friedman, David Greenberg, Jim Guercio, Al Kooper, John Mock, Laura Mullen, Jim Nagle, John Richardson, Ed Sutton and, especially, Frank Zappa.

PART TWO

Brown Shoes Don't Make It:

The Early Years

ARE YOU HUNG UP? (1993)

Dave Marsh is a prolific and provocative critic of popular music. He produced the following memoir for the professional newsletter *Rock & Rap Confidential.*

In 1967, I was finishing high school and watching any number of friends split for the Haight-Ashbury scene. I thought about going out there, too, but repeated listenings to Frank Zappa's preachments about the phoniness and ignorance dominating the "scene" convinced me otherwise. I can remember trying to persuade friends heading West that if America was going to experience a youth utopia, it had better be built right there in Detroit. (Well, we *tried.*) If it hadn't been for Zappa's *We're Only In It For the Money,* any of those drugged-out and disillusioned kids portrayed in its songs could have been me—and you could listen to the disasters portrayed on the album and visualize what happened to a lot of my Haight-bound friends.

Almost three decades later, *Money* sounds just as prophetic. Zappa's later satire often wore thin, but maybe that's because he never found his emotions so mixed as when observing all those genuinely idealistic, authentically dumb kids trying to forge *something* positive out of the plastic catastrophic America they'd inherited. Zappa savages the hippies, all right, but he's even more scathing about the parents and authority figures who made their all-but-pointless rebellions essential. Beyond the parodies of doo-wop, "Louie Louie," surf music, and "Hey Joe," the layered music and vocals in "Hey Punk" that anticipate hip-hop, there's a sense in which songs like "Concentration Moon" and "What's the Ugliest Part of Your Body?" stand the optimistic narcissism of the Beatles' *Sgt. Pepper's Lonely Hearts Club Band* on its head. For once in his career, Zappa's futuristic "serious" music not only perfectly complemented rock'n'roll accents, it also found subject matter as visionary and dangerous as the soundscape itself. His portrayal of kids murdered by cops in the park for making too much noise lets no one off the hook—parents, authorities, the "creeps" she was hanging around with, the would-be hippie herself. Just as important, the savage lyric is sung with tremendous compassion: Zappa stands for life, and by that he doesn't mean just breathing and stumbling through the world but living as consciously as you can.

The concentration camp for eccentrics, rebels and those who will not submit to becoming morons even has an appropriately contemporary name: Camp Reagan, the liner notes call it.

DAVID WALLEY
ONLY IN IT FOR THE MONEY (1972)

The first book about Zappa was David Walley's *No Commercial Potential* (1972), its title ironically referring to a thick record executive's mistaken estimate of Zappa's eccentric talent. Walley has since revised his book for subsequent editions; the most recent appeared in 1996. Walley has since published books on Ernie Kovacs and other way-out celebrities.

The days at the Garrick Theater, from late November, 1966 to the fall of 1967, were legendary times for the Mothers of Invention. Greenwich Village was in the thrall of post-Beat expansion. Coffee houses were closing, but the residue of the urban folksters lingered on. The West Village was experiencing the first stirrings of electric blues, acid, and flowerpower. The East Side was always experiencing a rebirth of some kind. On St. Mark's Place, now the DMZ of the hip scene, Andy Warhol's Exploding Plastic Inevitable, a mixed media dance joint, was working out of an old Polish dance hall named the Dom. The East Village was coming into its own, a new crop of suburban dropouts from Queens and Scarsdale mixed with the indigenous artists, hoboes, and Ukrainian immigrants.

A mild psychedelic haze hung over MacDougal Street. A select underground of college students was turning on to an intimate drug scene. Dylan was at his height of audience comprehension with albums like *Blonde on Blonde.* The Beatles had gone psychedelic with *Rubber Soul,* and later *Sgt. Pepper.* The Rolling Stones had just released *Aftermath* and *Between the Buttons,* and the Byrds were openly talking about LSD in "Eight Miles High" and "Younger than Yesterday". . . . And there was The War. New York was getting into the age of acid while the West Coast was into trips festivals, concept art, and the Velvet Underground.

A new generation joined hands tentatively. The movement in San Francisco, the band explosion, and the living experiments in Haight-Ashbury which had been brewing since 1964 were showing signs of going public. On more external levels, a language was being formed using symbols culled from West Coast psychedelia and Bob Dylan records. Strong communications developed between bands and their audiences. A concert was a cross between a celebration and a Be-In. The Jefferson Airplane had just taken off as an electric modal folk quintet. The Grateful Dead were playing trips festivals in San Francisco with Ken Kesey and the gang of Merry Pranksters. Country Joe and the Fish were tearing around Berkeley.

The term "head" was coined to connote special consciousness—a head was someone who had achieved awareness with or without drugs. No two heads looked the same way then—there were no uniforms and no psyche-delicatessens to cater to their needs. They were just there. Elaborate codes of behavior developed around the ritual of marijuana. The *East Village Other* and the *L.A. Free Press* and the San Francisco *Oracle* pooled the centers of energy on the Coasts. A new population, nurtured on Ferlinghetti's "Coney Island of the Mind" and Kerouac's *On the Road,* the children of Ginsberg's "Howl," were developing their own consciousness.

The dealer was a folk hero—the man who came with the good grass, who knew his product and his clientele. The transactions were personal, archetypal: the Man comes in. "Happen to have some stuff here." You smoke, talk about the political scene, something you've read—shoot the shit. Dealers improved their education by taking suggestions from each of their clients about books to read or movies to see—the culture was open-ended and transcontinental, fed by an enormous input of books, magazines, and music, all with its own special language.

It was that simple. Those looking into the scene knew it looked a little strange, but they couldn't decide what laws were being broken. It was 1966: the stirrings were turning into a rumble that would later turn into a generational movement. Time was accelerating.

No one was interested in heroin on the head scene. The basic staple was grass. Acid was for people who really had it together. There was a definite hierarchy in the psychedelic generation: acid on top, grass in the middle, depressants on the bottom. Taking LSD required meditation and reading. Relative time: "Don't say never, just say not right now." Guidance was the answer. Many acid dealers wouldn't sell to people they didn't think capable of handling the experience, and they would guide those whom they did on their first trips. A sense of responsibility marked the early stages of the psychedelic revolution.

Into the developing East Coast consciousness came the Mothers, fresh from the studio with their second album, *Absolutely Free*. This album was filled with images of Americana all reversed. It contained many of Zappa's classics: "Plastic People," about anyone willing to take it all seriously. Another classic, "Brown Shoes Don't Make It," encapsulated the American dream—"TV dinner by the pool, I'm so glad I finished school." Also the oft-requested "Status Back Baby," done with marching band strut and drum majorette whistles—very greasy and very visual.

Many of the songs on the first few Mothers' albums were written as much as four years before they appeared and had been merely rearranged. Zappa's themes key in to the later albums also. *Absolutely Free* was more musically complex than *Freak Out*. Except for the Beatles or the Stones, who weren't doing the same things anyway, no other rock artist could compete. Some of the songs were clearly a direct comment on what Zappa had been experiencing at the time—the rampant social stupidity of the Sunset Strip riots, for instance. From "Plastic People" (spoken): "I hear the sound of marching feet down Sunset Boulevard to Crescent Heights and there at Pandora's Box we are confronted with a vast quantity of plastic people;" (sung) "Paint the day and walk around, watch the Nazis run your town, then go home and check yourself, you think we're singing about someone else but you're plastic people oh baby now you're such a drag." Maybe a little heavy?

The album also saw the return of Suzy Creamcheese. The song entitled "The Return of Suzy Creamcheese" might well have been titled "Suzy Creamcheese Please Come Home"—Pamela was in Europe at the time.

Absolutely Free featured another magnificent two-part production number on Side Two: "America Drinks," and "America Drinks and Goes Home." First time through the number is scatjazz, a densely orchestrated piece with cheap cocktail lyrics: "I don't regret having met up with a girl who breaks hearts like they were nothing at all / I've done it too; now I know just what it feels like. . . ." Etc. The lyrics were incongruous given the musical setting. Second time through, the song is set in a cocktail bar, complete with clinking glasses, loud chatter, a tired cocktail combo, and a vocalist who sounds like he's half in the bag himself and bored to tears with his audience. Zappa explained it all in near pathological detail in a remarkable interview with Frank Kofsky in *Jazz and Pop* of October, 1967. In it one can see the remarkable lengths to which Zappa will go in visualizing his recording concepts.

"America Drinks" is based on the same subconscious formula that all those pukers use. You know II-IV-I chord progressions, modulating all the way around. They modulate normally in regular songs in a circle of fifths. But this changes key and modulates and it gets weird. There is something happening in all those changes. And the melody, if you were to play the melody as a straight thing, it's an interesting tune. But those stupid, stupid words, and in that setting, with the cash registers, and all that—we spent hours putting that together. Herbie was playing the cash register. We rehearsed the crowd noises. The talk track itself which is underplayed there, is funny because they're saying things like, "I got a new Mustang" and like the girls are saying, "Sally will you go with me to the bathroom?" You know that stuff?

You've got the song itself. And the tune which is a parody of all the lyrics. You've got the vocal performance of the lyrics which is a parody of everybody's closing bullshit. . . . You've got the sound of the setting . . . the crowd mumble which was carefully programmed, like choreographed. Then on top of that, which you can't even hear, there's a fight going on. We had the crowd separated in two rooms. In the main studio we had ten people sitting around the microphone, doing these lines on cue, with the cash register over here and the glass on one microphone. Then in the vocal booth off to the side we had Ray [Collins] and Jim [Black] and Roy [Estrada] going through this number. We had Bunk [Gardiner] trying to pick up two girls. You know, "What's a girl like you doing in a place like this?" All that stuff. And then Jim's an Okie wanting to beat up a Mexican, who is Ray. They start drinking beer together and find out . . . the Indian accuses the Mexican of going out with his wife and they punch it out. And meanwhile, the chicks tell this other guy to fuck off because he's coming on too strong, you know, "What kind of girls do you think we are!" And it's all happening in there, but you can't listen to it all. You've got to have it on ten tracks so you can walk around the room and see where it's all coming from.

Those things are so carefully constructed that it breaks my heart when people don't dig into them and see all the levels that I put into them.

The same holds for all Zappa productions. The energy Frank expends on all his albums, concerts, and projects staggers the imagination.

Absolutely Free impacted heavily on the growing freak culture. This Mother *was* serious by the time he got to the Garrick in November 1966.

The Garrick Theater sat on Bleecker Street, across from Village Oldies and down the block from the Village Gate. Downstairs was the Cafe A Go-Go. It was a small, sweaty little place with maybe enough room for 300 seats. At the time the Mothers were taken as a West Coast version of the Fugs, a group of East Village poets and artists who were committed cultural revolutionaries.

Zappa drew crowds with his little revue called *Pigs and Repugnant.* He went so far as to hire a press agent to get publicity for his spiffy combo, but critics were wary. Even before opening night the problems and games started. MGM rush-shipped to the theater about 300 new Mothers' albums of *Absolutely Free* to give the critics at least some idea of what they'd seen. The next day after the opening show, it was discovered that inside the Mothers' album was a recording of the Bill Evans Trio. Reviews ranged from no comment to mixed, but it didn't matter. The Mothers were a success. They more or less camped at the Garrick for six months, doing two shows a night, six nights a week. They did everything. "We performed a couple of marriages on stage. We pulled people out of the audience and made them make speeches. One time we brought thirty people up on stage and some of them took our instruments and the rest of them sang 'Louie, Louie' as we left."

What kind of a show was this anyway?

There were more Mothers now. Bunk Gardiner had joined the group for the recording of *Absolutely Free.* He played a variety of instruments including bass clarinet, soprano, alto, and tenor saxophones, flute, bassoon, and piano. He had distinguished gray hair and a manicured beard. Don Preston had joined in the summer of 1966. Since he was five years old, he'd been playing piano as well as bass; he now specialized in electronic effects and occasional transformations on cue into a monster figure. Jim Sherwood, alias Motorhead, former road manager and Frank's high school buddy, played baritone sax and tambourine. He could talk about cars for hours and possessed a certain amount of teen appeal. Billy Mundi, looking like a stylized Noh villain, was added as another drummer. It was some crew. Zappa sometimes performed in ruffled shirt, purple and white high school sweater, purple pipestem pants, and orange construction shoes. He was dressed to the height of absurdity.

No one really knew what was going to happen at the Garrick. Each show had its incidents—like the one with the Marines. One afternoon, when the Mothers were rehearsing, three Marines in full dress uniforms walked in. About a week before, a Marine had been killed in the Village, and there were rumors that every Marine within striking distance was aching for revenge. Frank was a little miffed at the time but politely invited them to sit down. After the rehearsal the Marines said, "We just bought your album and we really like it." Frank said, "Well, I'm glad you do. Hey listen, how would you guys like to work with us tonight?" Frank asked them whether they could sing; they said they knew "Everybody Must Get Stoned" and "House of the Rising Sun." They adjourned across the street, and while Frank and the band ate, the Marines rehearsed their big number. When they came back after dinner, fully rehearsed, Frank said, "Now look, there's one little thing I want you to do. When I give you the signal, I want all three of you guys to lunge for the microphone and start screaming 'Kill!'"

During the performance the Mothers played some dissonant jazz reminiscent of Archie Shepp. The Marines lunged forward on cue screaming "Kill!" The audience couldn't believe it. When it was all over they clapped. Then Frank said, "Thank you." Ray Collins said, "Thank you." When it got to the Marines, the first one said, "Eat the apple, fuck the Corps." The audience couldn't believe it. The second one said the same. More confusion. The third Marine capped it all with: "Hey, you know I feel the same way as my other buddies: Eat the apple, fuck the Corps, some of us love our Mothers more!" And that was only the first show.

Frank was astonished. "Don't you guys realize you could get court-martialed for that?" The Marines said they didn't care—the Corps could only court-martial them once anyway. Frank had another brainstorm—he told his wife Gail to run home and get a doll they'd been given as a present. Frank opened the second show with, "Hey ladies an' gennelmen, the guys are, uh, going to sing 'Everybody Must Get Stoned'." The Marines did as they were bid, then Frank said, "Now we're gonna have basic training. Uh, ladies an' gennelmen, this is a gook baby; and the Marines are going to mutilate it before your very eyes. Kill it!" Frank tossed out the big, plastic doll. The Marines ripped it apart, pulled its arms off, tore it to shreds. After they were done, with music and lights low, Frank held up the mangled doll by its hair and pointed out to the audience all the damaged parts as if it were alive. Frank reminisces: "There was one guy in the front row, a Negro cat just back from Vietnam, who was crying. It was awful; and I ended the show there."

When nights were slow other things could happen. From a wire system rigged up in the back of the theater the lighting man would send down an assortment of materials to the stage—first maybe a spread-eagled doll, then a salami. Sometimes the lighting guy would send down eggs and it would get messy. The biggest attraction of the show was the soft giraffe—the boys in the band had constructed a huge, stuffed giraffe with a hose running up to a spot behind the rear legs. Ray Collins ("an archetypal acid burn-out victim," says Frank) would climb up to the giraffe and massage it with a frog hand puppet. The giraffe's tail would stiffen and flop! the first three rows of the audience would get sprayed with whipped cream. All these little deals, accompanied by the appropriate music, were called atrocities. The audience loved it. "Music is always a commentary on society, and certainly the atrocities on stage are quite mild compared to those conducted in our behalf by our government," said Frank at the time.

Pigs and Repugnant was geared to vibrations and accidents—Zappa capitalized on coincidence and people's own weird trips. On occasion he could make people cry on cue, just by talking to them. He used certain items, noises, and songs as building blocks, arranging them differently to suit his own fancy or to suit the vibrations he was getting from his audience. It was all very scientific and funny. After a while he was playing to the same audience of weirdos. The people who showed up were the real show.

Frank had other schemes up his sleeve as well. While performing at the Garrick, he secured a contract with Merson/Unicord, makers of Panther organs and Haegstrom guitars. He was supposed to endorse their equipment, as well as design other equipment, in exchange for use. He even designed a few ads for them like the exciting "Long and Slippery" Haegstrom ad that ran in some teenage magazines. His ad for Panther organs was never run. It was a high contrast picture of Frank seated at the organ with the blurb, "This is the best fucking organ I ever played." Though the ad never got past the company, Frank did secure what he needed in the way of PA's, amplifiers, and column speakers.

After playing from Thanksgiving, 1966 through New Year's, 1967, the Mothers packed up their gear for two weeks in Montreal—then back to Los Angeles where it was warm. But the club scene in L. A. was taking a beating, and since Jimmy Carl Black, the Indian of the group, had five children to feed, they reluctantly moved back to New York to work Easter weekend. The management erroneously assumed that the Mothers could keep the gross up so they were booked through the summer. Although the band grossed over $103,000, the overhead was high—$15,000 a month with rent and electricity. It worked out to something like $200 a month for each of them, which wasn't much.

In addition to the work at the Garrick, Frank Zappa produced four albums of merit in the New York period: *Lumpy Gravy, We're Only In It for the Money, Uncle Meat* (the soundtrack for a movie which was never released), and *Cruising with Ruben and the Jets*—a spiffy parody of Fifties rhythm and blues tunes. They are all long stories.

Lumpy Gravy was originally commissioned by Capitol Records— though Capitol had no business contracting Zappa on any level. Still, Frank signed on as composer and arranger for the album, now an underground classic brought out by MGM. The record featured a studio orchestra called the Abnuceals Emuukha Electric Symphony Orchestra and Chorus. The front cover shows Zappa wearing a red jersey with the word "Pipco" on it—no one to this day knows what that means. On the back is a similar picture of Frank dressed in black magician's garb with a top hat and a cane. A little talk bubble near his mouth reads: "Is this phase 2 of *We're Only in it for the Money?*" Zappa's records were now being recorded in conceptual pairs. A talk bubble on *We're Only in it for the Money* reads: "Is this phase one of Lumpy Gravy?" Snatches of music from both coincide; on *Money* one hears one of the studio musicians grumbling, "Do we have to go through this again?" It seemed very funny at the time.

Lumpy Gravy was a monument to John Cage, coincidence, and audio found objects. It was also a monument to the engineers who put it together from the mess of tapes it once was. It was amazing that it came out at all considering the condition of those tapes once Zappa got them back from Capitol. MGM had finally bought back the tapes from Capitol whose business dealings with Zappa remain murky indeed. It was discovered that Capitol engineers had their own way of editing and splicing: one day's guitar track would be next day's percussion track. They had no standardized way of making splices; there were even holes in the tape. The job of putting them all together was monstrous, especially for a qualified engineer.

It was tougher for someone who didn't like Frank's music. Gary Kellgren was the man behind Zappa during this project, which was recorded at Mayfair Studios in New York. He was the one who was made to do all. Now he will admit that it was an experience.

Mayfair Studios were the best in New York, and Kellgren was king of the advanced eight-track board. He had just been working with Jimi Hendrix—Zappa was far the other side of Jimi. The whole production became even more interesting when Frank never told anyone which tracks were which. Gary had to familiarize himself with every note and every bar. They just about pasted the whole composition together bar by bar. "It made me the best," says Gary in retrospect. He may be right. Anyway, he now runs the Record Plant recording studio in Los Angeles and lives across the street from Herb Cohen in Hollywood.

Gary had a great opportunity to watch Zappa work. He thought Frank a considerate boss, but too much of an android, a machine. It was some match: Kellgren the psychedelic magician, and Zappa the straight arrow, Kellgren the sensualist and Zappa the ascetic—locked together for six months in a musty editing room. Gary still likes Frank, though he cordially hates his music. He said Frank ranks with Colonel Parker—Presley's manager—as a great exploiter. But then he also characterized him as the archetypal anarchist. Gary, through his close association with Frank, appropriated for himself some Zappaisms like "greed's the key." Gary also engineered some of the *Money* album; one can hear him on the opening cut threatening to erase all Zappa's master tape copies and adding, "I know he's sitting in there in the control room listening to everything I say but I sincerely don't care . . . hello, Frank Zappa."

Lumpy Gravy was a difficult album to make. There were many accidental splices on the tapes. "You'd be listening to a piece of tape and a bleep would go by and Frank would say 'let's edit that out.'" The record is not that flawed. *Lumpy Gravy* was by far the most ambitious project Zappa had worked on to date—he had worked with a pick-up twenty-seven-piece orchestra back in 1963 for an avant-garde music concert at St. Mary's College, but this was different. For this production he utilized the skills of no less than fifty-one musicians and a chorus made up of friends. It was a mixed media presentation. Zappa intercut spoken sections with musical quotes from Varèse, Stravinsky, some surf music—"a little nostalgia for the old folks"—and schlock symphonic treatments of old Zappa themes. The dialogue sections were especially interesting because they came out totally by accident. While recording one afternoon, Frank got bored and decided it would be fun to put microphones under a piano and have people talk randomly about whatever came into their heads—then Frank would cue them. He liked it so much that he spent three entire days working with different people, giving them subjects from "Everything in the universe is made out of one element which is a note" to "I hear you've been having trouble with the pigs and ponies" to "I'm advocating dark clothes." This last case ended with a surrealistic little dialogue between two male voices:

voice 1: How do you get your water so dark?

voice 2: 'Cause I'm paranoid, I'm very paranoid, and the water in my washing machine turns dark out of sympathy.

voice 1: Out of sympathy? Um, where can I get that?

voice 2: At your local drugstore.

voice 1: How much?

voice 2: It's from Kansas.

Lumpy Gravy also introduced Zappa's theory of the big note. He maintains that everything in the universe is made from one element which is a note—atoms are really vibrations and all part of the big note. Frank is working on the theory even now, using his ARP synthesizer as audio test equipment. Another theory of his holds that any one time, like any one wave, is equal to any other time. Music marks time too, and he has said that all his music is actually one piece of music. *Lumpy Gravy* was a quote using time and those vibrations. It was probably the most far-reaching of all Zappa's published works to date. Some people are waiting for him to continue in that vein. He does not seem interested quite yet.

Lumpy Gravy served as a cross reference to *We're Only In It for the Money.* Zappa the social critic again leaped into the generational breach. By 1967, psychedelia had blossomed full-blown upon an unsuspecting public. After the Easter Be-In in New York, came the Summer of Love. Everyone was going to San Francisco with flowers in their hair. Everyone was a hippie, even those with just long hair and a headband. *Money* was written in the spirit of that nascent commercialism. It had to come. "This entire monstrosity was conceived and executed by Frank Zappa as a result of some unpleasant premonitions August through October 1967." The cover of *Money* was a masterful parody of the Beatles' *Sgt. Pepper,* only reversed: on the outside individual Mothers in drag; inside, a distorted replica of the Sgt. Pepper Band picture. But instead of nice clean Beatles in Edwardian-cut uniforms there were the Mothers, with their name spelled out in carrots and watermelons, posing in front of notables like Harry Truman, Lyndon Johnson, Lee Harvey Oswald, Charles Lindberg, Rasputin, and other lesser luminaries.

The Beatles themselves weren't too pleased. When the album was finished, about the same time the Beatles had released theirs, Frank called Paul McCartney to ask permission for his parody cover. Paul said that's what business managers are for, and Frank said something like—that's what artists are for, to tell the business managers what to do. However Capitol objected, which is why the album arrived in the record stores late in 1967 with covers reversed. Frank maintains that it's not when a record is released that matters, but when it was recorded. Once done it's a fact. However, the Beatles controversy remains.

Money had an interesting impact. While everyone else was being self-congratulatory on finding a new nation-wide lifestyle with its own commercial conduits, and everyone was either in San Francisco, falling out in the East Village, or being spaced in L. A., Zappa was policing the scene with some direct head-to-head commentary. This during the Summer of Love?

Money contained the most biting satire—it was vicious and merciless. On one track one hears quite audibly, "Flower Power sucks." It not only castigated the phony freaks, but lambasted their parents for not understanding what was happening. No one was immune from this attack which lashed out to puncture the neat paisley bubble that was turning out to be a very lucrative business. Some of the songs were truly funny in a horrible sort of way. "Concentration Moon," for instance, provided a logical answer to the hippie problem—have the government lock them all up but grant them the freedom to carry out their own fantasies. It is a wistful look back from inside.

The music on the record ran the gamut from camped-up, psychedelic rock to Broadway show tunes to abstract impressionism. *Money* had no separations between songs: one had to listen to one huge block of time if the impact of the lyrics and the music and the third dimensional pictures were to have any effect. It was difficult to cue the record for radio station play—and there were all these dirty words which no one but Frank Zappa would deign to use. MGM retaliated by censoring *Money* when it was pressed again. For instance, they took out a word uttered by The Cheese and so changed the whole concept of a sentence. It went from "I'm not going to do any more publicity balling for you," to "I'm not going to do any more publicity for you." MGM didn't even tell Zappa what they had done. Soon MGM would have to go.

During this entire period, musicians were recognizing Zappa as a communications guru. He was deluged with offers to be a producer. The Jefferson Airplane wanted him to work with their third album, *After Bathing at Baxters,* but he was otherwise employed. He worked with Eric

Burdon and the Animals and helped produce a group called Auto-salvage. In spite of his wide and obvious influence on fellow musicians, he would get a little miffed when a "name" group adapted some of his musical characteristics. But on the whole, he was immensely pleased with what he was accomplishing personally and what he could see happening. "If they use that album [*Freak Out*] as Point Zero, that's dynamite, man. If every group in the industry would do that . . . the whole complexion of the music world would change in a hurry, and it would be gratifying to hear that weirdness coming from people other than us," he said in the middle of 1967.

By the latter part of 1967, success seemed imminent. Zappa was in the forefront of the musical explosion, though he was not getting that much media exposure because radio stations refused to play his music over the air. At this time the Garrick closed. He took a brief respite and toured Europe. During June, Pamela Zarubica had returned from Europe. Frank had married Gail in the meantime. Gail was expecting, and at first Frank wanted Pam to stay with Gail to help her take care of the baby that was soon to be born. "Frank called me and said that there was a great desire to see Suzy Creamcheese because the people in Europe couldn't imagine what kind of a chick to associate with the picture they had seen of these guys," she recalls. "He said, 'I'm going to Europe and they want Suzy Creamcheese, you come and stay with Gail,' and I said, 'Come and stay with Gail? I am Suzy Creamcheese and I'm going with you because if you take some asshole who doesn't know how to talk to the press [on the Mothers first promotional tour for *Freak Out,* Frank used another girl called Suzy Creamcheese who talked to promotional men at MGM throughout the country] that doesn't know how to talk to people, you're never going to talk to anybody, period.'"

Pretty strong words, but then The Cheese is strong. It was that simple. Pamela became THE CHEESE for Frank, his mouthpiece and screen. The tour covered England and the Scandinavian countries. Frank was violently sick on the road from tension and the food, and at one point he had to be carried offstage. Quoth The Cheese: "In Stockholm [they said] we're so sick of being neutral. America's obviously going to be first and he's got the answers, and if he doesn't want to give them out that's one thing, but if he would, we're behind you. So I said [to Zappa], 'These people want answers, give them to them,' and he said, 'I'm not here to give the answers.' He was scared. I knew him when he wasn't afraid. I knew him before he ever admitted a possibility of failure of what he really wants to do."

What Frank Zappa wanted to do was anyone's guess at the time; he wasn't talking, but what he did do in the next few years added another level. He was now dealing from a position of strength.

ROBERT LEVIN
ZAPPA INTERVIEWED (1969)

In part because he had the courage to be unashamedly provocative, Zappa was a favorite interview subject for both underground newspapers and record-based throwaways. The following interview appeared in 1969 in one of the latter, *Go Magazine*, that was published in New York City.

"The values of the people who consume music are so perverted and corrupted by ad men and that sort of crap," Frank Zappa said over the phone from Los Angeles, *"that they have no real criteria for what is good or real. The Mothers didn't sound like the stuff they heard on the radio so we weren't accepted as music."*

Zappa had taken time out from a heavy recording schedule to respond to questions about the recent disbandment of the Mothers of Invention. Reports which lay the blame for the group's demise on Zappa's private ambitions and which suggested the possibility of a law suit against Zappa by the other members of the unit, have apparently caused him no small vexation. Such stories, he asserts, are grossly untrue and typify, in their "idiocy and inaccuracy" the very circumstances which made it impossible for the group to continue.

"Our records sold well, but to the limited audiences that already liked us. We couldn't reach the people who needed to hear us. Radio stations wouldn't play us—even 'underground' stations which just play as many blues records as they can. Our stuff, without being listened to, was categorically thrown into the garbage can by radio station programmers. There was no alternative but for us to separately get into other things. I think the members of the group had talent that would have been very difficult to maximize in the Mothers where their talents were ignored by the public. One good thing is that they will now be able to bring what they learned with the Mothers—the skills they learned with the Mothers—to other groups and situations and help spread the word around a little bit.

"The problems," Zappa continued, expanding into the scene in general, "are ignorance, the church, greed, and complete misunderstanding of the word love. True, people are tearing this and that convention down, but they're not proposing valid alternatives. I would like to see changes that are better than what we have now, but I've seen no evidence of them.

"The majority of Americans still like to drink beer and watch baseball games on TV with their stomachs hanging out, or watch a good fight and see somebody win. People don't believe that peace is really good. At best if they want peace it's because it's fashionable. Even businessmen are making the peace sign now—and buying bush jackets. And the peace sign is something that a kid who feels alone and out of things can pick up easily and use just to be in. Most of the kids who are sticking up two fingers now were sticking up one finger not too long ago."

Didn't he see any genuine revolutionary energies and possibilities coming out of rock?

"The rock scene is absurd. I hate love songs—they gag me. It's very difficult for me to accept the love song as the ultimate art form. And a lot of these soul groups who talk about how much soul they have—like they're out there sweating—and looking at their watches.

"Yes, revolutionary things ARE happening in rock, but MOST of what passes as revolutionary is bullshit—tawdry stuff, the notion of an ad man. The Mothers were revolutionary. Captain Beefheart and his Magic Band—a lot of people aren't going to like this—is the only group I've seen that really makes it in terms of originality, devotion and intense feeling for what they're into. Most other rock groups belong to the entertainment syndrome.

"The blues thing in white rock is ridiculous and embarrassing. It's embarrassing to hear most white rock singers singing the blues. It's embarrassing that THEY aren't embarrassed. White blues players are deluding themselves—a Brooklyn accent singing 'Baaaby!' Agh! B. B. King plays and then he invites all these white musicians in the audience on up to the stage and they play all his licks and he pats them on the head. White players using Negroid mannerisms on the guitar is the same as the Japanese synthesizing miniature TV sets."

Zappa, although he admits to bitterness and exasperation about the failure of the Mothers to survive, has not retreated into brooding seclusion, but gone straight ahead with his work. The Jean Luc Ponty album, for which he has written all of the music and which will include numbers from the Mothers' repertoire as well as some "classically"-oriented pieces, is a project with which he is intensely involved at present. A number of good jazz musicians are participating in the sessions and Zappa is conducting them with, apparently, great pleasure.

"I'm getting a chance to work with other musicians and to bring some of the ideas and devices I developed with the Mothers to other musicians. I'm conducting the way I conducted the Mothers—using hand signals . . . and a lot of the musicians are very excited about the approach.

"But listen to this. I heard the other day that some bullshit girl singer is getting a hundred thousand dollars for an album! We're having five sessions for the Ponty album and with all the musicians who are on it we've got a budget of eight thousand dollars. Right? It's ignorance. The public is not ready to listen to long instrumental things. They can't hear them. They hear certain aspects of the guitar . . . fuzztones . . . but they can't hear plot or thematic development in a guitar solo. Drum solos they've always been able to hear—especially if they're loud and if you don't break meter. It's a problem of education. Education has to start in school. Radio stations have to do it."

Zappa is also preparing for a concert at Albert Hall in London in late April. The concert will encompass a broad representation of his music and include compositions from all the various forms—rock to ballet music—in which he writes.

Still another project is a television show.

"It will be shot in the basement of my house—so many weird things go on in my basement. People—friends, musicians—will simply do what they want to do. We're going to do it as a syndicated thing, not a network thing, so that we can have complete control over it. Someone has already agreed to shoot the pilot."

Zappa has been an important, if largely unacknowledged, force in contemporary popular music. The influence of his Mothers of Invention upon other groups (including the Beatles and the Stones) has been pervasive and profound and, with some dozen albums still in the can, the Mothers' influence should continue to be felt for some time.

Zappa on his own . . . well, there is no telling what a talent of the size and range which he commands might achieve. Certainly his future work will have wit, energy and weight. No less could be expected from him.

The Mothers of Invention, infamous & repulsive rocking teen combo, is not doing concerts any more. Jimmy Carl Black (the Indian of the group) has formed another ensemble which he calls Geronimo Black (named after his youngest child). Don (Dom De Wild) Preston is collaborating with avant-garde dancer Meredith Monk in performances of electronic music. Ian Robertson Underwood is preparing material for a solo album. Roy Estrada, Bunk Gardner, Buzz Gardner & Art Tripp are doing studio work in Hollywood. Motorhead (James Euclid) Sherwood is working on his bike & preparing for a featured role in a film with Captain Beefheart. Frank Zappa is producing various artists for his record companies, Bizarre and Straight (which he co-owns with Herb Cohen), working on film & television projects & is currently writing arrangements for a new album by French jazz violinist Jean Luc Ponty. This Ponty album, to be released on World Pacific, will mark the first attempt by any other artist to record a whole album's worth of Zappa's writing, exclusive of the Mothers of Invention interpretations.

It is possible that, at a later date, when audiences have properly assimilated the recorded work of the group, a re-formation might take place. The following is a brief summary of The Mothers' first five years of musical experimentation & development:

In 1965 a group was formed called The Mothers. In 1966 they made a record which began a musical revolution. The Mothers invented Underground Music. They also invented the double-fold rock album & the concept of making a rock album a total piece of music. The Mothers showed the way to dozens of other groups (including the Beatles & Stones) with their researches & experimentation in a wide range of musical styles & mediums.

The Mothers set new standards for performance. In terms of pure musicianship, theatrical presentation, formal concept & sheer absurdity, this one ugly band demonstrated to the music industry that it was indeed possible to make the performance of electric music a valid artistic expression.

In 1967 (April through August), the Garrick Theater on Bleecker Street in New York was devastated by cherry bombs, mouldering vegetables, whipped cream, stuffed giraffes & depraved plastic frogs . . . the whole range of expressive Americana . . . all of it neatly organized into what people today would probably call a "Love-Rock-Long-Hair-Tribal Musical." The Mothers called it "Pigs & Repugnant: Absolutely Free" (an off off-Broadway musical) . . . it was in its third month when "Hair" first opened.

The Mothers was the first big electric band. They pioneered the use of amplified and/or electronically modified woodwind instruments. . . . everything from piccolo to bassoon. They were the first to use the wah-wah pedal on guitar as well as horns and electric keyboard instruments. They laid some of the theoretical groundwork which influenced the design of many commercially manufactured electro-musical devices.

The Mothers managed to perform in alien time signatures & bizarre harmonic climates with a subtle ease that led many to believe it was all happening in 4/4 with a teen-age back beat. Through their use of procedures normally associated with contemporary "serious music" (unusual percussion techniques, electronic music, the use of sound in blocks & strands & sheets vapors), The Mothers were able to direct the attention of a large number of young people to the work of many contemporary composers.

In 1968, Ruben Sano lifted his immense white-gloved hand, made the fingers go "snat!" and instantly Neo-Greaser Rock was born. A single was released from Ruben's boss & tough album (remember "Cruisin' With Ruben & The Jets"?) called "Deseri." It was played on many AM stations (actually rising to 39 on the Top Forty at KIOA in Des Moines, Iowa) until programmers discovered Ruben & The Jets was really The Mothers under a disguise.

Meanwhile, the so-called Underground FM stations could boast (because they were so cool and far out) that they actually went so far as to play The Mothers of Invention albums on their stations. Yes. Boldly they'd whip a few cuts from "Freak Out" on their listeners between the steady stream of important blues numbers.

And then of course, there was "Uncle Meat," recorded back with "Ruben & The Jets" (a somewhat unusual production procedure). In spite of the musical merit of the album, the only thing that drew any attention was the fact that several words, in common usage, were included in candid dialogue sections.

Awaiting release is a collection of 12 complete albums of Mothers' music; a retrospective exhibition of the group's most interesting work, covering a span from two years prior to the actual formation of the ensemble through August 1969. Included in the collection is documentary material from first rehearsals, tracing the development of the group through to its most recent live performances in the U.S. and Europe, some of which have become almost legendary. To those people who cared at all about The Mothers' musical explorations (and also those who didn't care & who wish to be merely entertained), this collection will prove of great interest.

MILES

FRANK ZAPPA (1994)

Miles is a British biographer whose specialty is counterculture celebrities. He has produced books about Allen Ginsberg and

William Burroughs, in addition to Visual Documentaries about Frank Zappa, the Rolling Stones, and Pink Floyd.

I first met Frank Zappa in July 1967, outside the Garrick Theater at 152 Bleecker Street in Greenwich Village. He was standing on the sidewalk, turning in slow circles, barking the show and signing autographs for teenyboppers most of whom had no idea who he was. He was wearing floral patterned pants, so tight you could see he wasn't Jewish. I was introduced by Ken Weaver, the drummer with the Fugs, and his friend Pigpen from the Dead, whose first album had just been released. Ken and Pigpen, both in Hells Angels leathers and sweating profusely in the New York heat, tried to gross-out Frank by French kissing each other with a lot of tongue action and hog calling but he was un-moved. After all, gross-out was elevated to an art form in the Mothers.

I was the co-founder of *International Times,* known as *IT,* Britain's first underground newspaper and had read all about Frank's Freak Scene in Hollywood from the irregular newsletter that he ran for Mothers fans in the Los Angeles underground paper, the *Los Angeles Free Press.* He was very interested in hearing about the underground scene in Britain and invited us all to the show.

The set was dramatic for its day: the stage in complete darkness except for the little red lights on the amplifiers. Then a drum roll made itself heard above the noise of the audience and as it grew, Zappa was silhouetted, back lit against the stage curtain standing beside a large gong. I thought he might bang it, like the man in the J. Arthur Rank movies, but not so. The Mothers were less organized than they would become in later years, but many of the famous hand-signals were in use and worked very effectively. The group would get into an extended rock out, apparently totally improvised, when Frank would give an imperceptible hand signal and the music would change completely from, say 4/4 to 7/8. During the set, the members of the group performed ritual acts with vegetables: Don Preston lay down and celery, peppers and assorted fruit and veg were arranged artistically on his body. A groupie allowed herself to be dragged on stage and groped—the Mothers would not qualify as a PC group. Some of the vegetables were thrown at the audience, and while not being felt up, the girl swept up the squashed vegetation with a broom or played a tambourine. The Mothers did all their old favourites including "Brown Shoes Don't Make It" and, of course, "Call Any Vegetable." I was impressed. No one in England had such a theatrical stage act, not even Arthur Brown.

In September 1967, Frank came to Britain to play the Royal Albert

Hall [on the 23rd]. In those days the music press still ran the "it has a good beat and you can dance to it" type of review and since Frank, sensibly, didn't trust Fleet Street, he used *IT,* his local underground newspaper, as his main advertising vehicle, just as he used the *Los Angeles Free Press* back home. MGM Records had refused to include the lyrics to *We're Only In It For The Money* with the album on the grounds that they were obscene so *IT* published them, with additional comments by Frank. To illustrate the article, *IT* took the infamous picture of him sitting on the toilet which was made into a poster by Danny Halperin at Osiris Visions posters and then bootlegged all over the world, dogging poor Frank everywhere he went for a decade.

Frank wanted to meet the Beatles to get their permission to parody the *Sgt Pepper* sleeve on *We're Only In It For The Money.* I had been seeing a lot of Paul McCartney who was involved with *IT* and got him on the telephone so that Frank could talk to him and perhaps arrange to meet. But there was a communication gap between them. Back then the cultural differences between Liverpool and Los Angeles were so great that they talked entirely at *cross-purposes.* Paul was puzzled; he knew the Mothers' records very well and had been expecting someone very hip and amusing, the kind of person he could have over for a smoke and a chat. Instead Paul told me that Frank sounded like an American businessman, "He kept talking about 'product'," he said. Paul gave him his blessing anyway and telephoned Brian Epstein's office to ask if they would clear the way for Frank to do it, but obviously Frank encountered an EMI lawyer somewhere along the line. EMI, not the Beatles, owned and paid for the sleeve.

Frank was also puzzled, he told me, "But he's a Beatle! He can do anything! All he has to do is tell EMI he's said it's okay." This was probably true in the USA. To the rest of the world the Beatles were Gods and any record company exec would kowtow and perform unspeakable acts just to gain favor; but the Beatles were on EMI and EMI in those days was like the BBC, with men in white coats carrying clipboards and tea ladies pushing huge trollies around. The Beatles were just a nice little earner on one of their more obscure pop labels. Frank later told a journalist, "Paul McCartney was disturbed that I could refer to what we do as a product but I'm dealing with businessmen who care nothing about music, or art, or me personally. They want to make money and I relate to them on that level or they'd regard me as just another rock 'n' roll fool."

Frank went ahead and used Cal Schenkel's parody cover anyway but reversed the sleeve so the famous crowd scene was on the inside centre fold. He included the *International Times* IT-Girl logo among the crowd on his cover as a reference to his visit.

When I arrived in Los Angeles in 1969, Frank and Gail offered to put me up. They had not long moved to the large wooden house off Laurel Canyon Blvd, high in the Santa Monica Mountains overlooking Hollywood where Frank was to live for the rest of his life. The house was set back, cut into the hillside above the winding road. In a driveway shaded by trees was an old white English Jaguar he bought off Captain Beefheart. All the seats had stuffing sticking out where they been slashed by the LA police in an unsuccessful search for drugs—the LAPD never paid for the damage and it was never fixed. Next to it stood Gail's gleaming red Buick Riviera (the type referred to as a "soft car" by the GTOs) and a business-like panel truck for the Mothers' equipment.

Because the house was built into the hillside, the front ground floor was the back basement. The front windows were shuttered and the only indication that it was not a normal middle class Hollywood household was the double door on the ground floor which enabled bulky studio equipment to be brought in and out.

I had never seen a full-scale American dream kitchen before, though probably not exceptional by Hollywood standards—with surfaces littered with blenders, mixers, extractors and choppers, an eye level oven, a triple width fridge, deep freeze, twin sinks with garbage disposal units, and an ice water dispenser with its own little paper dixie cups. Such things did not exist in Britain in the sixties and are pretty rare even now. For some reason I had expected Frank to eschew all this side of American consumerism; but, after all, this was a court and there were lots of people to feed.

All around the walls and over the kitchen units hung Frank's ever growing collection of hotel keys. The walls were covered with weird photographs and drawings, many of them sent by fans to United Mutations, the nearest thing that the Mothers had to a fan club. There were Polaroids, clippings, and trivia including citations from the City of Los Angeles for putting his garbage out on the street TOO EARLY.

The kitchen was Gail's domain where everyone hung out. She kept control of the calendar of appointments and constantly checked with Frank on the phone, telling him who was there and what was happening. She never seemed to sleep. The kitchen served as an ante room to the presence. Everything was focused on Frank and his work and designed to make sure he could function smoothly and efficiently: food appeared when he wanted it, even at 4 am, roadies and business people were ushered in and out, and his appointments kept track of. Since Frank rarely went out, he encouraged people to come to him. He liked lots of people around the house in case he wanted to emerge from the basement and be sociable. "There are a steady stream of interesting people walking through the door—all I have to do is sit here, man," Frank told me. He tended to work until about 9 am, sleep through the day and make an appearance around 6 pm. His children kept virtually opposite hours and Gail made sure they did not disturb their father. Her strength and her dedication to Frank and his work was not something I noticed particularly at the time; but looking back, it was a wonderful thing and sustained a potentially difficult rock 'n' roll marriage for more than 25 years.

On the door leading to the basement was a small black card on which was written, in white, "DR ZURKON'S SECRET LAB IN HAPPY VALLEY." The room was huge, with very deep pile baby blue carpet, like walking through long grass. The intense California sunlight was completely excluded by shuttered windows covered by soundproof patterned screens. Two huge speakers, hissing quietly, stood five feet high either side of a large assemblage by Cal Schenkel made from plastic, wood and an auto hood which surrounded the hatch through which films were projected from an ante-room. The carpet was littered with instrument cases, an electric organ, an antique wheelchair and more assemblage material. Paintings, concert posters and a framed broken plaster plaque proclaiming "Zappa's Grubby Chamber" in large white paint on a green backing, covered the walls. Some areas of the room were very dark, particularly where people sat; I could not see to read while sitting on the settee. It had the usual recording studio feel of time shut out.

Crouched over the Scully 280 2-track tape machine, which was the center of Frank's life, like a black rook peering with large surprisingly gentle liquid brown eyes, sat Frank, staring hard at his little chalk editing marks as if the notes would suddenly emerge as actual musical notation on the smooth brown tape. The Scully was the same model as those he used at Apostolic Studios in Greenwich Village where he recorded parts of *Lumpy Gravy*, *We're Only In It For The Money*, *Cruising With Ruben & The Jets* and *Uncle Meat*. He was surrounded by piles of tapes on 10" NAB spools, tape boxes, leads, guitars, and more tapes: tapes of concerts. He grabbed one, "Here's one which has a crazed groupie from Miami." It was very similar to the tape which got Zappa jailed back in Cucamonga, except this time it wasn't faked. One huge pile of boxes contained test mixes, "Like to hear 'Absolutely Free' without the vocal overdubs?" Others were tapes of conversations and oddments, waiting for their day to come in the massive Zappa re-issue programme which he had planned even then.

A row of cupboards housed Frank's collection of 7,000 45s, mostly doowop and R&B. He was very sociable and played some: "Valerie" by The Starlites on Lana, The Gladiolas' "Little Darlin'" on Excello, The Spaniels' "Goodnight Sweetheart" on Vee Jay and even The Crystals' "Da Doo Ron Ron" on Philles. "I'm getting ready to put out an 'Oldie But Goodie' type album," he told me. "I've made a list of the songs I want to include on it and they're all obscure, but they're the weirdest of the weird things that were released during the fifties. Songs like 'Rubber Biscuit' by the Chips which was like a hundred years ahead of its time, man! There's no words to it, it's all chanting. The guys are sort of making it up with rhythm accompaniment and the only thing you can really hear when they're singing is the words. One guy says 'Woody woody, pecker pecker,' and the rest of it is all this bizarre mumbling and grumbling but all major and minor chords, and it's easy to listen to, it's happy and it's very surrealistic." He played it to me. It's terrific. I've almost worn my copy out since then though now it's available on Sequel's *The Ultimate Doo Wop Collection* CD.

Frank put on another '45: "Then there's another song called 'The Girl Around The Corner' which is the other side of 'Teardrops' by Lee Andrews and the Hearts and the lyrics to that are just incomprehensible, it's something like 'Butchy Stover makes love like Casanova, she fucked him five times in the eye, three times in the knee. Buddha McCray, she's crazy that way ! . .' Then there's a sax solo in the middle of it and he's honking away, sort of inanely and then this one guy starts to sing too soon and then he stops and then it's time to come back in. It's a great record. Really far out." It actually it sounds more like, "She says that Butchy makes love like Casanova . . . Butchy put a bucket on a bumble bee, it stung her three times in the eye and five times in the knee . . ."—but Frank's reading is a classic example of his thinking, and it *is* a great record.

"I'm trying to acquire all the masters right now. It's going to take a little checking around to see who owns them. You see, a lot of those companies went out of business. That one's from Chess, I can probably get that, but some of the other things are just very obscure. There's one called 'The Drunkard' by The Thrillers on Old Town which is a recitation record where this guy tells of the evils of drink and the corruption of a young lad at the hands of a fast crowd and a bottle. Oh man! It's *horrible!*" The compilation never happened.

I once suggested to Frank—in the sixties—that there were some parallels to be drawn between himself and Andy Warhol. Like Andy he encouraged freaks to hang out and taped their weird ideas for his various film and cultural history projects: the *Uncle Meat* film, the "field recordings" of Wild Man Fischer and the GTOs, the Lenny Bruce and Lord Buckley and the way his secretary and staff were all included in his films and projects. Frank rejected the idea totally and with some vehemence but I think this was because of the bad blood existing between himself and Lou Reed. There was a great animosity between the Mothers and the Velvet Underground when Andy brought his Exploding Plastic Inevitable show to headline at the Trip in Los Angeles in May 1966 with the Mothers as the opening act. The slick street-wise New York Velvets in their black outfits and shades thought the Mothers looked like country bumpkins in their gaudy flowery costumes and long hair and didn't appreciate Frank sitting in the audience making fun of them on stage.

I think Frank's approach to the Mothers did have some similarities to Warhol's Factory, particularly with the first line-up, who were encouraged to act out spontaneous plays, improvise with broken dolls, dildos, and vegetables and generally freak out. But Frank would not allow them to take drugs or get legless like regular sixties rock bands which is one of the reasons that they never made it commercially—the kids couldn't relate to it.

As with Andy Warhol, Frank's motivation was twofold: a combination of wanting to preserve popular cultural history, as well as gathering ideas for his own work. He has been criticised, as Andy was, for being manipulative but without Frank, much of it would not have happened in the first place, and without him it would certainly not have been preserved.

At the time it was not yet clear whether the Mothers of Invention were a group, albeit with a powerful leader—like fellow Los Angelinos The Doors—or if it was just Frank directing a group of musicians. I asked him about it.

"I give all the signals. But that's based partly on some crazed whim that takes place at the time, partly on the desire to create a musical composition instantly on stage and partly because I know the personalities of each member of the group, . . . Well, let's say I know that if Motorhead does a certain thing at a certain time and I gesture to another player that he has complete freedom to play whatever he wants, I just have to point to him and he'll play whatever comes into his head right then. I've got a pretty good idea what's going to happen, see. So I can play the personalities against each other to make different flavors of madness. It's pretty. It looks real simple but it's very complicated and the reasons for the choices, when they occur, are pretty complex. Some of it has to do with the way the audience is behaving and a lot of it has to do with how you feel that day."

When I first stayed with Frank, his current social anthropology project mostly concerned the fauna inhabiting the Landmark Motor Hotel—Groupie Central and home to many rock musicians as well as three of the GTOs. He was producing an album with the GTOs so the house was filled with girls. Gail made sure they stayed in the kitchen.

When Frank and Gail returned to L.A. from the Mothers' 1967 season in New York, they first moved into the $700 a month Tom Mix Log Cabin, which had a bowling alley in the basement, beneath which was buried Tom Mix's favourite horse. There was a stream and artificial caves in the garden and a secret passage connecting it to Harry Houdini's pad across the street. (All now demolished.) There he set up a commune with Gail, Miss Christine and Miss Sandra, two of the girls who later formed the GTOs, and various other freaks. The GTOs first began as the Laurel Canyon Ballet Company and rehearsed in Frank's enormous living room, dancing to Mothers of Invention records. Their uniform, designed by Frank, was a thin white t-shirt with no bra and a large nappy with G.T.O. written across the bottom. They danced with the Mothers at three concerts at the Shrine Auditorium before Frank decided that they really should be a vocal group and began rehearsing them. Their first singing gig was supporting the Mothers at a Christmas show at the Shrine Auditorium. When Frank and Gail bought their own place, Miss Christine moved with them to become Moon Unit's nanny and "governess."

There were still elements of a commune in the Zappa household when I first visited. Because the household ran 24 hours a day, it was hard to determine who was actually living there, and who was just visiting all night. One typical night the kitchen might feature the GTOs planning a concert, Frank's business manager Herbie Cohen demanding coffee and cupcakes and Captain Beefheart restlessly pacing up and down. I remember one conversation between Captain Beefheart and Frank Zappa held at 6:30 am:

Beefheart: "That was an earthquake. Did you feel it?"

Zappa: "Yes, but it was so small that it made the people seem enormous!"

There was a strong British presence there: Joey Gannon, the general manager of Zappa's production company, Bizarre, who used to do the lights at the UFO club in London before heading off to Hollywood, and Pauline, Frank's English secretary. Several other people lived there: Janet Ferguson, who helped Gail with the children, and Frank's brother Carl, as well as several visiting girl fans including one called Pete who had arrived from the Midwest "to be with my Mothers. . . ."

Janet Ferguson, known as Gabby, had taken over from Miss Christine on the afternoon/evening children shift and lived in the tiny garden house, the walls of which were completely covered with news clippings, photographs and pictures torn from magazines: Dylan, Beatles, Frank. She kept very late hours and members of the Mothers liked to hang out there. A joint would surreptitiously make the rounds if Frank wasn't about. Zappa discouraged dope in his house, partly because he was a sitting target for a drug raid and partly because "it stops people from being clearheaded." He never took it himself which is why, in many ways, he was so very much apart from most of the sixties youth culture. Several of the Mothers, however, quite enjoyed stopping themselves from being clearheaded and could often be found hiding in Janet's little house. She starred as the freckled red-head in the memorable topless scene in the film *200 Motels* where Keith Moon plays a groupie nun collapsing from a drug overdose.

Then there was Carl, Frank's younger brother, living in the changing rooms by the pool, doing all the things that Frank used to sing about: working at the car-wash and as a short-order cook. Frank got him to demonstrate the L.A. Flop and the Pachuco Hop for me, looking on adoringly as his brother flopped about, humming to himself. Carl played the role of Minnesota Tishman, the Ringo Starr looking character in the terrible *Uncle Meat* movie.

Some days I would take Moon Unit for a walk in the garden. We would walk round the pool and play with the kittens or Georgia, Frank's German Shepherd. On one occasion, I walked her down the street but Woodrow Wilson Drive has no provision for pedestrians so we didn't make it any further than the first intersection. Moon Unit's new baby brother, Dweezil, spent most of his time sitting in a plastic bucket seat on the kitchen counter, staring at a tiny flickering portable television. One day Gail and I and Dweezil watched in the kitchen as Americans landed on the moon and bounced about in slow motion on the sandy surface. Dweezil made no comment. I see now that it was a very sixties experience.

Frank made strenuous efforts to show me the sights. We went with Gail to his favourite drive-in taco stand for dinner and, more interesting, he took me to a recording session at TT&G Studios. He had hired veteran doowop producer Johnny Otis to lead the Mothers in the studio while he controlled things in the booth. I cannot be sure but I think they were cutting "Overture To A Holiday In Berlin."

Johnny Otis, whose only British hit was the 1957 "Ma, He's Making Eyes At Me", had a very slick studio technique. He would walk very quickly into the studio, shout, "Let's get this group moving," nod his head and stamp his foot ferociously just a fraction ahead of the beat, then, when the take was over, say, "Not bad. Now do another one." He wore shades, a late fifties Tony Curtis slicked into place with thick lacquer so not a hair moved out of place as he bobbed his head to the music, a knife-edge crease to his pants, and short black silk socks held up with black calf-suspenders, high shine shoes, black shirt and a little voodoo doll worn as a necklace. Johnny was cool.

A little bead of sweat appeared on his brow as he grinned and grimaced with the beat, leaning over and clapping his hands within inches of the drummer's ear, driving him into the music. Art Tripp did not look pleased but his massive injection of energy soon made the band move. Johnny had been working for the Musicians Union for the past few years but he was soon to make a comeback.

Frank's cigarette burned another brown line in the Formica top of the mixing board as he balanced the tracks. The Mothers were amazingly professional and unlike most rock groups could read music. At one point Frank interrupted Ian Underwood in the middle of a keyboard passage to rewrite the whole center section of the passage, telling him the changes over the slate. After a short silence Underwood called back, "Okay, I got it."

They played it through again with Underwood flawlessly playing the new score. On the second take Frank decided that he had master rhythm tracks and went into the studio to position the microphones for the next part. "We'll put the Electrovoice there, pointing upwards to catch the sound of the saxophone as it bounces off the wall. That's how they made it sound so greasy in the fifties!" He and Otis discussed the room sound of the fifties and did a test run. Sometime in the middle of the night, Frank was twiddling with the knobs on the mixing board and explaining, "I'll just make a test mix before we go."

I stayed with Frank again six months later and in the early seventies when I was living in New York I saw him whenever the Mothers played the Fillmore. I thought that the social anthropology aspect of his work got out of hand with the Flo and Eddy line-up because they inevitably dominated the whole set, giving the Mothers a reputation for puerile skits and jokes which Frank never lived down. Frank wanted to be known for his serious music and his contribution to getting rock recognized as a serious art form but his preoccupation with sexual devices, bondage, and other adolescent interests eventually alienated his potentially large audience who were, after all, growing old with him and most thirty-somethings with a family no longer found the humor very funny.

The problem was that Frank continued to think that it made the "serious" side of the music more accessible and commercial. He was probably right, but I don't think so. Initially he had little choice as he told me in 1969: "What we're doing now, which is a lot more like serious music, if you want to use that expression, and very little of it is vocal music, you see. A lot of it depends on how well 'Uncle Meat' sells as to whether or not we're going to be able to even survive continuing in that direction because if you stop singing, the audience stops listening. You have to either talk to them or sing to them but they're not prepared to listen to music at all, they just don't want to sit through it. They have a bad interest span for instrumental music unless it happens to be glandular music, you know, loud blues. They can dig it because they can tap their foot to it. But you whip a bunch of atonal 5 and 7/8s on 'em that they can't, uh, groove with and that you have to think about, then you're in dangerous territory when you consider that next week you're going to have to pay your rent."

I saw Frank on and off over the years and in 1979 I visited him at the Town House, Richard Branson's London studio where he was producing a solo album for the Indian violinist Shankar. He had just written a song called "The Dead Girls Of London" which he got Van Morrison to sing. This, for me, showed how out of touch Frank was getting, apart from being sexist, it was directed at the women who Frank met at Tramp—of all places. He had been several times, late at night looking for something to eat and been rebuffed by the women there. This was not surprising: they were probably richer than him, certainly better dressed, and the concept of groupies was probably completely unknown to them unless you were talking about being a "special friend" with a racing car driver or footballer. Frank couldn't get laid so he wrote a nasty song about them. The whole business of the women's movement and sexism was something we argued about several times—but Frank could not, or didn't want to see it. (For some reason Frank had to replace Van Morrison's vocal with his own when the record was released.)

Frank's great worth, in rock 'n' roll terms, was his insistence that rock was an art form and should be taken seriously by both the industry and the audiences. He was one of the first pioneers in this field and he went a long way to achieving his goal. Back in 1969 he told me, "Record industry executives need to find out what it is they're selling because, see, they don't know how important pop music is today. All they know is that that's what's making money this month. They don't really know what a revolution it is in terms of musical history because there are a lot of people working in pop music today who are doing things that are artistic, and actually mean 'em that way! There are also people who pretend to be artistic who are doing just complete bullshit, but this is today's serious music. I think it's living serious music!" A listen to his most recent release, *The Yellow Shark* played by the Ensemble Modern, produced and composed by Frank, will confirm this.

PART THREE

You Can't Do That on Stage Anymore:

Performer/ Composer

THE MOTHERS LIVE (1969)

The New York writer Doon Arbus contributed this pioneering appreciation of the Mothers' remarkable early performances to the rock monthly *Cheetah*. It stands now as a contribution to the literature recognizing that concerts were more than music; they were indeed performances. I was less than enamored with Frank Zappa's stage presence when I saw the group perform at the Fillmore East. Keeping note cards at the time, I wrote down my initial impressions which I present here unedited. (All of this material was later collected in *The Fillmore East: Recollections of Rock Theatre.*)

DOON ARBUS

In Person: The Mothers of Invention

The Mothers of Invention remember it well. They remember white bucks and pompadours and pimples and going steady. They remember rock-and-roll in the days of its innocence: songs of self-affirmation ("Rock-and-roll is here to stay/It will never die"); songs of adolescent agony ("I'm so young and you're so old/This my darling I've been told"); the shameless glorification of romantic woe ("Goin' to the river/Gonna jump overboard and drown"); and the eloquence of nonsense lyrics ("pa pa oom mow mow," "dombee doobee dom," or "*sha* da da da, *sha* da da da *da* da"). Alan Freed, the lindy, or even the real Elvis Presley already seem like part of history, but the Mothers were there in their late teens and *they remember*.

Frank Zappa, composer, conductor, lead guitarist and unquestionably the leader, ambles on stage. He is wearing a purple high-school cardigan, knit pants, and butterscotch-colored shoes with pointy, turned-up toes. His face is made of planes and angles, like a house of cards, and is framed by a mantle of squiggly, black curls. The mustache and abrupt goatee form an upside-down anchor. He is like a wild, woodsy hermit, either very benign or very ferocious.

The other six Mothers follow at their leisure. They make an incongruous group. Each seems a distinct, Technicolor character, as identifiable as Hollywood. Billy Mundi, the rotund, unjovial drummer, is a baker from the French Revolution. Roy Estrada, caressing his electric bass, looks perplexed and determined, like a Polish anarchist. Don Preston sits within the circle of piano, organ and clavichord, well intentioned and vague, a Don Quixote before the windmill encounter. Bunk Gardner, absorbed in his collection of wind instruments, appears oblivious to everything except the anticipation of playing music. With his silver hair and trim beard he exudes the unruffled elegance of a riverboat gambler. Jim Black, the wry-eyed, bowlegged beater-of-the-gong, looks like a Mexican *bandido*. Ray Collins, credited with lungs and ingenuity in the program, is a high-browed Viking.

Zappa has not even glanced at the audience yet. He has been adjusting dials and tuning his guitar. He has chatted inaudibly with Don, tied the shoelaces of his butterscotch shoes, and sipped pale coffee from a glass mug. His nonchalance is, of itself, a kind of frenzy. Finally he approaches the center microphone and peers past the lights, scanning rows like a surveyor.

"Hello, pigs." A few people giggle briefly.

Zappa speaks thickly, deliberately, like a 45 rpm record played at 33 1/3. It makes him seem supremely dispassionate.

"We're gonna lay some 'thick black sounds' on ya," he says, quoting a phrase from a *New York Times* review of a Mothers' performance.

It begins with a medley of "My Boy friend's Back" ("a rock-and-roll song which some of you may have gotten pregnant to"), followed by "I'm Gonna Bust His Head," and "Ninety-six Tears." Ray is singing and making literal, illustrative gestures. He hunches his shoulders and strides forward, the football-hero boyfriend coming back. He places one hand on his hip and swats the air as he sings, "I'm gonna give him such a *smack*." All the Mothers are ravenous mimics; the source of inspiration is not always detectable.

Between numbers a few Mothers wander around stage. Others carry on pantomime conversations with each other or exchange quips. Zappa often talks to the audience. "The *New York Times* said we show contempt for our audience. See," he says, holding up his mug of coffee, "contemptuously I drink this." He spews a mouthful out towards the audience. Most of it lands at the end of the stage. Ray, almost smiling, sweeps up the mess with a broom. They have made an art of silliness.

In the middle of the show Zappa introduces "this strange little person in her mod clothes," who is called Uncle Meat. She is a very young, expressionless girl with silky hair, who sings, sometimes in duet with Ray. They stand with their arms around each other rubbing chests and looking tender and mournful. They even dance with each other, separated by a century of style. Uncle Meat also gazes through a kaleidoscope or rattles a hypnotic rhythm on the tambourine or parries Ray's carrot swordplay using a lettuce leaf for a shield.

They are much more fun to watch than listen to, so that towards the end, when they begin to tire and the singing becomes sporadic and the kidding around loses its fervor, the music becomes relentless. It goes on and on, the volume and insistence making listening to it like a day at the ocean: Afterwards, nothing can be seen but waves. And when it is all over, ending very abruptly (Zappa says, "Good night," and all seven leave the stage), the music seems to go on without them, an engulfing, independent rhythm, like a complementary image of the show.

RICHARD KOSTELANETZ
At the Fillmore East, 20 April 1969

I'd not seen this legendary group before, even though they first came to New York, some two years ago, with enough advance publicity to persuade my leftish theater friend, Lee Baxandall, to see their premiere performance at Andy Warhol's Balloon Farm, on St. Marks Place. In spite of an extravagant eccentricity that would have been unacceptable to nearly everyone a decade ago, the Mothers have survived. From the music to the costuming to the choreography, everything here seems the creation of one Frank Zappa, a California boy about my age who obviously knows and cares a lot about modern music. At one point in the group's concert, he accused a fellow musician of stealing something from Pierre Boulez and then, after a pause, put down us "kiddies" for not knowing who Boulez was. Funny perhaps to some, this was distasteful, if not a bit arrogant, to me. Zappa presents himself as a complicated personality with contrary ambitions. He evidently despises capitalism and yet expects to make a lot of money. He has an "advertising agency" that so far promotes mostly himself; and in an interview I heard recently on WRVR-FM, his haughtiness was repelling.

At this concert, he told us "boys and girls" that this would be the Mothers' last New York performance. Then they did three long, complicated, difficult pieces that drew less upon rock than upon improvised jazz, with Zappa pointing to each man to do his riffs. Don Preston on the organ and electric piano was brilliant even, if a bit too improvisatory for my taste; and a gray-haired, gray-bearded fellow played in succession saxophone and flute quite spectacularly. Why this band should have two drummers I cannot figure, especially since only one of them, with a long face and mustache, is groovy-looking. It is hard to understand why Zappa should bother to employ as many as ten musicians, especially since two guys need not play sax, two guys need not sing behind Zappa, etc. Zappa himself on the guitar is inventive, though less than skillful; and he speaks where he should sing. His hirsute appearance, particularly beneath the shadows caused by overhead light, is a fantastic theatrical creation. In all, however, his music is rather boring, if not deliberately alienating (unlike most rock, which aims to seep into one's system); more than once I found myself dozing off. Partly this anti-effect stems from the lack of modulation; more likely it relates to the fact that, as John Cage has been saying for years, experienced musicians, when allowed to improvise, will make rather familiar moves that forbid surprise. (At more than one point, I swear the second saxophonist was stealing sequences from Charlie Parker.) I was very disappointed.

STEVE ROSEN

FRANK ZAPPA: GUITARIST (1977)

Writing for *Guitar Player,* a magazine for aspiring professionals, Steve Rosen had an elaborate conversation with Zappa about his favorite instrument prior to the latter's discovery during the 1980s of the Synclavier synthesizer.

Frank Zappa—guitarist, composer, producer, avid roller derby fan, and leader of the Mothers Of Invention—is, at 36, probably the elder statesman of progressive rock and roll. Though most people first credit Zappa for his advanced, avant-garde songwriting, it takes his own exceptional and original guitar technique to put forth those ideas.

In addition to leading his ever-changing, ever-expanding Mothers—which has included such notables as French jazz violinist Jean-Luc Ponty, multi-keyboardist George Duke, drummer Aynsley Dunbar (now with Journey), and Mark Volman and Howard Kaylan (presently known as Flo and Eddie)—Zappa has continually served as one of the most articulate and controversial satirists on "pop music weirdness." Some of the Baltimore-born artist's side projects have included: producing an album by Grand Funk Railroad; leading a Fifties rock revival put-on called Ruben & The Jets; and producing several films, such as *200 Motels*.

Here then is the unexpurgated story of Frank Zappa—his early influences, his guitar technique, his equipment changes through the years, and his approach to producing his own sound on record.

• • •

When did you start playing guitar?

I began when I was eighteen, but I started on drums when I was twelve. I didn't hear any guitarists until I was about fifteen or so, because in those days the saxophone was the instrument that was happening on record. When you heard a guitar player it was always a treat—so I went out collecting R&B guitar records. The solos were never long enough— they only gave them one chorus, and I figured the only way I was going to get to hear enough of what I wanted to hear was to get an instrument and play it myself. So I got one for a buck-fifty in an auction—an arch-top, f-hole, cracked-base, unknown-brand thing, because the whole finish had been sanded off. It looked like it had been sandblasted. The strings were about, oh, a good inch off the fingerboard [laughs], and I didn't know any chords, but I started playing lines right away. Then I started figuring out chords and finally got a Mickey Baker book and learned a bunch of chords off that.

Who were some of your early guitar influences?

I used to like Johnny Guitar Watson, Clarence "Gatemouth" Brown, Guitar Slim [Eddie Jones], Matt Murphy.

Were there bands playing in your town that you could go and see "live"?

Yeah, sure. In San Diego when I was in high school down there, they had plenty of rhythm and blues bands. Most of them played instrumentals, only a few had singers.

Were your parents musical at all?

My father played guitar when he was in college. He had an old one sitting around the house, but it didn't feel as good to me as the one for a buck-fifty. He played it about once every three years; he'd pick it up and go wank-wank-wank, *but that was about all.*

How long did you keep playing drums?

I still play a little bit now. I had a few lessons. I went to a summer school once when I was in Monterey, and they had, like, basic training for kids who were going to be in the drum and bugle corps back in school. I remember the teacher's name was Keith McKillip, and he was the rudimental drummer of the area in Pacific Grove. And they had all these little kids about eleven or twelve years old lined up in this room. You didn't have drums, you had these boards—not pads, but a plank laid across some chairs—and everybody stood in front of this plank and went rattlety-tat *on it. I didn't have an actual drum until I was fourteen or fifteen, and all of my practicing had been done in my bedroom on the top of this bureau—which happened to be a nice piece of furniture at one time, but some perverted Italian had painted it green, and the top of it was all scabbed off from me beating it with the sticks. Finally my mother got me a drum and allowed me to practice out in the garage— just one snare drum. Then I entered my rock and roll career at fifteen when I talked them into getting me a complete set, which was a kick drum, a rancid little Zyn high-hat, a snare, one floor tom, and one 15;dp Zyn ride cymbal. The whole set cost fifty bucks. I played my first professional gig at a place called the Uptown Hall in San Diego, which was in the Hillcrest district at 40th and Mead. I remember it well, going to my first gig: I got over there, set up my drums, and noticed I had for-gotten my only pair of sticks* [laughs]. *And I lived way on the other side of town. I was really hurting for an instrument in those days. For band rehearsals we used this guy Stuart's house. His father was a preacher, and he didn't have any interest in having a drum set in the house, but they allowed me to beat on a pair of pots that I held between my legs.*

And I'm sitting there trying to play shuffles on these two pots between my legs!

When did you buy your first electric guitar?

I didn't get my first one until I was 21, when I rented a Telecaster from a music store. Then I bought a Jazzmaster which I used for about a year and a half. I used to play, like, lounge jobs—you know, sit on the stool, strum four chords to a bar, "Anniversary Waltz," happy birthday, one twist number per night, don't turn it up. All that kind of crap. Nobody else in the band really knew what the chord changes were to these dumb songs; they were all trying to figure out what was going on. I played places like Tommy Sandy's Club Sahara in San Bernardino, some clubs around West Covina. Really boring, miserable places. I worked with a group called Joe Perrino And The Mellow Tones. Then I got a chance to write some music for a movie and actually earned something doing that. So with the money I got from the film job I bought a Gibson ES-5 Switchmaster, which I used for about five years. I recorded the first three albums with that guitar.

What movie was that?

It was called Run Home Slow. *It was a western starring Mercedes McCambridge and was written by my high school English teacher. It's been on TV a few times. I've done music for four films. The first one was called* The World's Greatest Sinner, *starring Timothy Carey, about a guy who thinks he's God and then later on has doubts. Then* Run Home Slow, *and a short called* Burnt Weeny Sandwich, *then* 200 Motels.

Were you involved in any serious music before the Mothers of Invention?

I had a three-piece power trio called the Mothers, with Les Papp on drums and Paul Woods on bass, and we were working at a place called The Saints & Sinners in Ontario, California. It was, like, mostly Mexican laborers, a go-go bar, lots of beer, and a few waitresses who would jump on the tables—that type of thing.

Did you begin singing around the same time you started playing?

Well, I used to have to sing with that trio at the Mexican place. But that was mostly blues-type songs. I did a little bit of singing on and off on the first few albums, but I never thought that I could really sing. The problem was, with the lyrics I was writing, it was hard to find anybody else who felt comfortable singing those words. They would never get it across right. So I figured if I was ever going to get the intention of the lyrics out I'd better do it myself. I still have a horrible time singing and playing at the same time—just ridiculous. I can barely strum a chord and say one word over it; that's hard coordination for me. I'd never make it in country and western music.

Besides the Switchmaster guitar, what equipment did you use on *Freak Out!?*

Just a Fender Deluxe amp, that's all. After the Switchmaster I got a Les Paul gold-top and used that for a couple of albums. And eventually I got a Gibson SG.

Are you still using an SG?

I'm using a variety of things now; I've branched out quite a bit in the last couple of years. I've got a couple of Strats wired up funny ways. Both of them have preamps built into them, and one has a special tone control switch which lets you put each of the pickups out-of-phase and that kind of stuff. The other Strat has a Barcus-Berry located in the neck, which gives it a really interesting sound, because I do a lot of stuff with my left hand, and it helps the notes speak a lot faster. It's like the whole guitar is alive; you can touch it anyplace and hear where you touch the guitar, because the Barcus-Berry hears all of it.

What specifically do you do with your left hand?

If I pick one note with my right hand, I'm playing five with my left. I don't pick everything that I play, and consequently the action is kept down pretty close on most of the guitars. I also do some stuff where I use the pick on the fingerboard, pressing down and hitting the string at the same time. It gets kind of a Bulgarian bagpipe sound. An example of that is on the end of the solo in "Inca Roads" and also on "Po-Jama People" [both from One Size Fits All*].*

Are you still using the SG pictured on the cover of the "live" *Roxy & Elsewhere* album?

No, I have another SG that I'm using. The one that's on the Roxy *cover has since been thoroughly injured by an airline company—oh, they beat the hell out of it. They cracked the neck, and the most recent time it came back from Europe the binding was off the fretboard. I had the neck repaired, but it's never been the same; it flexes so much that it's hard to keep in tune, so I hardly use it anymore. But one time we were working down in Phoenix, and this guy came to the dressing room after the show with this guitar he'd built and wanted to sell. He had copied a Gibson [SG] except he'd added one more fret so it went up to an Eb, and it had an ebony fingerboard, humbucking pickups, and some inlay, and some real nice wood-work on it. He wanted $500.00 for it, and I thought it was a real nice guitar, so I bought it. I had [guitar maker] Rex Bogue do some stuff to it, add a preamp and snazz it up, and that's the one I'm using now. Another one of my Strats is the one Hendrix burned at the Miami Pop Festival; it was given to me by this guy who used to be his roadie. I had it hanging on the wall in my basement for years until last year when I gave it to Rex and said, "Put this sucker back together," because it was all tore up. The neck was cracked off, the body was all fired, and the pickups were blistered and bubbled. That's the one that's got the Barcus-Berry in the neck. A lot of people thought I had Hendrix' guitar from Monterey, but it was from Miami; the one at Monterey was white, and this one is sunburst.*

Do you use the vibrato arm on the Stratocaster or the SG?

Well, I used to use it on the SG a little bit, but I took it off because it was too hard to keep the instrument in tune, especially the one with the soft neck. But I use the vibrato arm quite a bit now on one of the Strats. I don't even have a vibrato arm on the Hendrix Strat. You can hear it on Zoot Allures.

What type of wah-wah do you use?

*I have a Mu-tron and the Oberheim VCF [voltage control filter]. I've got an example of that on this new album [*Zoot Allures*]. I'm starting to use some Echoplex now, which I've generally avoided in the past.*

You use the wah-wah a lot in its bass position where it acts as a sort of fuzz boost.

Yeah, I use it for a tone control. Very seldom do I just step on it on the beat like on the old Clapton records where he goes wacka-wacka-wacka, *just to tap your foot on it. Usually what I do is shape the notes for phrasing with it, and the motion of the pedal itself is very slight. I try to find one center notch in the thing that's going to emphasize certain harmonics, and ride it right in that area. Because if you put it all the way to the top it's too squeaky, and if you put it all the way back it's too blurred.*

Had you heard Clapton or Hendrix using the wah-wah before you started?

As a matter of fact, I think I was one of the first people to use the wah-wah pedal. I'd never even heard of Jimi Hendrix at the time I bought mine; I didn't even know who he was. I had used wah-wah on the Clavinet, guitar, and saxophone when we were doing We're Only In It For The Money *in '67, and that was just before I met Hendrix. He came over and sat in with us at the Garrick Theater that night and was using all the stuff we had onstage. Seems like every time I went to Manny's [156 W. 48th St., New York, NY 10036] there'd be some new gizmo that we'd try out, so we were always into the hardware of the rock and roll industry.*

How did Eric Clapton come to appear on *We're Only In It For The Money?*

I met him someplace in New York; I can't remember where, maybe at one of our concerts. He played with the Mothers once at the Shrine in Los Angeles and came over to my house, but I haven't been on speaking terms with him for some time now. He was just in New York one day hanging out, so I invited him over to the studio to do the rap that's on We're Only In It For The Money. *People think he's playing on it, but he's not; the only thing he's doing on there is talking.*

Did the two of you ever sit down and trade ideas on guitar?

No, he wasn't that kind of musician as far as I could tell; he wasn't the jamming type. When I used to live in a log cabin I had some amps set up in my basement, and he came over one day and played during one of our rehearsals. But he didn't like the amp; we were using Acoustics then, and he didn't like them. And remember when he came onstage at the Shrine? Nobody knew who he was. He came out and played the set, and nobody paid any attention to him at all, until he walked off, and I told the audience that was Eric Clapton.

What is an "octave bass" [used on *Hot Rats*]?

It's a bass that's been speeded up an octave to put it up into guitar range. Speeding it up not only changes the rate that you play the notes, but it changes the envelope of the notes and gives a punchier attack. And you know how a bass will ring for a long time? It gives you a different kind of sustain; the sustain comes out an octave higher.

Are there any devices which you've developed for the guitar?

There's one thing a guy named Bob Easton constructed for me called the Electro Wagnerian Emancipator. It's a very attractive little device that combines a frequency follower with a device that puts out harmony notes to what you're playing. You can have your choice of any twelve chromatic notes in four parts following your runs. You can't play chords with it, but linearly it'll follow you whether you bend or what-ever. It's main drawback is that the tone that comes out of it is some-what like a Farfisa organ.

What kind of picks and strings do you use?

I use Fender Heavy picks, and I use a different set of strings for each guitar, and I have about 22 guitars. To give you an idea, I use either an .008 or .009 on top [E], an .011 or .012 on the B, a .016 or .017 on the G, a .024 on the D, anywhere from a .032 to a .038 on the A, and any-where from a .046 to a .052 on the low E. So it's medium on the bot-tom strings, and they're mainly all Ernie Balls.

What is your amp setup?

I have a Vox cabinet with four JBLs in it [12;dp each] and another Marshall cabinet with JBLs. I use a 100-watt Marshall and an Acoustic

*270, but I'm going to redo all that stuff for the next tour. I'm trying to
optimize the sound, trying to get more of the kind of sound I like
onstage out into the audience, and you can't always do that just by
putting a mike in front of the amp.*

Are there certain settings you use on the 270 equalizer in conjunction
with the guitar to achieve certain sounds?

*It depends on what kind of hall I'm playing in. I'm real fussy about
equalization, and sometimes there's a compromise between the kind of
sound I want to get onstage and what the mixer needs to hear out in
the audience, and I'll change things around like that. But I've used the
100-watt Marshall with the volume at about 4; I double the inputs into
the bass channel (with a connecting cord), and the treble is on about 4,
and the bass at about 3; midrange will be anywhere from 6 to 8; and
the presence will vary from 6 to 10. This is the average—the bass could
be as high as 10 or as low as 0 depending on how much bottom is
needed. And on the 270 the volume will be on 4; treble all the way up;
the bright switch is on; the midrange will be on about 75%; the bass
will be about 80%; the graphic equalizer is all the way up at 80 cycles,
about 80% at 160, all the way up at 320, just about flat at 640, and
maybe a little bit of boost at 1250.*

Is this the same equipment you use recording?

*In the studio most of the stuff is played through a Pignose. I've done
all kinds of things with a Pignose; I've taken it and put it in a 'live'
chamber and taken an [Electro-Voice] RE-20 and stuck it right in
front of Pignose, and that will get one kind of sound. It's actually the
sound of an amp, but you can hear that it's in a room, and the room
is resonant, so it's a realistic sound. On Zoot Allures about the only
thing I used the Vox bottom and the Marshall top for was to get feedback on a song called "Filthy Habits." There's another song called
"The Torture Never Stops" where it's just Pignose. Another thing I've
done with the Pignose is just put it out in the middle of a dead studio,
put two mikes on it, and mike it in stereo. It gets a good sound. Put
one mike behind the other so there's a slight spread to it. I've also put
the Pignose in an echo chamber and miked it, but not too close,
because the echo chamber is real resonant. Since the amplifier isn't
real loud, if you put the mike a foot away from the amp, you're going*

to get a sound that really approaches what you hear in a hockey rink. *Anybody who's working in a studio and wants to try this, just tell the engineer to disconnect the speaker cables in the echo chamber and put a plug [phone jack] on the end of the echo send, and plug the echo send into your Pignose. Then you can sit in the control room, plug your guitar directly into the board, send it to the echo chamber on the echo send, and hear yourself coming back—and it sounds like you're in a hockey rink. You can even make it feed back by long distance. I've been using a Pignose for about the last three or four years. I think I started using it the most on* Apostrophe ('), *but there is some on* Over-Nite Sensation, too.*

Do you feel more comfortable playing in a "live" situation as opposed to the studio?

Yes. I mean, I have had a few laughs in the studio, but the problem is that in a studio I'm my own producer, and I've got so many other electronic things to worry about that it distracts me from just getting in there and playing the instrument. You can go out on the road, and once the houselights go down, and the red light comes on, it's a different story. I usually play my best stuff on the road.

Are your solos on record improvised first takes, or are they conceived beforehand?

It depends on what the song is; very rarely are they first-take things. But they aren't things where I'd sit down and work out the whole solo in advance before I played it. I can't do that, I can't remember it. Usually what I do if I get something going, I'll lay down twenty bars or so, and stop the tape, back it up, and punch in, and take up where I left off. I try to have the event that's going on the record make musical sense and fit in with what's going on; because a record is a fixed object, it doesn't change. It's not a song anymore, it's an object. If you're playing a song on the road it can change every night. It can be something, it comes alive each time you play it, and it has its own existence. But once you've committed it to wax, it never changes. So if you're going to leave your guitar solo on, you're stuck with that for the life of the record. I'm fairly fussy about it, but I'm sure I let a few go out on record that I could probably do better now. But I hope that's the way it's always going to be.

Have there been songs in the past that you've written specifically as guitar vehicles?

Not really, no. There are a few now that I've designed that way. I figure that since I've been playing for about twenty years or so, I might as well start doing that.

What scales do you work from?

My solos are speech-influenced rhythmically; and harmonically, they're either pentatonic, or poly-scale oriented. And there's the mixolydian mode that I also use a lot.

You don't really play a lot of blues licks in your solos.

I can, I have, I started off that way. But I'm more interested in melodic things. I think the biggest challenge when you go to play a solo is trying to invent a melody on the spot. I also think that a guitar player can only be as good as the band that's accompanying him. If the people backing you up are sensitive to what you're playing, you'll sound great; if they're just note-mashers, then you'll always sound mundane.

Are those the qualities you look for in a backing musician?

I've always had good rhythm section players, but I wouldn't say that they've always been too enthusiastic about what I was playing, or understood it very well, or really got into it. Because if a person's from the jazz world they're going to play worlds of gnat-notes, clouds of pentatonic gnat-notes that really don't amount to shit. Or if they're from the blues world they want somebody who gets on three notes and goes squirm-squirm-squirm. It's hard to explain to guys just coming into the band, the rhythmic concept I have about playing, because it's based on ideas of metrical balance—long, sustained events versus groupettoes that are happening with a lot of notes on one beat. Like a lot of sextuplets, septuplets, and things like that. A lot of times I'll play thirteen notes over a half note and try to space it evenly so it flows. This is sort of against the grain of rock and roll which likes to have everything in exactly duple or triple, straight up and down, so you can constantly tap your foot to it. But I prefer to have the rhythm section be aware of where the basic pulse of the time is and create a foundation that won't move, so I can flow over the top of it. It's hard to do, it's hard to get people to do that. And it's also hard to get them to leave some space for where the fast notes occur. Rhythm sections always have a tendency to copy: if they hear somebody else playing fast notes they want to play fast notes, too, and then you can't hear any fast notes any more. I've always had good rhythmic rapport with Aynsley Dunbar—I thought he was really good, drum-wise. And Terry Bozzio, the drummer in the group now, is excellent. He has a tendency to frenzy out a little bit, but I just figure that's because he's from San Francisco.

What about playing with [bass guitarist] Jack Bruce on *Apostrophe (')*?

Well, that was just a jam thing that happened because he was a friend of [drummer] Jim Gordon. I found it very difficult to play with him; he's too busy. He doesn't really want to play the bass in terms of root functions; I think he has other things on his mind. But that's the way jam sessions go. On that solo on "Apostrophe" I'm using an SG with a Barcus-Berry on the bridge, and that's being sent to one of the channels, then the other side is coming out of a Pignose. And there's an attack differential between how fast the Barcus-Berry speaks and how fast the Pignose speaks. So you've got a sharp attack on one side and then the rest of the note following it on the other. And on "Stink-Foot" [Apostrophe (')] there's an interesting sound where I'm using an acoustic guitar with a magnetic pickup on it and a Barcus-Berry on the bridge. The Barcus-Berry is going into one channel, and the magnetic pickup is going to a Mu-tron and the other chan-channel, so you have a sharp attack and an enveloped attack. It gives a lot of space.

You don't play a lot of acoustic guitar.

No, but I like it. Since most of my life is oriented toward the road, rather than the studio, there's not much opportunity to play sensitively on your acoustic guitar except in a hotel room. The rest of what we do is high volume stuff. I have a real nice Martin—I don't know what that model number is, but it has a classical-width neck that joins the body right at the 12th fret, in a jumbo shell. I also have an Ovation and a bouzouki with a Barcus on it. I've recorded some stuff with that, but it hasn't been released yet; I have some duets I did with [violinist] Jean-

Luc Ponty that turned out real nice. I also have a Gibson round-hole acoustic with a pickup right next to the fingerboard—I don't know what model number it is either. I like that guitar, it's got a good neck on it. I just lucked out, because I don't think all the necks are good on Gibsons. In fact, they're usually a little too pudgy for my hand; I like to get them shaved down.

Since you've used both Fender and Gibson guitars, do you have any preference for one over the other?

I use them for things that they're good for. The Strat has a drier sound—it has more of an acute, exact sound—and I use the Gibson for more of a sweat-hog type of sound.

Is there any reason why you don't often work with other guitarists?

Well, I have. [Lowell George, and others for example, have appeared on past LPs, but not in multi-lead situations.] But double leads just never seemed appropriate to what I was doing. Sneaky Pete [Kleinow] was in the band for a while, but he couldn't stay; he had too many other appointments.

Do you ever play slide guitar?

No, but I do have a fretless guitar, and I'm pretty good on that. At one time Acoustic manufactured a fretless guitar; they made a proto-type and tried to interest people in it, but nobody wanted it. So the prototype ended up at Guitar Center [7402 W. Sunset Blvd., Hollywood, CA 90046]. I walked in there one day and asked them if they had anything new, and they said, "Have we got one for you!" And they brought out this thing, and it was really neat, so I bought it for $75.00. The only restriction was they had to take a chisel and some black paint and scratch off the word "Acoustic" on the head-piece, because Acoustic didn't want anybody to know that they had made such a grievous error as to make a fretless guitar. I've put a Barcus-Berry on that, too, and I send the magnetic pickup to the left and the Barcus on the right. The thing that sounds like a slide guitar on "The Torture Never Stops" is actually a fretless. It's also on "San Ber'dino" and "Can't Afford No Shoes" [both from One Size Fits All].

It's different than a regular guitar; you don't push the strings to bend them, you move them back and forth like violin-type vibrato, which is a funny movement to get used to. But you can play barre chords on it—it's fun.

Are there guitar players you listen to?

There are a few that I've heard recently who I think are real good. I like Brian May of Queen—I think he's really excellent. And I always did like Wes Montgomery until they started smothering him with violins. I think his best album is one on Fantasy that just has him and his brothers playing "Lover Man" and "Monterey Blues" [The Montgomery Brothers, Fantasy, 3308]. I like the Johnny Guitar Watson records from the early Fifties; they're really good. And I especially like Guitar Slim. His solo on "The Story Of My Life" [The Things That I Used To Do, Specialty, SPS 2120] is one of the best early distorted guitar solos; it really sounds like he's mad at somebody.

What about the contemporary heavies, like Jeff Beck or John McLaughlin?

I like Jeff, yeah. I've listened to Wired [Epic, PE 33849], and there are a couple of solos on there that I like. And I like some of his stuff on Rough And Ready [Epic, KE 30973]. A person would be a moron not to appreciate McLaughlin's technique. The guy has certainly found out how to operate a guitar as if it were a machine gun. But I'm not always enthusiastic about the lines I hear or the ways in which they're used. I don't think you can fault him, though, for the amount of time and effort it must have taken to play an instrument that fast. I think anybody who can play that fast is just wonderful. And I'm sure 90% of teenage America would agree, since the whole trend in the business has been "faster is better."

You're pretty fast yourself.

Well, I'm not really a fast guitar player, because I'm not picking everything I play. I only play fast when I think it's appropriate to the line I'm doing.

How do you see your role as a guitarist different from that of a Beck or a McLaughlin?

I think that's a matter of advertising more than anything else. Once I get out onstage and turn my guitar on, it's a special thing to me—I love doing it. But I approach it more as a composer who happens to be able to operate an instrument called a guitar, rather than "Frank Zappa, Rock And Roll Guitar Hero."

How does your playing differ in your current four-piece band as opposed to the larger orchestrated groups you've worked with in the past?

It differs quite a bit, because with a larger group you have to play less—there are a lot of people waiting in line to play solos. That's one of the reasons I've got a smaller group now, because I happen to like to play solos, and I happen to think I'm in a specialized category from the stuff I play, and I don't think there's any reason why I should have to wait in line [laughs]. I have some stuff to say, and I'm going to get out there and do it.

Have you ever thought of using another producer, to allow yourself more time with the guitar?

I would if I thought I could find somebody who would produce things the way I want to hear them. But the details that I worry about when I go into a studio are how the board is laid out, what EQ is going to be on the stuff you're listening to in the headphones, what kind of echo you're going to be using, how long you should be taking to do such-and-such a thing because at $150.00 an hour you don't want to be wasting your time in there. It's hard once you've got all that stuff set up to just walk in and play and forget about it. I'll spend anywhere from three to nine hours just getting the sound on the rest of the band right before I'll record. On this new album [Zoot Allures] it's different, because I did a lot of tracks just starting with a Rhythm Ace and building all the stuff up from there. What I usually do is, play the guitar from the control board while the band is playing, or else have the band lay down a track and then put mine on later.

Are there songs where you've recorded more than just a rhythm and lead track?

Yes, "Po-Jama People" [One Size Fits All], and there are a couple on the new album that have anywhere from three to five guitar parts. "Filthy Habits" [Zoot Allures] has five guitar parts; and then there were also a few multiple-guitar-part things on We're Only In It For The Money *and* Uncle Meat.

You've been playing for two decades now. What else do you plan to do with the guitar?

The hardest thing for me to do is play straight up and down, absolutely the hardest to do. Stuff that everybody else does naturally just seems as impossible as shit to me. I don't think in little groups of twos and fours and stuff; they just don't come out that way. I can sit around and play fives and sevens all day long with no sweat. But the minute I've got to go do-do-do-do, do-do-do-do it feels weird, it's like wearing tight shoes. So I'm going to keep practicing. It's like learning how to speak English—if you've been speaking something else all the time. It's like trying to develop a convincing English accent.

BEN WATSON
IN RESPECT OF RUBBISH (1982)

A Zappa FANatic since his days as a student in Cambridge, England, Ben Watson (b. 1956) is a British poet and critic who has contributed regularly to marginal literary magazines. His summa opus, *The Negative Dialectics of Poodle Play* (1995), is probably the most extravagant book on any contemporary popular artist, drawing as it does upon Shakespeare, Baudelaire, and other literary heavies to illuminate its subject. Watson's inspired commentaries are radical in the ways that Zappa's music was radical; so that any "companion" lacking Watson is ipso facto not worth reading. Instead of reprinting from that book, this collection favors contributions written before and since. For this elaborate appreciation of Zappa's principal film, Watson designed pages along with providing commentary.

IN RESPECT OF RUBBISH

Rubbish is pertinent ; essential ; the most intricate presence in our entire culture ; the ultimate sexual point of the whole place turned into a model question.

OUT TO LUNCH ON 200 MOTELS

In writing on <u>Shut Up 'n Play Yer Guitar</u> I've already argued that Zappa is at his most original and interesting when he's not blithely showcasing his considerable talents as composer, arranger, producer and guitarist (Willie The Pimp) but when he chucks it all away (A Little Green Rosetta). THERE IS PERHAPS NO SINGLE FACTOR WHICH DISTINGUISHES SCHOENBERG SO BASICALLY FROM ALL OTHER COMPOSERS AS HIS ABILITY TO DISCARD AND REJECT ALL HE HAS PREVIOUSLY POSESSED (Theodor Adorno, <u>The Philosophy of Music</u>, p122) Zappa is aware that all sound is sociology: everything we hear has become totally humanized, hums with the grand (class) conflicts of the epoch. All human products are charged with meaning: meaninglessness is hence strictly impossible; significations will swurl and flicker whatever our attempts to limit the ferment - from Zen to Alcohol negation falls short. It follows from this short person dilemma that RUBBISH must occupy a paradoxical position. Rubbish is value denied, it is rendered universally meaningless, but since this is impossible, its meaning returns in an INVERTED or REPRESSED form to haunt us in disguise, in the form of daydreams, faint odors, noxious pollution. The readers of Society Pages will I am afraid be the last to confess what everyone else acknowledges: namely that 200 MOTELS is a load of RUBBISH. With the pungency of a putrid pizza and the cantankerous contiguity of a crumpled coca-cola can in your back yard, 200 MOTELS boggles the mind, a concentration at once fetid and prismatic of the problems of the age, a wince-worthy whirlpool of closeted desires, flush with queasy nuggets of totemic sexuality. How this obviously cheap and indulgent concoction can prompt a Special Issue on the part of SOCIETY PAGES (thus engaging the passionate interest of all addicts of The Big Note) presents indeed A Model Question.

Interviewer: Mr Zappa, is it possible to be free? FZ: Well, at least you can be cheap.

200 MOTELS was - quite literally - a cheap film. United Artists supplied a budget of £200,000 and it was shot at Pinewood Studios in 5 days after only 5 days rehearsal. It was filmed on 4 simultaneously running video-cameras. One third of the 320 page script was never shot: but this didn't deter Zappa from putting out what did get done in the 5 days. This attitude towards the integrity of the art object is well illustrated by the quote in the top right hand corner, which succinctly lays down the parameters of Zappa's output macrostructure. There's no attempt to disguise the cheapness of 200 MOTELS: it's quite clear for instance that the entire film's shot in the same warehouse, the sets are deliberately fake. Props are reminiscent of Claes Oldenburg's Store Days, when the Pop Artist set up 'shop' in an art gallery and sold papiermaché brooms and mops (but did the mob turn round 'n bite him? ... no chance. It can't happen here... Brixton maybe, or Chapeltown) paint splashed phones and burgers. You get the feeling that the collapse of every bit of scenery is imminent, the waking quakery of of the dream landscape in fact, the disturbing erotic quiver which shatters the object of guiltless contemplation.

From this epoch spring the arcades and the interiors, the exhibition halls and the dioramas. They are residues of a dream world. The utilization of dream-elements in waking is the textbook example of dialectical thought. Hence dialectical thought is the organ of historical awakening. Every epoch not only dreams the next, but while dreaming impels it towards wakefulness. It bears its end within itself, and reveals it - as Hegel already recognized - by ruse. With the upheaval of the market economy, we begin to recognize the monuments of the bourgeoisie as ruins even before they have crumbled. WALTER BENJAMIN - Charles Baudelaire, A Lyric Poet In The Era Of High Capitalism

YOU GOTTA WADE THROUGH PILES OF SHIT TO GET TO PARADISE

Hence Zappa's particular skill: to encourage real flaws in the technical illusion, extend them into flaws in the real world, so that the fault and the guilt become seamless, a seamless presentation of reality through a shoddy shambles. The wobbling walls of REDNECK EATS are signs of insufficient budgeting from United Artists and a criticism of the pennypinching functionalism of those who design our mining community's facilities: the contrast between the might of the machinery that digs profit out the earth and the temporary arrangements that provide accomodation and leisure gratification for people - who are after all temporary arrangements too (as my Dad used to say) compared to the timeless accumulation of Capital that insists on mass unemployment, baby murders in Iran, the locking up of Poles.

Zappa was particularly excited with a new technique that enabled him to make moulds of real objects and reproduce them using some resinous matrix. This fascination extends to the protagonists as well: we get, for instance, Zappa himself (well, briefly: playing guitar like a jackass on Magic Fingers; grinning as Howard describes how he wants to 'wee wee in your hair' and finally staring at the camera in the grand chaotic finale - brown eyes don't make it/ so what is the meaning of this?), Ringo Starr dressed up to look like Zappa and a Zappa dummy; we get the two groupies, Flo & Eddie dressed up to look like them and two dummies - at one point (during Daddy, Daddy, Daddy) we see both sets of replicas sway together (a remarkable prediction of the Really Saying Something Bannanarama/Fun Boy Three video).

"that which withers in the age of mechanical reproduction is the aura of the work of art"

"the technique of reproduction detaches the reproduced object from the domain of tradition"

"the instant the criterion of authenticity ceases to be applicable to artistic production, the total function of art is reversed. Instead of being based on ritual, it begins to be based on another practice - politics."

in - The Work of Art in the Age chanical Reproduction (1936)

One of Zappa's favorite artists is Brittini (a sample of whose work is displayed over the bed on the cover of Overnite Sensation).

Brittini's prints appear on the walls of motel rooms throughout America. He paints trompe-l'oeil pictures of Venetian blinds to give closed off rooms a sense of fresh air (as this page is aerated by pretty girl pneumatics): a model of the trumpery production

under capitalist relations entails.

"The satire-collage is the form taken by artificial epic in the degraded world of commodity production and of the mass media: it is artificial epic whose raw materials have become spurious and inauthentic, monumental gesture replaced by the cultural junk of industrial capitalism. So it is that the most authentic realization of the epic voice in modern times – an ideal of many centuries of western culture – yields not some decorative and beautiful pastiche, but the most jarring and energetic mimesis of the mechanical, and breathes a passionate revulsion for the standardized manipulations of contemporary existence." Frederic Jameson – 'Wyndham Lewis As Futurist' in the Hudson Review 1973/4 page 325

200 MOTELS is dream; it is also artificial-epic/satire-collage; and on top of that it is also that ever recurring horror at the heart of the modern imagination, the concentration camp. As Maggie Thatcher and her right-wing cabinet win the British electorate to her unpopular policies by sinking ships full of Argentinian teenagers, all the while denouncing the enemy as a Fascist junta, it's as well to remember that credit for creating this piquant little hell on earth must go to the British: the first concentration camps were set up by Her Majesty's Army in South Africa during the Boer War. Perhaps that's why Zappa chose to film 200 MOTELS in England. The concentration camp is the final solution to the main problem of the present-day world system – ie, people. Used most notoriously in the Nazis' massacre of Jews, Socialists, Gays, Adherents of Wilhelm Reich's Sex-Pol and Feminists, they have also been used against insurgent populations in Northern Ireland, Chile, Poland. The death camp has a relationship to rubbish: it is where power would put all who refuse its pressure. Here people become mere refuse, for ready conversion to

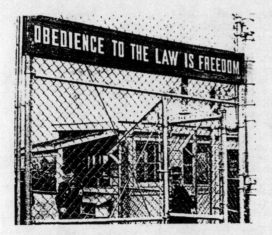

soap and lampshades. In comparison to its horrors the world of disinterested art and beauty becomes callous rubbish. Zappa's inversion of values is necessary in an upside-down society: the revered monuments of art are so much rubbish/ rubbish is pertinent because in it we can read the social unconscious:

ALL POST-AUSCHWITZ CULTURE, INCLUDING ITS URGENT CRITIQUE, IS GARBAGE   ADORNO – Negative Dialectics page 367

"Arbeit Macht Frei" was wrought in iron letters over the entrance to the Auschwitz death camp. Zappa had "Work Liberates Us All" written over the entrance to his disaster area.

Zappa's politics are a strange kind of pre-Marxist, post-situation materialism: they basically define themselves in opposition to social control through ideas. The great bogey is religion, hotly followed by Fascism and Television, its latter day derivatives. Possible members of this current include the Marquis de Sade, Johnny Rotten, Killing Joke (before they became a Rock Band) and Crass. Obsessed by the religion he's rejected Zappa secularizes religious themes. In 200 MOTELS heaven and hell are presented simultaneously and in forms which stress their material possibility: be free to dance and sing or watch the Nazis burn your town, innocent tomfoolery or Auschwitz. The word Auschwitz contains the German for 'joke', 'Witz' - the Sex Pistols (like Killing Joke) stressed the proximity of horror and fun in their slogan "Belsen Was a Gas" - predictably misunderstood by Nazi shitheads in this country and probably, on balance, a mistake. Social democratic imagination keeps the two poles apart, thus

exorcising and repressing the disturbing fact that under capitalism
mass murder bubbles below consciousness as a constant possibility
for entry on the charts - with a bullet. In 200 MOTELS - and, for
instance in The Torture Never Stops - FZ alerts us to these
unsavoury truths. Zappa was doing the same thing when he directed
listeners to Kafka's 'In The Penal Colony' on Money. Adorno said of
Kafka that he 'sins against an ancient rule of the game by
constructing an art out of nothing but the refuse of reality' (Prisms
page 251): like Zappa and Uncle Meat, he's another alchemist of the
dustbin and scrapheap. Lest it be thought eccentric that I use Adorno
- an obscure Hegelian Marxist Frankfurter - to explain Zappa - a
popstar - I append two quotations:

collage techniques, musical density, etc. In the early fifties, Zappa,
then unknown and unnoticed, attended the *"Kurse für Zeitgenös-
sische Musik"* (Courses in Contemporary Music) in Darmstadt, Germany, where almost all the composers who have so radically changed
the contemporary avant-garde music scene lectured or studied: Boulez, Stockhausen, Nono, Zimmermann, Ligeti, Henze, Kagel, Berio.

JOACHIM BERENDT -
THE JAZZ BOOK
PAGE 343

GILLIAN
ROSE -
THE MEL-
ANCHOLY
SCIENCE
PAGE
110

ADORNO TAUGHT MUSIC AT DARMSTADT IN THE 50s AND 60s

This would mean that FZ was imbibing the principles of negative
dialectics sometime between the ages of 10 and 15 - someone should
ask him if Frankfurt School Crtical Theory wasn't a bit much at
that age. Anyway, the Captain got it wrong: the two real people
in the world weren't hamburgers, they were frankfurters.

An example of the real flaws that prise apart Zappa's oeuvre
like the real world is the moment where Flo and Eddie lead the
chorus on 'Penis Dimension'. Though they play up their embarassment
with the words, their response is recorded as documentary, not
acting. This playing up, making a virtue of necessity (the mother
of them all) is characteristic of everything in 200 MOTELS. Lack
of rehearsal was inevitable given United Artists' budget, because
Time Is Money. In that track (off Sleep Dirt) FZ questioned the
so-called freedoms of the fuzztone heavy guitar solo (freedoms
highly questionable since the demise of Hendrix - see OTL in
SOCIETY PAGES no 9) by following each 'expressive' note with a
meticulously scored accompaniment by assorted percussion. All that
time in the studio, such expense: the freedoms of FZ's guitar

underlined by WORK. Under capitalism, work has to be expressed in
terms of time in order to translate it into money: any 'freedom'
we possess is constrained by these limits, the cost of production.
FZ's entrepreneurial view of limits doesn't lead him to solidarity
and socialism, but it leads him to concentrate on his music's
relationship to the economic sphere (at the end of 200 MOTELS he
rolls the accountant's paperwork; the bootleg Greggery Peccary
includes announcements of meal breaks) which makes it universal
- in a material, non-ideological sense. 200 MOTELS was in its
production constrained by the twin tormenting calipers of time
and money, but far from letting them pinch him, Zappa uses them
to tweeze us: uses them as metaphor for _our_ activities ("Is this
waste of time what makes a life for you?"). True imagination is
indeed infinite, but it proves itself in delineating real
boundaries, not in daydreaming it's absolutely free. For the
purposes of shifting product, toy manufacturers would have the
child dress dollies, but we all know that the child strips the
doll, tears it apart. Adorno approved of this impulse in the
composer and consumer:

Flo & Eddie's
grimaces and
giggles at the
script have another
function besides
adding a 'live',
'cheap' quality:
they also provide a
model for the musical
score as obstacle race,
task master, to which resistance
and mistakes appear as the voice of
the unconscious. It's not just the
Penguin that has to jump through a hoop
of real fire, it's as though every
performer is pushed through unnatural

> ADORNO RECOMMENDED THAT REHEARSALS OF MUSIC
> SHOULD BE BROADCAST AND MUSIC MADE AS
> ACCESSIBLE AS POSSIBLE BY EXPOSING AND
> EXPLAINING THE PROCESSES OF COMPOSITION AND
> PERFORMANCE, NOT BY THE PROCESS OF
> STANDARDIZATION (THE "SWEETENER").
>   Gillian Rose - The Melancholy Science
>   page 134

acts. To hear a horn section follow an arrangement scored from an FZ-
guitar-solo-transcription (eg Redunzl) is to hear a madcap chase after
an impossible order, a scramble after the recreation of a once-only
improvisation that is doomed to failure. Zappa has commented how he
loves to hear a group of musicians desperately pursuing an eccentric
melody line - he finds the inevitable inaccuracies exciting. The

orchestral music of 200 MOTELS puts the entire Royal Philharmonic
Orchestra in the Mothers' predicament: the radical dislocation of
musicians faced with scores and duties that undermine their dignity
and rationale. Jeff Simmons might have said of the LA Philharmonic
"those dudes are really out of it, man. It's like working with people
from another planet" (Time Magazine 1st June 1970) but finally he
found FZ's recreational reorientation facility harder to take than did
the classical musicians, as the cartoon section of 200 MOTELS explained.
Lucille Has Messed My Mind Up is a great LP, but it's dated (zap me
with your hair dryer, Jeff - I'll let you feature your hurt). Zappa's
music on the other hand never dates because it never commits itself
to a fashionable style, locks itself into a period. It stands above
and pares its nails. In this hostility to music Zappa has rediscovered
an element central to his hero Stravinsky (an element which the late
"neoclassical Stravinsky" also forgot):

THE MODERN ASPECT IN STRAVINSKY IS THAT ELEMENT WHICH HE HIMSELF CAN NO
LONGER BEAR: HIS AVERSION, ACTUALLY, TO THE TOTAL SYNTAX OF MUSIC. ALL
OF HIS FOLLOWERS - WITH THE POSSIBLE EXCEPTION OF EDGARD VARESE - ARE
COMPLETELY VOID OF THIS SENSITIVITY.
Theodor Adorno - The Philosophy of Music   page 153

This 'possible exception' was the transmission link that created the
presentday composer who refuses to die. Zappa's importance to western
philosophy can hardly be overrated. Music is philosophy made concrete,
philosophy become sensually available. Good music isn't a pleasure, it's
a necessity. Zappa provides the sole link between this tradition -
western classical music, in which musical composition is judged by its
success in siting the correct position of subjectivity vis à vis the
social totality - and Black music, in which a social process extrudes
itself into aesthetic commodities. This is a fancy way of saying that
Zappa represents a uniquely successful marriage of classical and pop.
Mingus, for instance, falls short, because his classical input stops
at the romantics (though Dolphy's solos prefigured atonality, these
were lapses not statements). Anthony Braxton's dissolution of melody
into rhythm, and the
whole range of conscious
Afro-percussion - Olatunji,
Trane, Blood Ulmer,
Ornette Coleman and his
Harmolodics - work in
parallel to FZ's explor-
ations (cf Uncle Meat/

Harmolodic headaches

Black Page no 1/ BeBop Tango, not to mention the Wet T-Shirt Nite chord
progression) but they don't take on the philosophical problem of the

classical domination present in the relationship between conductor and orchestra. A relationship FZ maintains for his own reasons - Captain Beefheart calling him a sexual fascist, purveyor of red-in-the-face, erection-at-all-times, nose-to-the-grindstone ethics - but this relationship allows FZ to carry through a project which is <u>not</u> to provide an alternative but a <u>model</u> (a model question) of forces operating in society. Artworks which perpetuate the social order invariably disguise its workings; the danger of alternative representations is that they can be used by affirmative thought as cosmetic daydreams, consolation for the also-rans. The trendmongers brandish Kid Creole & the Cocnuts as a multiracial, polysexual dance troupe - but what's the difference between this and the Black & White Minstrels, apart from the fashionable seal of approval? This hapless beast had better watch out, the furtrapper from Strictly Commercial is out and about. In 200 MOTELS Zappa doesn't appeal to the authoritarian authenticity of the symphony orchestra like Deep Purple or Andrew Lloyd Webber, he pursues its inner logic to the ultimate sexual point of absurdity and destruction.

TRUTH IS OBJECTIVE, NOT PLAUSIBLE
ADORNO - NEGATIVE DIALECTICS p41

The only previously published statement on 200 MOTELS by Out To Lunch is this: "In respect of rubbish, Zappa's 200 MOTELS does all that The Waste Land pretended to." (from Out To Lunch: 'Erogenous Sewage In The Work of Hart Crane' in <u>HERETIC</u> vol I no 2, available from Paul Brown, I76 Peckham Rye, London SE22 9QA, England - £2.50 including postage) I've been asked to clarify. I see The Waste Land as a shot at garbage-epic that failed because TS Eliot lacked contempt for the refuse he mucked about in: what we have is decorative pastiche and sententious pronouncement. THROUGH HOSTILITY TOWARDS ART, THE WORK OF ART APPROACHES KNOWLEDGE - Adorno, The Philosophy of Music, page 124 - and TS Eliot never got near. The Waste Land cracked itself up to be a central work of high modernism, but the images aren't broken they're crazy-paved. It's become the consolatory humbug that allows America to feel "profound" about the atrocities committed in Vietnam (Apocalypse Now). True works of modernism resist recruitment by reactionary currents. 200 MOTELS is such an irregular, monstrous artefact; its putrescence can only be faced on its own terms, the specific materials from which it's constructed: the ideologies of heavyrock and classical music (neither of which survive), the place of the Mothers in society.

> MUSIC OF THE DISRESPECTFUL ABYSS, ANTI-HUMAN RHAPSODIES
> OF THE WASTE PIPE AND WATER CLOSET
> NIGHTLY THE GROPING FINGERS OF THIS VULGAR INTRUDER
> HAVE STRUMMED THE TOPPLING BYZANTINE ORGAN OF HIS
> MIND
> BLACK FUGUES RESULTED - RESOUNDING DOWN THE EWIGKEIT
> Wyndham Lewis - Enemy of the Stars, 1932

Like Enemy of the Stars, 200 MOTELS revolves around some hidden and
hideous primal scene. When Rance asks the groupies if they will trade
what lies behind the curtain for what Howard has in his pants we see
a glimpse of a Nazi in uniform (well, some unfortunate symphony
percussionist). This is a reference to the idea that sexual repression
lies at the root of fascist psychology, the authoritarian personality.
You betta know now <u>all</u> your education, or you'll wind up workin' in a
gas station - and that's not petrol he's referring to. This is why FZ
told the baby held aloft in the aisle at Hammersmith 19/2/79 to listen
to the words of Dirty Love, so maybe the baby'd grow up straight:

> Reich has written about the repression
> of sexuality in the white man, and how
> this blocking of natural emission and
> other violent energies causes cancer
> and madness or white Americans. And
> this sexual energy is a dirtiness,
> an ecstasy, which always threatens
> the "order" ie "rationalism", the a-
> human a-sexual social order the
> white man seeks with all his energies
> to uphold.
> Leroi Jones <u>Home, Social Essays</u>
> (1968) page 233

We don't have to endorse Leroi Jones' suspect commitment to 'natural'
sexuality to see that in 200 MOTELS Zappa indeed presents a load of
rubbish whose intricate presence turns the ultimate sexual point - and
here I am of course talking of the PENIS - into a social, and hence
political question.

OUT TO LUNCH would be delighted to hear from readers of
SOCIETY PAGES who have something to say about
the above, or weird discoveries, or poems or *N.G.*
tapelists or whatever: OTL, 29 Glossop St. Leeds 6,
United Kingdom.
DON'T WORK

HOTCHA!

ORCHESTRAL MANEUVERS (1984)

Zappa discusses his career as a "classical" composer in this Bill Milkowski interview.

After 18 years of playing practically every concert hall and hockey rink in the free world, Frank Zappa was nearly ready to call it quits. Disgusted with the whole exhaustive prospect of touring and playing before legions of rowdy, potentially violent fans, Zappa decided to shelve his rock career in order to concentrate on other pursuits, namely, symphonic music.

Phase One of Zappa's new career began last year with the release of a digitally-recorded album of his ambitious contemporary symphonic pieces, performed in concert by the London Symphony Orchestra. That program was conducted by 31-year-old Kent Nagano, of the Berkeley and Oakland symphonies. The recording session was produced and engineered by Zappa for his own Barking Pumpkin label.

Phase Two occurred in February 1983, when Zappa shared the baton with maestro Jean-Louis LeRoux for a 100th anniversary celebration of the music of Edgard Varèse and Anton Webern, which was performed by the San Francisco Contemporary Music Players at the city's War Memorial Opera House.

Zappa's burgeoning interest in symphonic works continues. This past January, three original Zappa chamber compositions were performed by conductor Pierre Boulez's prized chamber orchestra, the Ensemble Intercontemporain, with Boulez himself conducting the proceedings at the Theatre De La Ville in Paris. An album on EMI Records is forthcoming.

Last spring, Nagano and his Berkeley Symphony presented the world premiere of Zappa's "Sinister Footwear," a ballet performed by the Tandy Beales Company and featuring the puppet creations of Ron Gilkerson.

And there's more. Zappa has been invited to guest conduct at the prestigious Magghio Musicale Fiorentino in Florence, Italy, and has also been asked to guest conduct for the Honolulu Symphony 1984/85 season and to conduct his own music and selections from Edgard Varèse at the University of Buffalo in 1985.

All this from the man who brought you such irreverent rock classics as "Don't Eat The Yellow Snow," "Dinah-Moe Humm," "Illinois Enema Bandit," "Half A Dozen Provocative Squats," "Help, I'm A Rock," "Saint Alfonzo's Pancake Breakfast," "My Guitar Wants To Kill Your Mamma" and the notorious "Stink Foot," to mention just a few in his discography of hundreds of recorded compositions.

Zappa has not abandoned his rock career. He's just put it on the back burner for a while. This summer he plans to release *Them Or Us*, the 36th album of his career. Besides featuring his regular band of Steve Vai and Ray White on guitars, Chad Wackerman on drums, Bobby Martin and Tommy Mars on keyboards, and Scott Thunes on bass, it will be something of a family affair. His oldest son Dweezil will be making his debut with daddy, playing some insanely wicked wang-bar riffs on "Stevie's Spanking" and a reggae remake of "Sharleena," a love ballad that originally appeared on Zappa's *Chunga's Revenge* album. Daughter Moon Unit will also make an appearance on the new LP, offering up a Valley Girl rap for a mock aerobics tune called "Hoznia." And Zappa's youngest son Ahmet Rodin actually penned one of the tunes, "Frogs With Dirty Little Lips," which is a little ditty he dreamed up at the age of six and sang around the house every day. Johnny Guitar Watson also makes an appearance on the new album. Other tunes include "Baby Take Your Teeth Out," "In France," "He's So Gay," "Won Ton On" and "Planet Of My Dreams."

And as if that weren't enough . . . there's also a book in the making and a Broadway musical in the offing, a production called *Thing Fish*, which Zappa has been working on for some time now. While in New York recently, Zappa talked about his music, his career and where he's headed.

Modern Recording & Music: I understand that you had a harrowing experience in Palermo, Italy, the last date on the last rock tour you did. Was that something that turned you off to touring?
Frank Zappa: I would say so, yes. What happened in Palermo was . . . we were working in a soccer stadium, it was the last concert on the tour, and I had been looking forward to playing in Sicily because my father was born there. And that afternoon I had taken a drive over to his hometown, this horrible little village called Bartenicco. So I checked that out, you know, getting into the Sicilian vibe of it all. There's this Italian schmaltz connected with Sicily for all people of Italian extraction.

So anyway, I was in a pretty good mood after exploring these old haunts. I get to this gig, had a great sound check, I had written a song that afternoon and taught it to the guys in the band . . . everything looked like it was going to be fine. We start the show and within 10 minutes of the beginning of the show there's this weird something going on, but you can't see the audience. It's totally black out there. They're a million miles away cause we're out in the middle of this soccer field. And I hear some disturbances. Suddenly, they got the army there and the police department and they're all fucking armed to the teeth. The next thing I know, the tear gas starts going off and guys are kneeling down with rifles, like mortars, shooting this tear gas into the stands. Bricks start flying. It turned into chaos. And we kept on playing through this. But it got so bad that we had to put wet rags on our faces to keep the tear gas out of our eyes. And we kept playing on and on.

Finally, the lights start going on and we see that the place is being emptied out. They're firing tear gas all over the place and they're clearing these people out of the stadium. We played for about an hour and a half during this thing. And we found out later that some kids had brought guns to this concert and the cops had guns and they were shooting at each other like cowboys and Indians. Meanwhile, we're trapped in the stadium downstairs, some gangs had broken into the tour bus, there's rocks flying all over the place and it's like a little war going on. And what the fuck for?! We go there to play some music and it turns into a situation where people are injured.

MR&M: And you lost money on that tour besides.

FZ: *Oh, yeah. The complete tour was financially very problematic, to the tune of $160,000. So after that whole experience there I'm saying, "Look, I am 42 years old, I like music a lot. But I don't believe that subjecting yourself or the audience to that kind of potential abuse is something that you have to do in order to make music. I think it's quite enough to make records. And I've got at least the next five records already on tape, 37 tunes ready to mix, with the last road band. And I'm not saying that I'm never going to go on stage again because I've done some conducting since that tour of Italy was over. But to go out there with an electric guitar and play rock 'n' roll music on a regular basis night after night in town after town . . . I don't want to do that. I've done it . . . 20 years of it. It's enough.*

MR&M: Would you agree that what did happen in Palermo is an extreme example of the potential for violence at any rock concert today?

FZ: *Anyplace, but especially in Europe. There's a large amount of anti-American sentiment over there as a result of the actions of the present administration. It used to be that if you were an American, your name was mud. Now your name is shit. Because, if they see you on the street, you are the visible manifestation of everything they hate about a regime they don't understand, located someplace else, that threatens their country. There's so much distrust and distaste for American behavior and ideals right now. It's a bad time to tour.*

MR&M: What about the American concert circuit?

FZ: American concerts are dangerous to do also because the Americans don't have any money to go out and buy tickets. So, the only things I'm really interested in doing on stage now are things with orchestras or chamber groups.

MR&M: You have no degrees, no mentor or no formal music training, yet you're composing this incredibly difficult music. How did you teach yourself?

FZ: I went to the library. It's free and it's there. And until they close down the public libraries in the United States, everybody has access to the same information. Just go and do it.

MR&M: So you were hungry for this sort of information at an early age?

FZ: Yeah, I started when I was about 14. I was writing symphonic pieces before I ever wrote a rock 'n' roll song.

MR&M: And throughout your career it's been trial-and-error with the various projects you've undertaken?

FZ: Yeah. I don't think I've mastered any of the techniques but I've gotten to a point where I'm severely competent. And in order to master the things that I've set out to master, the main thing that stands in my way is the budget to do it, because the stuff I'm working with is all expensive machinery and expensive personnel and things like that. I mean, I'm at the stage now where in order to do the things that I need to do, it requires resources beyond what I'm capable of providing for myself. Remember, it's my money that makes these things. I'm not funded by grants or foundations or anything. If I get a sales of a concert ticket, part of that money goes back into buying equipment and the airplane tickets for the next tour and paying the salaries of the people who go out. And the costs of making records keeps going up too. So I operate just like any other small business. The capital comes in to keep the business running so that people can consume it. I mean, I don't stick the money up my nose and I don't buy a yacht. It goes right back into the music. It's like converting the income I made from "Valley Girls" into this orchestra album. But I see no way in the future that I can continue funding such projects. This orchestra album is as much as I can spend, and it's kind of a dead-end project at that because we only pressed 6,000 copies of the album and it cost so much to do it that it's already a net loss as a project. So that gives me a number of problems for future projects.

MR&M: I understand you had a number of problems in getting this orchestral project together. What happened?

FZ: Wanna know why we didn't do this thing in the United States?

Besides the bad attitude we encountered, it was a money situation. We were originally going to record this with the Syracuse Orchestra with Christopher Keene conducting, and it was going to be premiered at Lincoln Center in New York City. We had made a deal with the Syracuse Orchestra and within a matter of days they managed to double the price. It started out at $150,000 for the whole project and then somebody in the orchestra union had found a whole bunch of extra rules that brought the cost up to $300,000. So I said no way.

MR&M: This project has gone through a lot of sidetracks along the way. You mentioned that at various times it was going to be done with the Krakow Symphony Orchestra, then the Mexico City Symphony, then Syracuse. How did you end up with the London Symphony Orchestra?

FZ: *Well, as soon as we got this extortionary message from the Syracuse Orchestra we decided to try to contact a British orchestra. First we called the BBC Orchestra but they were booked solid for the next five years. Then we called the LSO and they said, "Well, we don't know whether we can do it because we're just finishing off a film score and the musicians have one week off before they have to do another film score." And since they get to vote on everything they want to do, they put it to the orchestra and the orchestra members chose to record my stuff rather than take a vacation. They went directly from* Return Of The Jedi *to my stuff to another film. We had just a certain number of days to do the whole thing, and they were rehearsing their butts off. We had 30 hours of rehearsal for one concert and three days to record.*

MR&M: They probably didn't have to rehearse that much for *Jedi.*

FZ: *Well, they didn't have to because it's more traditional notation. It's not that hard to read, no difficult counting involved.*

MR&M: What were the problems you encountered with the Krakow and Mexico City orchestras?

FZ: *I went to Mexico City and actually conducted their orchestra for a little while. They were very interested in doing the project, then after we had the rehearsal and we got down to what it would cost, the guy I dealt with added it up and wanted $400,000. He had somehow gotten a hold of what the scale would have been if I had done it in New York City. And there was no way that they were as good as the New York Philharmonic and no way that I was gonna give them $400,000 . . . so I said, "Thank you, goodbye."*

As far as the Krakow Orchestra goes, they had been after me for

years and at one point last August, right at the end of a European tour,
I was supposed to go from Sicily to Warsaw to start this project. It had
all been set up at the beginning of the tour. Two weeks into the tour,
martial law broke out in Poland and all this other crap was happening
over there. So I said, "I don't think I want to take my recording truck
into Poland next to the tanks. It's crazy to do that." So we passed.

MR&M: Can you tell me about the problems you encountered in dealing with the orchestra unions in America?

FZ: *You have problems with the unions because of the way the union*
scale works and the cost per musician to do these projects and the fur-
ther entanglement of union regulations that you have to wade through
in order to do the project. That's only part of the problem. The other
part of the problem is the attitude of the people on the board of direc-
tors of the various orchestras as to what they will or will not program.
Then you have the economic constraints placed on the orchestral busi-
ness in the United States by the concertgoers themselves. Concertgoers
will only buy tickets to certain types of events because they haven't been
educated to new music. Most concerts of orchestral or chamber music in
the United States are devoted to regurgitation of artifacts left to us by
dead people from another country. That's classical music in the United
States. If you're not dead and you don't come from someplace else, then
obviously you're no good and your music shouldn't be played. That
pretty much sums up the attitude of the people who make the decisions
as to what orchestras play. And part of that decision is based on how
many tickets they can sell to the concert.

The economics of the business are totally different from what peo-
ple think of in rock 'n' roll. I'll give you an example: If by some strange
coincidence you are a composer and an American orchestra wants to
play your piece, something that you may have worked on for five years,
in order to just get the parts copied for the orchestra it might cost you
thousands of dollars. And do you know what you receive from the
orchestra for playing your music? $300 to $500 for the rental of the
materials to play it. That's how great the business is from a composer's
point of view. The only time a composer has a chance to earn anything
above and beyond that is if the piece gets recorded and he gets publish-
ing royalties from those records. But those records don't sell in the huge
quantities that rock records do, so the publishing royalties aren't that
great. The other way composers stay alive in the United States is with
grants or with teaching positions. But it's very difficult to see why any-
body who is studying music now would ever want to become a com-

poser. It's pretty much a dead-end street in the United States. And if you become a composer, you have to know in advance that what you're doing will probably never be played. The only person who will ever hear it is you, in your head.

MR&M: Why is that?

FZ: Because most symphony orchestras in the United States are simply doing what amounts to cover tunes of the greatest hits. Guys in orchestras have been playing Bach and Beethoven and Mozart and all that stuff since they were in the conservatory. They already know all the hits, so when a guest conductor comes to town, all he has to do is go out there, wave his stick and look romantic and it sounds perfect. It's like bar bands. Everybody knows how to play "Louie Louie." No problem. But if you hand them a piece of music they've never seen the likes of before, they'd have to learn it. So in a situation like that, if you want to try and get something brand new played, you're not going to get a good performance. For an orchestra to sound like a unit, playing something that is totally unfamiliar to them, it has to be rehearsed. So usually they won't touch a new piece because it's too much work, and also because the cost of rehearsal is so high.

For instance, some of the material I have written would take four weeks of rehearsal—that's eight hours a day, five days a week. In Europe you could get that, but in the United States you couldn't afford it. No way. And I've had offers from orchestras who want to play my music. They say they'll give it two days' rehearsal, and they make it seem like they're doing me a favor. Two days? They're crazy!! I would rather not hear it played at all than to hear it played wrong. Then you have to sit there while the newspaper critics say how shitty it was when what they have heard is not what I wrote. If it's going to come out, I want somebody to hear what I wrote and I want it played correctly.

MR&M: I've heard stories about the unions being so strong in some American orchestras that they were able to keep musicians who were completely incompetent due to alcoholism and were just faking it on stage, hidden within the orchestra. I understand that these people can't be fired because they are under binding contracts, yet the London Symphony Orchestra has no contracts and forces players to maintain a high degree of competence or else get booted.

FZ: The London Symphony Orchestra owns itself, it's an associative orchestra. The members own the orchestra, they hire their own conductor, they run their own business and they share in the profits. Consequently, an average guy in the London Symphony Orchestra will play 90 recording sessions a year while the average guy in the Boston

Symphony Orchestra, for example, will only do 17. See, the union scale in England is lower than in the United States so it costs you less to do a project with a British orchestra. And they're eager to do work, whereas the U.S. orchestras want to raise their pay scales up to the point where it's so sky-high that they're really not doing very many recording sessions. So ultimately their gross at the end of the year is less than what the British orchestra is going to get. On top of that, the attitude of an American orchestra seems to be: the smaller the amount of work you do, the better it is. It's really a lazy mentality, and it's the same kind of mentality that exists in other unionized industries like the auto industry. I mean, it makes me laugh when people complain about, "Hey, Japan is kicking our ass!" Yeah, they're kicking our ass because the American workers are getting all these benefits and big prices per hour for doing work, and they don't care about their job. All the quality control is gone. Craftsmanship isn't a part of your life anymore, you just want to get as much as you can from the evil capitalist pig who owns the factory, you wanna rip off the management, give them the big hose job, go on strike all the time and then when the stuff that you don't do well on the assembly line turns out to be a lemon and people don't buy it anymore and the company has to shut down, you just cut your own throat.

MR&M: By not putting back in.

FZ: Right. I just think that things would be a lot better if you are productive if you have a job, if you put in the effort and you do more work without ever having to go on strike. Then your boss, as a gesture of fairness and recognition, should give you more money . . . but for doing more work, not because 100 guys say, "We won't work at all unless you give us more money!" Because what happens then is the boss says, "OK, you think you got my balls in a bear-trap? I'll do this: I'll give you more money, but I'm raising the cost of my product 20 percent above what it was and I'll wind up making more profit." So the worker goes home with one dollar more in his pocket but the thing he needs to buy on the street is now costing him two dollars more. And every time there is a strike, there is this effect. That's the economic spiral that happens. You want more money? There's no free lunch. The guy who owns the thing is not gonna take less profit. Believe me, he'll find a way to make more profit. And strikes have been so prevalent that the product keeps going up in cost, a little bit and a little bit . . . and the next thing you know a jar of peanut butter costs five dollars!

MR&M: The Minneapolis Symphony went on strike earlier this year.

FZ: Yeah. I can just see it: "We will now withhold culture from the entire Minneapolis area until we get more pay for fewer concerts."

More orchestras have this cold what-can-I-get-outta-this attitude today. The Chicago Symphony is an exception. But you have to recognize that the Chicago Symphony is generally regarded as the best in the world. They sound good and they play like they really mean it, whereas, most of the other orchestras in the United States are not really serious about doing it. I mean, just because you have a tuxedo on doesn't mean that you're into something. They wear tuxedoes in Las Vegas, ya know.

PART FOUR

The Best
Band You
Never Heard
in Your
Life:

On Record

STEPHEN PAUL MILLER
PERFORMING QUOTATIONS: FRANK ZAPPA AS *FREAK OUT!* APHORIST

When I told my colleague Steven Paul Miller that I wanted to write an appreciation of Zappa's aphorisms, which I would have done, had the estate's lawyer had more respect for Zappa's work, Miller replied with the following fresh essay. A widely published poet and critic, Miller is also an assistant professor of English at St. John's University in New York.

Freak Out! was arguably the first concept album. The 1966 double album preceded the Beach Boys' *Pet Sounds* and the Beatles's *Sgt. Pepper's Lonely Hearts Club Band*, and Paul McCartney said that *Freak Out!* and *Pet Sounds* were models for *Sgt. Pepper's*. In what way? What is a concept album? A concept album might better be called an icon album or totem album. The concept is really a token that can interact with all the semiotic exchanges within the album's parts. This token potentially modifies everything else on the album. The reprise of "Sgt. Pepper's Lonely Heart's Club" and the quirky instrumentals of *Pet Sounds* are the informing tokens that render their respective albums conceptual. In other words, they are constant background possibilities. Before the Beatles' and Beach Boys' albums, the interjection of the performative of "freaking out" rendered Frank Zappa and the Mothers of Invention's *Freak Out!* conceptual.

Zappa was among the first to use *freak* as a verb. "Freak outs" were originally Los Angeles performances by the Mothers of Invention in the midst of happenings, or be-ins. To "freak out" was then a pleasant activity. However, a newer, younger version of the beat underground made its presence known to mainstream media, and a heavy ambivalence set it together with a sense of this underground as a movement that could affect widespread social change. In 1966 and 1967, to freak out began to take ominous overtones. Zappa's *Freak Out!* album reflects this shift. The inside of the double album cover of *Freak Out!* includes this definition of freaking out, titled "What is 'Freaking Out'?":

> On a personal level *Freaking Out* is a process whereby an individual casts off out-moded and restricting standards of thinking, dress, and social etiquette in order to express CREATIVELY his relationship to his immediate environment and the social structure as a whole. Less perceptive individuals have referred to us who have chosen this way of thinking and FEELING as "*Freaks,*" hence the term: *freaking out.* On a collective level, when any number of "*Freaks*" gather and express themselves creatively through music or dance, for example, it is generally referred to as a *FREAK OUT.* The participants, already emancipated from our national *social slavery,* dressed in their most inspired apparel, realize as a group whatever potential they possess for *free expression.* We would like to encourage everyone who HEARS this music to join us . . . become a member of the United Mutations . . . *FREAK OUT!*

This definition has it both ways. Freaking out is a pleasant and sociable expression that becomes ugly when seen through the filter of its "less perceptive individuals" who see freaking out as a threat. It is as if Zappa intended his group's 1966 album *Freak Out!* to be a challenge to American teenagers, an invitation that he did not expect to be accepted. After all, to "HEAR" the music was to freak out, to in a sense go native, to become the enemy.

As Zappa often reminds us, there was a limited commercial potential for such political sentiment or overt musical experimentation in 1966. Freaking out could not be apolitical. It was inherently subversive. By definition communal, it involved moving the avant garde to the mainstream and thus it was inherently political. To market an album called *Freak Out!* is to have an agenda, albeit an agenda that cannot be separated from its irony. It arouses by debunking its audience which, in turn, debunks itself.

Freak Out! is laced with slogans, conceptual tags, and general quotable quotes that self-satirize as they advertise. Social, artistic, and professional irony is Zappa's truing mechanism. With it, Zappa writes many of the era's most revealing lyrical aphorisms. *Freak Out!* begins by simplifying the ideologically confused vehicle of Bob Dylan's "Mr. Jones" into a more repressively cocksure "Mr. America": "Mr. America, walk on by the minds that won't be reached . . . the emptiness that's you inside . . . all the corny tricks you tried will not forestall the rising tide of hungry freaks, Daddy." "Hungry Freaks, Daddy," the album's first song, is its anthem. It characterizes the "rising tide" to "Mr. America." Zappa seamlessly extends the slogan "Make Love, Not War" into an individualistic program of discovery: "They won't go to war no more, great midwestern hardware store, philosophy that turns away from those who aren't afraid to say what's on their minds, the left behinds of the Great Society." The Great Society is equated to cultural tyranny: "Your supermarket dream . . . The liquor store supreme . . . Mr. America, try to hide the product of your savage pride, the useful minds that you denied. You saw their clothes and then you cried 'Those hungry freaks, Daddy!'" To be a freak is presumably to value inner substance over economic and social appearance. However, Zappa seems to doubt its inevitability. As the album continues, we consider that the speaker/singer of "Hungry Freaks, Daddy" is as ironic as the speaker/singer of the proceeding songs. Perhaps freaking has become one more posturing activity. The strongest line of the next song, a love ballad entitled "I Ain't Got No Heart," is "I ain't got no heart to give away." The internal begins to be ceded as a valid position. The song clearly suggests a credibility gap ("I don't believe in what you say") that affects the speaker.

The album's third song, "Who Are the Brain Police?," posits an affinity between art and state ideology: "Who are the brain police? What will you do when the label comes off and the plastic's all melted and the chrome is too soft?" "Plastic" and "label" imply that the record itself is surveying its audience, perhaps through a kind of commodity fetishism at work through flash and protective "chrome." However, the organizing mechanism of the commodity is apparently melting and dying. We become aware that its audience indeed contained these commodities: "What will you do if the people you knew were the plastic that melted and the chromium too?" Appropriately, the next song, "Go Cry on Somebody Else's Shoulder" provides an occasion for do-whop genre/audience lambasting. In the liner notes for the song, Zappa says, "You should not listen to it. You should wear it on your hair." The song ends with a talk over listing all the purchases that the speaker has made, such as khakis and a pompadour haircut. The speaker wonders why his former girlfriend does not "dig" him. This provides an interesting lead into "Motherly Love," which portends to be a sexual advertisement for the band: "Your mother's going to love you . . . Send us up some little groupies and we'll take their hands and rock them till they sweat and cry." "Motherly Love" translates unconditional motherly love into the sexual realm. The only truly virile love is motherly love.

The album then presents five consecutive uncommercial commercial songs: "How Could I Be Such a Fool," "Wowie Zowie," "You Didn't Try to Call Me," "Any Way the Wind Blows," and "I'm Not Satisfied." In a sense, the next song, "You're Probably Wondering Why I'm Here," comments on these songs. What is this band up to? Why are they working in a mode they do not seem to respect? "Just as much as you wonder 'bout me being in this place, that's just how much I marvel at the lameness on your face. . . ." The band would seem to be professional musicians who are merely making a living as best they can. They are not there for their audience and marketability but in spite of them. Thus "Trouble Every Day" follows "You're Probably Wondering Why I'm Here." The speaker of "Trouble Every Day" can relate to inner city riots: "You know something, people, I'm not black but there are a whole lot of times I wish I wasn't white either." The market economy is not working: "No way to delay that trouble coming every day. . . .Take your TV tube and eat it. . . .No one blabs it faster, their coverage can't be beat."

After "Trouble Every Day," *Freak Out!* explodes and leaves traditional lyrical structure. The voice-over of "Help, I'm a Rock" moves from a meditation on what a "drag" it is being a rock, policeman, and mayor. "It Can't Happen Here" then asks the musical questions "Who could imagine that they would freak out in Kansas?" and "Who could imagine that they would freak out in the suburbs?" "The Return of the Son of Monster Magnet" is addressed to Suzy Creamcheese: "Suzy Creamcheese, what's got into ya?" Suzy's repetition of "Flashy, Man" leaves us certain that something has indeed gotten into her. The album convinces us that one way or another Suzy Creamcheese and the rest of America will attend a freak out and "hear the music."

MIKE FISH AND BEN WATSON
FRANK ZAPPA ON DISC (1991)

The most elaborate commentary on Zappa's CDs comes from Ben Watson, here working with Mike Fish, in the British magazine *Wire*.

Frank Vincent Zappa was born on 21 December 1940 in Baltimore, Maryland. His parents were second-generation Sicilian Greeks and he grew up in California. His father moved a lot for work and he had a hard time at school. His gypsy good looks were not the American ideal, and he developed an outsider bitterness that led to an affinity for black R&B and a critical view of the American way.

Frank Zappa has not been served well by the rock press. Central to the 60s "underground" who sought to extend the scope of pop into art and politics, he is almost punished for surviving. It is so much more convenient to lionize dead heroes—Jim Morrison, Hendrix, Janis Joplin—than artists who are still productive. People who like music, though, are grateful that he is still there.

He learned rock music by collecting R&B records, something unusual for a white teenager before the advent of Elvis. He and Don Van Vliet, a high school friend (later to become Captain Beefheart), would listen to records together far into the night: Howlin' Wolf, Muddy Waters, Sonny Boy Williamson, Guitar Slim, Johnny "Guitar" Watson, Clarence "Gatemouth" Brown.

This was some education. Zappa's integrated high-school band The Black-Outs required defending from indignant racists after playing to a packed crowd in Sun Village, a mainly black area, in 1957. Like Johnny Otis, the West Coast drummer and 40s bandleader, Zappa's involvement with black culture meant that he could say (as he does on "Trouble Every Day" on *Freak Out*): "You know, people, I'm not black, but there's a whole lot of times I wish I could say I wasn't white", with an edge of honesty.

When the rock explosion of the 60s hit, both he and Beefheart were poised to create music that burned with subcultural riches. No wonder they thought San Francisco and its hippies were a bunch of fakes: when did Jefferson Airplane ever learn to play a stomping riff like "Metal Man Has Won His Wings"? You would need to have known James Brown's "Top Of The Stack" to play that one!

Then Zappa heard a record that changed his life: Edgard Varèse's *Ionisation,* a percussion/siren piece from 1931 that put Dada and Futurism into sound. It was being used as a demonstration record in a hi-fi shop (he had gone there looking for second-hand Joe Houston records). Zappa has subsequently broadened his interest in modern classical music, but his commitment to Varèse's explosive yet rhythmically defined soundworld remains undimmed. Rock music gave Zappa the ideal environment in which to explore the new sonorities Varèse dreamed of.

The Beatles and Stones and Bob Dylan arrived, making all sorts of people feel that pop music could become a new true culture. Zappa's background in marketing—he worked in an ad agency, designed greeting cards—enabled him to put together a band that turned current LA "freak" manifestations into a personal recording machine: the Mothers of Invention. An exceptional rhythm section—Jimmy Carl Black and Billy Mundi on drums and Roy Estrada on bass—provided a ponderous, unstoppable beat that no one has since managed to emulate (unless it is Bill Laswell's Material). Zappa's guitar developed from razorsharp R&B stylings into gorgeous psychedelia via the wah-wah pedal (which he was onto before Hendrix).

The Mothers were interesting people. Don Preston came from Herbie Mann's band, had played with Carla and Paul Bley and Charlie Haden in the 50s. Ian Underwood played bebop with bassist Steve Swallow in college. Ray Collins was a veteran doo-wop vocalist. Percussionist Ruth Komanoff was a Juilliard graduate. Elliott Ingber was the R&B guitarist who became Winged Eeel Fingerling. Jim Sherwood was a roadie who learned to play tenor on stage. Art Tripp was previously a percussionist with the Cincinnati Symphony Orchestra. These Mothers were old and could *play*.

Unlike the English muso bands of the 70s who harked on such amazing facts (*Keith Emerson was classically trained!* etc.), you have to dig around to find out these things. Zappa presented The Mothers as a circus, the apex of late-60s hairy anti-establishment Stop the War anarchy. People were disconcerted. André Previn said they were a con.

On "Little Green Rosetta" on *Joe's Garage* in 1979 Zappa sang, *"They're pretty good musicians/But it don't make no difference/If they're good musicians/Because anybody who would buy this record/Doesn't give a fuck if there's good musicians/On it/Because this is a stupid song/AND THAT'S THE WAY I LIKE IT"*. Mass-marketed virtuosity has never been able to equal the appeal of inspired amateurism. This was a doo-wop truth punk rediscovered. Zappa has always known it.

Zappa's critical stock fell in the 70s when he recruited two ex-Turtles to give his band teen-appeal (they also sang background vocals for Marc Bolan). He came back with two superb jazz albums (*Waka/Jawaka* and *The Grand Wazoo*—see below) that were generally ignored, and then initiated the DiscReet label with the notorious "pornography" of "Dinah Moe Humm". Yet he was all the while running perhaps the most explosively creative jazz band in the rock arena.

Zappa's commercialism has a venom that many listeners find offensive. It is problematic. Songs like "The Illinois Enema Bandit" and "The Torture Never Stops" make the sexist offence of Guns N' Roses seem childish, almost benign. Zappa is interested in shock as part of his aesthetic schema. Zappa has no qualms about taste, and really the game has always been the *documentation* of his musicians' behaviour—we decide what to think.

The 70s and 80s have been a continuous stream of tours, recordings, interviews. To create art using the forefront of technology—always one of Zappa's obsessions—requires that the artist become a businessman. The on-the-road rock-arena perspective meant that punk, for example, meant nothing to him (though he did admit to liking the UK Subs' classic "Live In A Car"). Sometimes the work schedule and isolation seem to condemn him to an ivory console. John Peel called it "building dungeons in the sky". But then he arrives with some vast composition like *Drowning Witch* and everything seems worth it.

There are flashes of openness which—for a major composer in his 50s—are quite unusual. The new enthusiasm for Conlon Nancarrow, for example, or inviting Archie Shepp on stage. Wonder what he thinks of Giacinto Scelsi and Michael Finnissy?

Now that Phil Lesh of the Grateful Dead has stood up to be counted as an enthusiast of modern classical music, Zappa no longer looks like a misfit and an outcast. Seems he was right all along. It is not weird to like Pee Wee Crayton *and* Pierre Boulez, Eric Dolphy *and* Elliott Carter—in fact it is common sense (and *Wire* philosophy, too). Zappa as patron saint of modern musical criticism?

Zappa is not going to hand the baton to John Zorn yet. His creativity is in full swing (witness the promised Synclavier cornucopia, the free-improvisation of *Make A Jazz Noise Here*). Zappa has been invited, alongside Stockhausen and Cage, to attend Frankfurt's 1992 Music Festival. This is a mark of honour for the younger man, a composer who has done so much to break down barriers of class and race in exploring what sound can mean. About time people started listening.—BEN WATSON

Rare Meat (1962–63)

A collection of pre-Mothers singles, absurdist versions of R&B that show Frank Zappa was a true connoisseur of doowop in all its primal weirdness. Two tunes feature Bob Guy, a local TV horror movie host. On "The World's Greatest Sinner" Zappa lets rip a guitar solo that rocks against the rhythm in a manner worthy of Johnny "Guitar" Watson: no other white bluesboy got *this* close. Pity the collection merely skims the surface of Zappa's juvenilia.—BW

Freak Out! (1966)

One of the most bedazzling debuts in music (daddy-o). Two sides of pop tunes disfigured by guitar noise and general craziness, two sides of extended weird, culminating in the closing "The Return Of The Son Of Monster Magnet". The Mothers were essentially a quintet of FZ, Roy Estrada, Jimmy Carl Black, Elliot Ingber (later Winged Eeel Fingerling of The Magic Band) and doo-wop voice Ray Collins. Zappa's career-long interests are already manifest: blasted satire, political contempt ("Trouble Every Day"), Elvis ("Help, I'm A Rock"). Also, "I Ain't Got No Heart" is a melancholy autobiography. The sleeve lists scores of influences. Other sleevenote: "Sometimes he (Zappa) sings. Sometimes he talks to the audience. Sometimes there is trouble."—MF

Absolutely Free (1967)

The first side, despite such subsequent raves as "Call Any Vegetable", is a little too fragmented, but the second is Zappa's first conceptual masterpiece, culminating in the scathing assault on middle-America in "Brown Shoes Don't Make It". The horn section of Buzz Gardner and Motorhead Sherwood arrived, as did keyboard whiz Don Preston, but it's Zappa's songs which cut the mustard. The CD reissue includes two extra songs which weren't on the original LP, "Big Leg Emma" and "Why Don't You Do Me Right".—MF

We're Only In It For The Money (1967)

Relentless, dark, angry, this grim answer record to *Sgt. Pepper* is Zappa's parting shot as a counterculture figure. It starts by poking fun at fake hippies, then stares at cops shooting kids and ends in a Californian version of Franz Kafka's *In The Penal Colony*. Some of the freewheeling energy of *Absolutely Free* is traded for structural detail, but the record remains a shocking experience. Zappa begins to unleash his toughest time signatures and charts, but the recording on the original is rather muzzy, and the controversial remix—substituting new bass and drum parts for those on the damaged master tapes—will sound uncomfortable to anyone who knows the original. Now doubled with *Lumpy Gravy* on one CD.—MF

Lumpy Gravy (1967)

No surprise that Zappa is currently planning a *Lumpy Gravy Phase III* (*Money* was "Phase I"). This record represents Zappa at his most outrageously creative, combining classical charts, bandmember mumbling and noises via a tape-slice technique that stands comparison to the work of Luc Ferrari (the king of European *musique concrète*). Because it only justifies itself via a keen sensitivity to contrasting timbre (whatever the sound source), this record has a purity that makes it a classic for Zappa addicts. When the later concerns—religion, alienated sex, exploitation, music-biz trivia—are mere history, maybe all the albums will sound like this. The Mozart of post-Capitalism states his case.—BW

Cruising With Ruben & The Jets (1968)

Zappa's tribute to the "cretin simplicity" of 50s street love songs. Recorded with the same primitive excitement with the multi-track as *Uncle Meat,* it is in fact a careful study of repetition and sonic levels. Minimalism that understood black music, this record looked forward to the knowing post-modernism of Chicago's House music. "Stuff Up The Cracks" is a suicide song (suffocation the social equivalent to the musical claustrophobia of endless piano triplets). Ray Collins sings so slimy it makes you cry. It's great. As with *Money,* new bass and drum parts on the CD change its impact.—BW

Burnt Weeny Sandwich (1969)

A more successful instrumental set than *Uncle Meat,* perhaps, since The Mothers play as a band—the massive "Little House I Used To Live In" is prototype jazz-rock that ought to be boring but isn't, thanks to the suave energy of Preston, Sugarcane Harris and Zappa—and the briefer pieces on side one find the present-day composer flexing genuine muscle. What might be doo-wop outtakes from *Ruben And The Jets* open and close the record, with the lovely "Valerie" acting as Zappa's farewell to the rock-'n'roll era. Currently unavailable.—MF

Uncle Meat (1969)

Sorry Mike, but *no record* is "more successful" than *Uncle Meat* (even *Burnt Weeny Sandwich*). This record set the agenda for art rock: everyone from the Soft Machine to the Hornweb Sax Quarter, Henry Cow to John Zorn, owe Zappa for this one. Multi-tracked Ian Underwood and Bunk Gardner substitute for horn sections in creating West Coast abstractions that put Stravinsky on a par with the Beach Boys. "Basically this is an instrumental album" runs the sleevenote, and "Pound For A Brown" and "Uncle Meat" are mighty compositions. The essential companion to *Trout Mask Replica*. (The CD contains 45 extra minutes—disappointingly not music, but dialogue from the *Uncle Meat* film).—BW

Hot Rats (1969)

A hit in England, this was "straight-ahead" music: driving instrumental rock with mesmerising, lopsided tunes and rich arrangements out of Rimsky–Korsakov and Richard Strauss. Captain Beefheart sang, Sugarcane Harris played searing violin, Zappa played monster solos. The cascade of musical ideas made all subsequent jazz-rock sound impoverished. The CD re-issue adds back all sorts of embellishments vinyl could not cope with.—BW

King Kong (1970)

Issued under Jean Luc Ponty's name with liner notes by Leonard Feather, this is a Zappa album in all but name. Some of the tunes degenerate into pleasant jazz (Ernie Watts and George Duke in romping form) but "Music For Electric Violin and Low Budget Orchestra" is a 19-minute epic, riding on Buell Neidlinger's bass and Art Tripp's drums and the cream of Hollywood session staff (Donald Christlieb on bassoon, Gene Cipriano on oboe, etc.). Burlesque acoustic music with a sick sense of humour. Jean Luc Ponty's surreal violin never sounded better.—BW

Weasels Ripped My Flesh (1970)

An amazing cut-up that might have been a seminal influence on everyone from Coldcut to Zorn—if they'd only heard it! Essentially no more than offcuts and loose ends from Zappa's workbench of the previous three years, the music covers the most ludicrous and most serious aspects of The Mothers Of Invention, often in hair-raising juxtapositions. Side two of the original LP is as great as any Zappa music: a tribute to Eric Dolphy, studio squeaks and gargles, the punk classic "My Guitar Wants To Kill Your

Mama", the irresistible "Oh No", a Glenn Miller-meets-Link Wray instrumental and the feedback gross-out of the title piece (recorded in Birmingham!) It rocks!—MF

Chunga's Revenge (1970)

I hadn't listened to this one for maybe ten years: it's an indulgent mess, even by some of Zappa's standards, but an entertaining one. There are chunks of heavyweight guitar on "Transylvania Boogie" and "The Nancy & Mary Music", which is a nonsense jam with great audience participation; "Road Ladies", a dull groupie song; skirling electric sax by Ian Underwood on the title track; fake 60s punk on "Tell Me You Love Me"; and lots more. Forgotten gem: the three a.m. jazzbo smooch instrumental "Twenty Small Cigars".—MF

200 Motels (1971)

Marketed as the "soundtrack" to the film, this double album was actually an excuse to release orchestral Zappa music—played by the Royal Philharmonic under Elgar Howarth. Tony Palmer mixed the visuals, then denounced the entire project as "self-indulgence" in *The Sunday Times*. Film and rock reviewers also registered irritation. So the music got ignored and Zappa, as the post-68 rock critics joined with the record companies in bad-mouthing anything that did not suit radio formats. "Magic Fingers" delivered everything Led Zeppelin ought to have done; "A Nun Suit Painted On Some Old Boxes" definitively parodied post–*Pierrot Lunaire* vocalese. "Little Green Scratchy Sweaters and Corduroy Ponce" is sublime.—BW

Fillmore East June '71 (1971)

Not much fun, and it sounds as if Zappa knows it. Having drafted Flo and Eddie (Mark Volman and Howard Kaylan) into the Mothers full-time, he made them the linchpin of this distended suite of rock-star-meets-groupie songs. It was mildly amusing 20 years ago, and it's quaint and tedious today. Even the other Mothers sound sloppy here, although there are knockabout bits of "Peaches En Regalia" and Don Preston gets to do an encore on Moog synthesiser.—MF

Just Another Band From LA (1972)

The intolerably laboured and tedious "Billy The Mountain" skit represents the nadir of FZ's work at this period, a collection of music-biz in-jokes grafted on to a mini-operetta. But "Magdalena", on the second side, is actually quite funny, and BW insists that the record is worth having for Zappa's snorting guitar improvisation on a revised "Call Any Vegetable". Well, maybe it is. Final appearance by Flo and Eddie with the group, fortunately.—MF

Waka/Jawaka (1972)

Made, along with *The Grand Wazoo*, following Zappa being injured at a London concert, this is a neglected and very fine record. Robert Christgau's opinion that it was made after Zappa had been listening to a lot of Miles Davis seems to be based on the presence of a trumpeter, Sal Marquez, in the band. It's a crisp, gleaming rock-jazz, decked out with strong modal solos (Zappa, Marquez, Preston) and horn charts which map out FZ's labyrinthine melodies and make them sound guilefully easy. Plus a couple of oddball songs, one of which features Sneeky Pete Kleinow on pedal steel. Great studio sound.—MF

The Grand Wazoo (1972)

A companion piece to the above, almost all-instrumental, and delivered by a full West Coast big band. If Shorty Rogers had breakfasted with Uncle Meat, this is what it would sound like (and the sleevenotes continue the Uncle Meat mythology). Some of the playing is so cool it anticipates 80s lite-jazz, but the long title track is a kind of rock-swing that nobody else, Zappa included, has much looked into since. George Duke appears; Don Preston is still on hand; the bassist is someone named Erroneous. Zappa directed from his wheelchair. Later, he confessed to little regard for the two records: "They were hits in Scandinavia."—MF

Overnite Sensation (1973)

The reformed Mothers included Ian and Ruth Underwood, Tom and Bruce Fowler, George Duke and Jean-Luc Ponty—a team of virtuosos and a remarkable *playing* band, which gets to show off its chops on full-tilt showpieces like "Fifty-Fifty" and "Dirty Love". But Zappa filled the record with his most scabrous pornographic lyrics, and what you hear is a brutal contempt for sex, which takes the energy out of the playing too. Duke gets off some crazy stuff and FZ is spirited, but this is the point where his music starts to sound as cold and heartless as his detractors suggest—MF

Apostrophe (') (1974)

Mike is not the only Zappa fan to register reservations after *Overnite Sensation*. It initiated a new label, DiscReet, and an overtly commercial blatancy. However, unprejudiced by an underground-rock Mothers-fan perspective (how old were you in 1968?), viewed in its own terms, *Apostrophe (')* is stunning. A mercilessly supercilious Zappa (people were calling him "Uncle Frank") takes us on a trip to the North Pole via religion-baiting and poodle-discipline. The title track (the only one without words, of course) was a jam with Jack Bruce and Jim Gordon. Fido was Plato's Phaedo, and the words—dismissed as "trivial" by the reviewers—actually concern mortality, materialism and masturbation. Heady stuff to reach number ten in the *Billboard* chart (June 1974).—BW

Roxy And Elsewhere (1974)

A quickie double-live set which manages to capture some of the tremendous gusto of this edition of The Mothers, jazz chops and little-big-band attack coupled with rock drive. Frank's skit on B-movie horrors, "Cheepnis", is priceless, there's a monolithic revision of *Freak Out*'s "More Trouble Every Day", and "Be-Bop Tango (Of The Old Jazzmen's Church)" brought forth Zappa's immortal line, "*Jazz is not dead, it just smells funny!*" Napoleon Murphy Brock replaces Ian Underwood on sax and is an inspired new straight-man foil for the leader. Beautifully crisp and crunchy sound.—MF

One Size Fits All (1975)

Highly rated by Zappaphiles and ignored by everyone else, this skintight sequence of songs in sumptuously hi-fi sound spotlights lots of fancy playing, sewn right into the fabric of the tunes, which give up on mere scatology and extend Zappa's private mythology to new extremes of obscurity. "Inca Roads" seems to be a poke at Eric Von Daniken, "Can't Afford No Shoes" blasts Nixon's recession, and Johnny "Guitar" Watson inexplicably gets two walk-on parts as guest vocalist. The Mothers sounded to be moving towards a hyper-slick jazz-rock, though all jazz-rock was getting hyper-slick in 1975.—MF

Bongo Fury (1975)

Captain Beefheart had appeared on the last one as "Bloodshot Rollin' Red". Here he was a front-line partner, though his appearances were mainly as Zappa's stooge, mumbling lyrics that scarcely added to the poetic treasury he'd already fostered. Cut mostly live in Texas, the music rocks—"Advance Romance" is a wild blues fantasy and "Muffin Man" shows off Zappa's guitar prowess—but the material is rather tired and shoeless: "200 Years Old" is about as weak a snook at the American bicentennial as you could imagine. The last album with "Mothers" on the masthead, and the last with the old crew of George Duke, Napoleon Brock and the Fowlers.—MF

Zoot Allures (1976)

A new chapter. The major player, besides FZ, is drummer Terry Bozzio, whose skilful playing is remote from jazz time: Zappa was getting back to rock. A neat, curt set of songs gives nobody much to bite on, with softcore porn, winos, disco boys and dead-end jobs the subject matter. "The Torture Never Stops" is ten minutes of orgasmic groaning and Vincent Price-monologue from the composer. Not bad, but the point remains that this period of Zappa's work seems much more dated than his 60s records, as timelocked as they are.—MF

Zappa In New York (1977)

Like all Zappa's double LPs, an album of vast musical and conceptual proportions. The word is opera. "Titties 'n Beer" rewrote Stravinsky's *Soldier's Tale* into B-movie cameos and verbal improvisation. The "Black Page" gave hapless individuals (including this author—Hammersmith Odeon 1979) the chance to dance onstage to rhythms of a complexity unsurpassed outside Brian Ferneyhough. "The Purple Lagoon" had the Brecker Brothers playing as if their lives depended on it. Some buyers got "Punky's Whips" (others did not). Hopefully the CD release will have it, as it achieves live word/sound surprise that was previously a tape-slice feature.—BW

The next three releases deserve explanation. Originally there was *Lather,* a four-record set that mixed live rock, tape-spliced *musique concrete,* orchestral music and jazz into a two-and-a-half-hour blockbuster. Warner Bros would not release it. There were lawsuits. Zappa salvaged the live rock as *Zappa In New York:* Warners released the rest with covers by Gary Panter (of *Raw Comix* fame) and no personnel details. This has "Redunzl" with some great Zappa guitar and George Duke keyboards; "Let Me Take You To The Beach", sublime idiot pop; "Greggary Peccary", a cartoon score that predates the current interest in Carl Stalling by over a decade.—BW

Sleep Dirt (1979)

"Filthy Habits" perpetuates the lascivious feedback of *Zoot Allures.* "Flam Bay" dissects cocktail jazz in the manner of "Twenty Small Cigars" on *Chunga's Revenge.* Intimate chamber jazz bass interacts with arena rock guitar and scored drum patterns. Some of the oddest music ever recorded, in fact. If you like interesting music, start here.—BW

Orchestral Favourites (1979)

There have been criticisms of Zappa's orchestral works by those who appreciate the avantgarde tendencies of his rock output: he is not challenging the composers he admires—Edgard Varèse, Krzysztof Penderecki, Pierre Boulez, Elliott Carter—with the music here. However, the instrumental burlesques and surreal takes on Western-movie pomposity are informed by a sharp ear for colour, and a sense of humour that is quite unique. This album is buoyed by electric bass and non-classical drumming (and a guitar solo on "Duke Of Prunes"), so it has a punch the later LSO albums lack.—BW

Sheikh Yerbouti (1979)

Zappa's apparent taste for hiring musicians who could simply play all his notes, rather than act as creative foils, tells against this double-LP. It's a series of nasty, tasteless attacks on John Doe which are no different to what was usually going on in 'punk' at the time, except for one thing: there is ice in Zappa's heart. Which makes the otherwise almost hilarious

"Bobby Brown" into something sarcastically horrible. Plus: "Baby Snakes", the near-hit "Dancin' Fool", the monumental guitar solo on "Yo' Mama".—MF

Baby Snakes (1979)

Live versions of songs from *Live In New York* and *Sheik Yerbouti*, the soundtrack to the video. Ripping stuff, recorded with maximum energy.—BW

Joe's Garage Acts 1, 2 & 3 (1979)

Two hours of songs segued into a "narrative" by Zappa speaking down a plastic megaphone (as "The Central Scrutinizer"). Production of bass and drums is ambient in the style of late 70s soul records and guitar solos are usually xenochronous, giving them an airy lack of propulsion. "A Token Of My Extreme", a song from the 1971 Flo & Eddie Mothers, is intriguing: others are less inspired. Side one, sex with a robot called Cy Borg, is magnificently brutal, and includes a Peter Wolf synth solo that expertly duplicates the sensations of oral sex. "A Little Green Rosetta" is, depending upon your position, (a) a laugh, (b) awe-inspiring commodity degradation, (c) a waste of time.—BW

Tinseltown Rebellion (1981)

Too much time on the road documenting his male musicians' foibles can give Zappa's lyrics a relentless sexism that is wearing. Covers of old songs proliferate. The musicians—by this time including future metal star Steve Vai, keyboardists Tommy Mars and Peter Wolf, and percussionist Ed Mann—are certainly blindingly proficient, but when their personalities are revealed in song (e.g., the cover of "Brown Shoes Don't Make It"), they sound nerdy, lacking the original Mothers' pachuco charm. Zappa's "attack" on LA Punk in the title track sounds misinformed as well as unkind. "The Blue Light" is dead peculiar, though, and the one guitar track is a stonker.—BW

You Are What You Is (1981)

Again, big on vocals—the only "music music" (Zappa's phrase) is "Theme From The 3rd Movement Of Sinister Footwear". Maybe the callousness of "Jumbo Go Away" is its saving grace, but the jaded nature of the subject matter (band-members bored with groupies) seems to invade the tune. The laborious choral workouts seem endless. The political comments are worthy but heavy-handed, lacking the paranoid urgency of yore. Even loyal fans looked forward to the next instrumental album.—BW

Ship Arriving Too Late To Save A Drowning Witch (1982)

This was nearly it. A new richness of multiple event made even the singing sound direct. "Valley Girl"—Zappa's daughter Moon mocking the phrases of Hollywood's monied youth—was the hit. As usual, Zappa's instinct for the cheap and amusing financed the abstruse musicality: "Drowning Witch", kicking off with *sprechstimme* nonsense, is a compendium of avantgarde composition (see Out To Lunch's review in *Hawaiian Picnic,* the short-lived new music journal). "Teen-age Prostitute" documented the other side of LA life. Classic stuff.—BW

Man From Utopia (1983)

This developed Zappa's *sprechstimme,* frequently "backed" by over-dubbed instruments which are following Steve Vai's transcriptions of Zappa's freeform gibberish. The results on "The Dangerous Kitchen" and "The Radio Is Broken" are a fantastic collision of discipline and randomness. There are three crucial instrumentals, a union-bashing song ("Stick Together") that reflects Zappa's petit-bourgeois composer aspirations and an R&B medley. Patchy, but an exciting indication that "Drowning Witch" was no flash-in-the-pan: Zappa was brewing up something new in his compositional schema.—BW

London Symphony Orchestra Vols 1, 2, 3 (1983)

An article in Oslo's *Society Pages* (the Zappa fanzine since relocated to New York) likened Zappa's orchestrations to a dinosaur's brain. Fine for small ensembles, it argued, it cannot animate a full symphony orchestra. "Bogus Pomp" (on vinyl vol 2 and the CD) was intended to parody movie clichés with "cheesy fanfares, drooling sentimental passages and predictable 'scary music'," according to Zappa. If you are not expecting the futurism of, say, Giacinto Scelsi or Michael Finnissy, the scores are great, a luxuriant swamp of quintessential Zappa. Vinyl vol 2 has two tracks—"Bob In Dacron" and "Strictly Genteel"—left off the CD.

Recording quality is exemplary. Sleevenotes include a characteristically spiky criticism of the LSO trumpet section by the composer.—BW

Francesco Zappa (1984)

Baroque trio sonatas by Francesco Zappa who (according to *Grove*) flourished between 1763 and 1788, realized on the Barking Pumpkin Digital Gratification Consort (i.e., Zappa's Synclavier) with the assistance of clarinettist David Ocker, who also provides some excellent demystificatory notes on the function of Baroque music ("sawing away while noblemen ate dinner"). It sounds like a musical Christmas card. The machine rhythms add a worrying mechanical slant.—BW

Them Or Us (1984)

Frank's "rock" albums—those collections without some specific thematic/musical intention—had by now become lighthearted patchworks where the master jumped from tune to tune just as in the very early days, yet without the most jarring of juxtapositions. Here there are instrumental excerpts full of glittering finesse, Steve Vai outdoing even the leader on his "Stevie's Spanking" showcase, and the first evidence of FZ's new interest in cover versions, with a reading of the Allmans' "Whipping Post" that outfries any boogie music the South could have served up. The title refers to Zappa's moral outrage at fresh attempts to censor music. And so say we all.—MF

The Perfect Stranger (1984)

Rumour has it that Zappa fell out with Pierre Boulez on this project, explaining the four (excellent) Synclavier incursions on an album ostensibly performed by Boulez's Ensemble Intercontemporain. *Freak Out*'s list of "influences" had included Pierre Boulez and, whatever the rumours (and Zappa's disgracefully funny "Down In France" on *Them Or Us* should be taken into account—mind you, he is very respectful towards Boulez in the *Real Frank Zappa Book*), the music is terrific. As everyone grows up, such fusions are more and more smiled upon. The point is that *this* collaboration produced important modern music. (Defensively?) Described by Zappa as "preposterously non-modern", it is Desert Island fare nonetheless.—BW

Zappa has always recorded his concerts. Now he decided to unleash a set of pure guitar solos, leavened with acoustic studio items. A lot of the tracks were derived from "Inca Roads", a jazzy number peculiarly suited to Zappa's melodic, claustrophobic guitarism (a full analysis was provided by Out To Lunch in *Society Pages* no. 9). Someone was actually using the rock machine to improvise music of gobsmacking originality. Until *Guitar* arrived it looked as if *Shut Up* was Zappa's *Interstellar Space*. No other guitarist has paid such acute attention to rhythmic separation. Phew.—BW

Guitar (1979–84)

Probably the best music available on CD, 132 minutes of live Zappa guitar with a band that really moves to his extensions. Fabulous sculptural sound quality makes *Shut Up* sound weedy. Chad Wackerman (drums) and Scott Thunes (bass) are really something. As John Swenson pointed out in *Guitar World*, Zappa has boxes and boxes of this stuff. Utterly spiffing.—BW

Jazz From Hell (1984)

A mere seven of the "five hundred or so" Synclavier pieces Zappa has been working on. The Synclavier is the computer-to-digital interface used by Miles Davis on *Tutu*. The bell-like purity of the *Perfect Stranger* fillers has been superseded by more carnal sounds. Interestingly, Conlon Nancarrow (the astonishing Mexico-based composer who resorted to piano-roll punching to instigate his "unplayable" ideas—namechecked on *Tinsel Town Rebellion*) provides Zappa with a guide to such bypassing of musicianship. For light relief there is a realtime guitar showcase, "St. Etienne" (perhaps named for Pierre Boulez—it is the "cultural desert" he grew up in). With *Jazz From Hell* Zappa leaps to the top of the list of worldclass futuro-composers. He has bought still more RAM to further digital realism. The mouth waters.—BW

Thing-Fish (1984)

Scabrous vision of Broadway rubs our noses in AIDS, racism and yuppie emptiness. Johnny "Guitar" Watson guests on vocals. Every home should have one.—BW

Frank Zappa Meets The Mothers Of Prevention (1985)

For non-American consumption Zappa omitted "Porn Wars", a cut-up of sensational pronouncements on rock music censorship, replacing it with a protest song delivered by Johnny "Guitar" Watson called "I Don't Even Care" and two abstract instrumentals. The CD has the lot. Zappa views the PMRC as endangering freedom of speech with their attacks on the so-called "bad language" of heavy metal and rap and has campaigned vigorously against them. "Yo Cats" is a tirade against the session-musician mafia sung beautifully by Ike Willis; "We're Turning Again" pans the 60s revival (Hendrix, Doors, etc.) with remarkable prescience. "Aerobics In Bondage" is more Synclavier lunacy. A classic.—BW

Broadway The Hard Way (1988)

This collected together the new songs from the 1988 tour, attacking business-class feminism, Republicans and TV Evangelists. The band included a nonpareil horn section (Walt Fowler—trumpet, Bruce Fowler—trombone, Paul Carman—alto, Albert Wing—tenor, Kurt McGettrick—baritone) but we do not get to hear them a great deal. Sharper politically than "You Are What You Is", the whole affair is like an updated *Money*. Some of the vocal writing—"Jesus Thinks You're a Jerk", "Any Kind Of Pain", "Rhymin' Man"—has the haunting, cynical beauty of Kurt Weill.—BW

You Can't Do That On Stage Anymore Vol I (1969–88)

The first in a series of six double-CDs that present live Zappa from the last 20 years. The reworking of themes and the customizing of composition for different individuals begs comparison to Duke Ellington. This includes a version of "Louie Louie" recorded at The Factory in the Bronx in 1969 with Lowell George on guitar and vocals, "Sofa #2" from Genoa and a storming "Zomby Woof" from Milan.—BW

You Can't Do That On Stage Any More Vol 2 (1988)

This one is a complete concert from Helsinki, July 1974, by the quintet from *Roxy And Elsewhere*, a superbly accomplished band playing music they knew backwards and could therefore have maximum fun with. The guitar playing is fierce even by Zappa's standards—sample "RDNZL" for a relentless yet somehow luminous improvisation—and George Duke adds virtuosic underscoring, Napoleon Murphy Brock (suffering from pneumonia!) comic relief. It plays for two hours and nothing gets boring.—MF

You Can't Do That On Stage Anymore Vol 3 (1971–88)

The 1984 band (Ike Willis—guitar and vocals, Ray White—guitar and vocals, Bobby Martin—keyboards and vocals, Alan Zavod—keyboards, Scott Thunes—bass, Chad Wackerman—drums) predominates here. A great vehicle for Zappa's guitar solos, there is rather too much from *You Are What You Is* for my taste. High points are a staggering "Drowning Witch", edited together from versions by two different bands (according to Zappa the 1984 band *never* played it correctly and the 1982 band "only managed to get close on *one* occasion"), a blues about Nixon performed by the *Roxy* band, a riotous Terry Bozzio drum solo, a magnificently decadent sounding "Zoot Allures" and a 24-minute "King Kong" that fuses solos from 1969, 1971 and 1982.—BW

You Can't Do That On Stage Anymore Vol 4 (1969–88)

A jolly song-oriented collection, notable for a tenor sax solo by Archie Shepp (!!) on "Let's Move To Cleveland" in 1984, some tunes from *Thing Fish* that might remind people how well Zappa writes opera, the brilliant Varèse-like "Approximate", a well weird "Florentine Pogen" and a hilarious yet painful rap from Zappa in 1969 called "Tiny Sick Tears". The Shepp showcase appropriately segues into some free-form Mothers Of Invention from 1969, "You Call That Music?", that demonstrates how much Zappa learned from late-60s revolutionary jazz. It also has Captain Beefheart on a nine-minute "The Torture Never Stops" from 1976, utterly different from its final form, the band stomping out a Howlin' Wolf riff with the sheer venom Hubert Sumlin brought to his guitar.—BW

The Best Band You Never Heard In Your Life (1991)

BW has already raved in these pages over this memento of Zappa's 12-piece touring band of 1988, which fell apart mid-schedule and cost its leader a lot of money. Considering the quality of the band, as evidenced by this recital, you can't blame him for feeling bitter: a horn section of huge panache lends added fire and soul to Zappa nuggets like "Who Needs the Peace Corps" and "Eric Dolphy Memorial Barbeque", the government sends a spokesman, Jimmy Swaggart is torn to pieces, a batch of covers runs from "Bolero" to "Sunshine Of Your Love", the likes of "Zoot Allures" are granted sumptuous new textures and everything ends on the horns playing Jimmy Page's guitar solo from "Stairway To Heaven". More!—MF

Make A Jazz Noise Here (1991)

A musical blockbuster, allowing the 1988 horns room to stretch out on music that sounds like an unholy alliance of sleazejazz, free improvisation, avantgarde classical, Knitting Factory samplers and guitar mania. Walt Fowler's trumpet on the "Royal March" from Stravinsky's *Soldier's Tale* is astonishingly fleet. One is used to hearing music on this creative level played to audiences of 20-plus (Leeds) or five (London): that Zappa can play such material to audiences of thousands is remarkable. Adorno noted that the avantgarde is frequently tainted by being deprived of the technical excellence afforded to commercial ventures. *Jazz Noise* is an act of defiance to the poverty-programme dealt more creative musicians. Mighty.—BW

Beating the Bootleggers

Frank Zappa has been mercilessly bootlegged throughout his career. He has decided to issue eight famous bootlegs himself. Prices are reasonable (£8 for CDs). As he says "If you must have crap, you can now get fully affordable crap and maybe put some sleazebag out of business". They are all on the Foo-Eee label.

As An Am-Zappa—New York, 31 October 1981.
The Ark—Boston, July 1968.
Freaks And Motherfuckers—Fillmore East, 11 May 1970.
Unmitigated Audacity—Notre Dame University, 12 May 1974.
Any Way The Wind Blows—Paris, 24 February 1979 (double).
'Tis The Season To Be Jelly—Sweden, 30 November 1967.
Saarbrucken 1978—Saarbrucken, 3 September 1978.
Piquantique—Stockholm, 21 August 1973 & Sydney 1973.

If you have difficulty obtaining releases, G&S Music is a mail order service that deals exclusively with Zappa's music. They are reliable and are genuine enthusiasts: G&S Music, 7 Ullswater Road, Leverstock Green, Hemel Hempstead, Hertfordshire, HP3 8RD, UK. Telephone: 0442-63287.

Fanzines operating at the moment are: *T'Mershi Duween,* 96a Cowlishaw Road, Hunters Bar, Sheffield S11 8XH UK; *Society Pages,* recently somewhere in America.

Recommended reading: *The Real Frank Zappa Book,* Frank Zappa with Peter Occhiogrosso (Poseidon Press, 1989).

ART LANGE

FZ ON CD (1988)

Art Lange, based in Chicago, has long been one of the most astute reviewers of avant-garde music of various kinds. Here he reviews for *down beat,* whose editor he then was, the initial Zappa CDs.

It's hard to believe that Frank Zappa, guitarist, composer, bandleader, social critic, studio engineer, marketing strategist, filmmaker, defender of democracy, and inventor of the term "hot and bulbous," among other things, has been hanging around the fringe of the musical world for over 20 years now. But it's true; I've got the proof right in front of me—the first 12 CDs in the projected Complete Works Of Frank Zappa to be issued by Rykodisc, an adventurous CD-only company.

I say that Zappa's been on the fringe because he's always been an outcast; he's never had a hit single or (to my knowledge) a gold LP, if any of his music gets played on the radio it's only his most innocuous pop confections, and his attitude has been, over the years, one of, shall we say, dislike, for the record company execs and industry business types who often decide what music we hear—or don't hear. But make no mistake— Zappa's one shrewd hombre, and for years he's milked his "outcast" status and created a cult niche for himself, one which has evolved and grown so that today he stands as a "serious" composer and musical/social commentator. He appears frequently on tv talk shows (and he was rumored to replace Joan Rivers as host of her nationally syndicated *Late Show.* The mind boggles.).

It all began in 1965, with *Freak Out!* (Ryko RCD 40062, 60:34 minutes), a real shocker on its release. The Mothers of Invention (Zappa's band at the time) were the weirdest-looking band in rock, and the songs— blatant pitches for nonconformism, anti-censorship ditties, parodies of pop love laments, and a couple of long acid-noise jams full of pounding drums, tape manipulations, psychedelic Mideastern drones, and drug-induced hallucinatory raps (probably imaginary—Zappa's always had a strong anti-drug stance)—were simply ahead of their time. Which is probably why, for the most part, they sound so good today. Musically, Zappa's borrowing of easily recognizable elements from r&b, doo-wop, teenybopper pop, L.A. barrio rock, and contemporary classical styles fits comfortably into today's neo-trad mood of rediscovering roots music for fun and profit, and the grungy, sloppy, garage band sound of the Mothers (reproduced well-enough on CD) was totally calculated, actually masking sophisticated arrangements and excellent musicianship (augmented by some of L.A.'s top studio cats).

Absolutely Free followed *Freak Out!,* but it was the third album which helped cement Zappa's reputation. *We're Only In It For The Money* (combined with *Lumpy Gravy* on one CD, Ryko RCD 40024, 70:54), with its killer *Sgt. Pepper* parody cover, took Zappa's satire into the realm of sarcasm, as the lyrics registered disgust at cops, politicians, hippies, parents—virtually every layer of late-'60s society. Was it crude? Certainly. Vicious? Maybe. Effective? Well, in retrospect, it varies. But there's no doubt that *We're Only In It For The Money* is a period piece today, suffocating under the weight of '60s cultural references and icons. Musically it's much less interesting than *Freak Out!,* though here are the seeds (via song segues, interludes, interjected dialog, and the use of the studio as instrument) of many later, more successful sonic pieces.

Rykodisc has generously paired *We're Only In It For The Money* with *Lumpy Gravy,* probably Zappa's most ambitious and least commercial LP—a 32-minute montage (in Zappa's words, "a curiously inconsistent piece which started out to be a Ballet but probably didn't make it.") recorded by a small orchestra of L.A.'s finest. The quick cutting layered snippets of Zappa's musical world (echoes of Varèse, Stravinsky, r&b, surf music, muzak, and jazz), with more (parody?) dialogs of drug-induced paranoia, and plenty of pig noises. Actually, there's more than curiosity value here—if you're looking for the structural model for John Zorn's collage pieces like *Spillane* and *The Big Gundown,* this is it.

Ruben And The Jets (Ryko RCD 10063, 41:28) is another conceptual album, but completely without pretension (save perhaps the almost unnoticeable reworking of the opening bassoon phrase from Stravinsky's *The Rite Of Spring* into a doo-wop chorus)—a slice of Zappa's high school nostalgia, a paean to East L.A. '50s r&b-flavored rock. Zappa obviously loves this music, while he so deftly parodies it, though in 1988 it's a one-trick pony.

By 1969 Zappa's interest in jazz began to manifest itself to a greater degree; live concerts by this time featured plenty of hot soloing, and fans wanted to hear Zappa stretch out on guitar. *Hot Rats* (Ryko RCD 10066, 47:16) was the initial result, showcasing the proficient jazz-rock chops of Zappa, saxist Ian Underwood, and violinist Sugar Cane Harris. With the exception of one riveting vocal by Capt. Beefheart, this is a strictly instrumental outing that sustains listening today because of the quality of the solos and the distinctive nature of the compositions/arrangements. I have one nit to pick, however. While digitally remixing the music for CD, Zappa added a few minutes of music to the original and rebalanced a few instruments, to no great gain or loss *except* for the three-minute *Little Umbrellas*. Originally a slow, moody Mideastern melody exquisitely textured and orchestrated, this piece lost a great deal of its exotic charm in the remix, where Zappa brought up a number of inconsequential secondary parts out of the mix (piano comping here, a recorder part there) and obscured or buried evocative textures under too much busyness. I'm holding on to my LP for when I want to hear this cut.

Uncle Meat (Ryko RCD 10064/65, 57:23/63:26) dates from about the same time as *Hot Rats,* though the two-LP set contains a fascinating—and equally frustrating—potpourri of studio jams, carefully orchestrated interludes, random gab, written dialog, noise, improvisation, idiocy, banter, and excerpts from live concerts, sliced, spliced, chopped, channeled, reupholstered, and polished (in the CD mix) to a sheen. The three saxes in the band instigate a lot of jazzy soloing (especially on the sidelong *King Kong*), but much of the material is interrupted by Zappa's typical fragmented sense of montage. Added to the program for CD consumption is some 45 minutes of sound track (dialog only, no music) from the film *Uncle Meat.* These interviews, rehearsals, scripted passages, and asides were edited documentary-style (CD verité?) with the effect of us eavesdropping on the making of the film. Textual motifs reoccur throughout in musical variational fashion, but only the hardcore Zappaphile will listen to this more than once.

Despite its sloppiness and periodic inanity, there's much of bizarre interest on *Uncle Meat*. Unfortunately, Zappa cleaned up his act on 1972's *The Grand Wazoo* (Ryko RCD 10026, 37:11). Apparently aimed at the fusion crowd, *Wazoo*'s clean, crisp sound delivers some rather bland instrumental arrangements and jazzy solos of marginal heat (none of the sizzle of *Hot Rats* here). George Duke energizes one cut, but most of the music is too ordered, too controlled, too (unthinkable for Zappa!) mellow. Hopefully Rykodisc will repackage *Burnt Weenie Sandwich* and *Weasels*

Ripped My Flesh, two uneven but infinitely more exciting LPs from the period between *Hot Rats* and *Grand Wazoo.*

Jump to 1979 and *Joe's Garage Acts I, II, & III* (Ryko RCD 10060/61, 58:36/56:52), an ambitious musical (songs carrying the unified dramatic thread) decrying censorship in a futuristic society that tries to outlaw music. It's well crafted in terms of dramatic variety and scene setting (though given its, shall we say, risqué subject matter, it's doubtful to replace the next Andrew Lloyd Webber extravaganza on Broadway), the production is first-rate, Ike Willis has an expressive voice, and there're long guitar solos symbolizing the protagonist's sense of mental escape from his fascistic environment. There's also the usual digs at organized religion, record industry execs, music critics, and lotsa lewd language. Not for the kiddies.

Public clamour for more guitar apparently forced Zappa to release the multi-disc *Shut Up 'N Play Your Guitar* (Ryko RCD 10028/9, 53:23/54:13), longish instrumental excerpts from live concerts (sound quality is top-notch). Zappa *is* an extremely fine guitarist (for a revealing look at this aspect of Zappa, see the interview in *db,* Feb. '83) capable of anything—bluesy, modal, melodic, patterned, hot, cool, complex, convoluted, grotty, ad infinitum. With strong support from his circa '79–80 band (MVP honors go to drummer Vinnie Colaiuta), this is worth discovery by fusion fans, guitar fans, and Zappa fans; others are advised to marvel in small doses.

The most recent development in Zappa's multi-faceted musical career has been the emergence of his "serious" classical compositions. One senses that, given the fragmented orchestral interludes on so many of Zappa's rock LPs, this is the direction he's always wanted to go in. The three compositions on *Zappa/The London Symphony Orchestra* (Ryko RCD 10022, 62:16) reveal how Zappa's writing has grown much more assured over the years; themes are given real development, and sectionalized episodes hang together and flow naturally. Zappa has mastered the syntax of contemporary classical music, and you can hear traces of Varèse, Bernstein, Copland, Ives, Stravinsky, and many more, but with a distinctive twist that is Zappa's contribution to the genre. There's a perhaps not surprising sense of ominousness to the music—danger and wariness fuel his drama—plus more than a few characteristic satiric touches deflating classical pretensions. Highly recommended for the adventurous listener. (Note: This CD represents the biggest programmatic change from the LP: two shorter pieces, *Pedro's Dowrey* and *Envelopes,* are dropped in favor of the long *Bogus Pomp.*)

BEN WATSON
FRANK ZAPPA AS DADAIST: RECORDING TECHNOLOGY AND THE POWER TO REPEAT (1996)

Ben Watson returned to Zappa again in the late 1990s, this time to make a case for his music in a magazine otherwise devoted to musicology. James Grier, recently at Yale University, gave a persuasive paper about Zappa at the 1995 New York meeting of the American Musicological Society. It would have been reprinted here, did its author not, as a good academic, want it to appear first in a "refereed journal," which this book ain't. Such reservations don't bother Watson, thankfully.

Frank Zappa's work has been persistently misconstrued by the pop industry. This paper seeks to relate his music to the tradition of the European avantgarde (especially Dada). Using the film theory of founding dadaist Hans Richter, Zappa's much criticized "self-indulgence" is interpreted as sabotage of commercial manipulation. Zappa's attention to the technical aspect of recording is examined, along with his concern to disrupt conventions of representation. He is compared and contrasted to the post-war classical composers Stockhausen, Cage and Boulez. A case is made for him as a composer who refused compositional ideologies, adopting instead a collage aesthetic. It is also argued that his eclecticism avoids the "mildness" that has been noted as a feature of postmodern polystylism.

Introduction: Zappa and Dada

Frank Zappa's death in December 1993 ended a career spent subverting the commercial culture in which he operated. By close attention to the way in which music manipulates its audience, Zappa played with parameters—musical, technical, social and sexual—that are usually left unexamined, sacrosanct. Nowhere is this clearer than in his use of recording, the essential means by which twentieth century music reaches a mass audience. Zappa was fascinated by the power relations of recording technology; indeed, his whole *oeuvre* may be viewed as a meditation on the consequences of being able to spool other people's time on pieces of plastic. Questions of propriety and property—the encounter of the individual with the social—were raised with unnerving persistence.

The pop press has not been kind to such tampering with the rules. Since the early 70s, Zappa's experimentation has been repeatedly attacked as "self-indulgence".[1] It is necessary to go outside pop to discover the spirit that animated him. His fusion of technical and social transgression is best understood as proceeding from the avantgarde of the early twentieth century—Futurism, Dada and Surrealism.

In *The Real Frank Zappa Book,* he had this to say about Dada, the "anti-art" movement that rocked the cultural establishment during the first world war.

> INTERCONTINENTAL ABSURDITIES (founded 1968) is a company dedicated to *Dada in action.* In the early days, I didn't even know what to *call* the stuff my life was made of. You can imagine my delight when I discovered that someone in a distant land had the same idea—AND a nice, short name for it. (Zappa, 1989, p. 255)

Dada was characterised by an impatience with separations between different artistic "specialties": painters incorporated words and letters into their artwork, poets banged drums. The recent reconstruction of Dr. Otto Burchard's Berlin gallery at the First International Dada Fair (Pachnike and Honnef, 1991) indicated how ambivalent Dada was to art values: next to placards ("Down with Expressionism!" "Take Dada seriously, it's worth it!" "Dilettantes, rise up against art!"), paintings with their own letters and slogans look more like hoaxes than genuine, purchasable artworks—jolts of provocation rather than objects for contemplation.

The Dada revolt was also marked by an extraordinary extension of technical means: it previewed nearly the whole of twentieth century art (including such diverse entities as Surrealism, Bebop, Blue Note record covers, Pop Art, conceptual art, punk, Smart Art, Damien Hirst). Dada rearranged artistic materials—letters, photographs, objects—with a freedom of invention that still giddies the mind. It is this emphasis on innovation, an advance that wilfully flouts social codes and moral values, that finds an echo in Zappa.

In the late 1930s, Hans Richter—a founder dadaist and its finest historian—wrote a book called *The Struggle For The Film.* It was first published in German in 1976, and only translated into English as recently as 1986. Richter made some pertinent observations about the avantgarde and the mass audience. He describes how European modernists made some of the crucial technical advances in film (Eisenstein's discovery of

---

1. The one exception being *Hot Rats*; in his review in *Rolling Stone* (7 March 1970), Lester Bangs praised its lack of "self-indulgence".

montage, Vertov's visual rhythms, the rediscovery of "film poetry" by dadaists like himself, René Clair, Ferdnand Léger and Man Ray). He also admits that the economic hegemony of post-war America allowed Hollywood to outflank European cinema. Keeping to a stringently technical analysis—this is no high-minded attack on Hollywood "vulgarity"— Richter shows how Hollywood's ideological strictures limit its capacity to represent the world.

> While in the cinema's earliest days, it was underdeveloped forms of
> expression and technological means that restricted the ways content could
> be presented, today it is the content that is inhibiting the development of
> the forms of expression. (Richter, 1938, p. 105)

Producing escapist dramas about the rich for the masses, postwar Hollywood suppressed film's potential for *documentary collage* (something pioneered by Dada) in favour of an illusionistic "realism" derived from already existing bourgeois forms: light opera and theatre. Richter does, though, grant that Hollywood has produced some masterpieces, particularly in its more extreme moments.

The history of the cinema becomes incomprehensible when it is written as a history only of the official production—within which a few extravagant artists have made interesting deviations from the norm. For it is precisely in these "extravaganzas" that an unusual content first finds its expression (Richter, 1938, p. 113). Zappa is just such an "extravagant artist", someone who can tell us more about recording in the twentieth century than more "mainstream" commercial artists.

Richter is writing in the context of an urgent and complex debate. In the 1930s, intellectuals were concerned to explain what had gone wrong with the left: how Hitler had managed to come to power, how Stalin had managed to destroy the best hopes of the Russian revolution, how capitalism appeared to have a new lease of life. Richter is contributing to a discussion already underway between Georg Lukás, Bertolt Brecht, Theodor Adorno and Walter Benjamin.[2] Unlike Theodor Adorno, who dismissed Hollywood and the mass culture industry as proto-fascist manipulation, Richter echoes Benjamin and Brecht. He called for a radical, populist art which could harness styles and techniques thrown up in the commercial sphere. Richter praised Robert Flaherty's documentary classic *Nanook Of The North* (1931) because it connected social behaviour to actual conditions.

---

2. A debate usefully anthologised by Ronald Taylor in Bloch et al. (1977).

The historical task of the progressive cinema is to develop a dramaturgy that arouses this kind of receptivity and turns people with quite primitive ideas into spectators who look for such a diet in the cinema and regard it as preferable to the other kind. (Richter, 1938, p. 135)

Because of Adorno's pre-eminence as a musicologist—his extraordinary knack for interpreting the *minutiae* of a composer's musical decisions as socially symbolic acts—it is often assumed that his despair with the culture industry (and his championing of the high-art avantgarde) is the only course for those who oppose capitalism. In 1938 he wrote an article condemning all "jazz" as "regressive listening" (Adorno, 1938). Hans Richter's analysis of film—which foregrounds technical advance and issues of manipulation and consciousness—provides a better model for approaching Frank Zappa's use of recording technology than Adorno's expressionist disdain for mass art.

The progressive cinema can no longer be identified simply with the artistic cinema. On "the other side", too, there are masterpieces of techno-artistic form. (Richter, 1938, p. 29)

Like Richter, Zappa was attracted to the extremes of pop culture—science fiction, monster movies, R & B—seeing in them potential for new content; he also had a strong pedagogic streak, hoping to introduce his mass audience to the joy of music as an end in itself. All this was to be achieved by emphasis on the material means of musical production—amplifiers, guitars, tape-recorders, mixing, record-production, touring—rather than moralising about "higher" artistic values.

Zappa's roots

Like many intelligent, solitary American boys growing up in the 1950s, Frank Zappa was fascinated by technology. He read popular magazines that mixed science fiction stories with teach-yourself science. His initial encounter with the European avantgarde—a record by Edgard Varèse—is described in images derived from this sub-culture:

I noticed a strange-looking black-and-white album with a guy on it who had frizzy gray hair and looked like a mad scientist. I thought it was great that a mad scientist had finally made a record. . . . (Zappa, 1989, p. 31)

Zappa's response is naively stated, but perceptive nonetheless. In 1928 Varèse's *L'Astronome* (documented in Ouellette, 1973, pp. 115–17) envisaged a performance event that is like a cross between Wyndham Lewis's *Enemy Of The Stars* (first printed in *Blast*) and a 50s science-fiction film. Indeed, it is because both the high-art avantgarde and the mass culture industry demand technical innovation that Zappa was able to set off a productive ricochet between the two. Interestingly enough (especially for those swayed by Philip Glass's assertions that non-tonal music is "unnatural" and "creepy"), he loved the music of Varèse straight away.

At High School Zappa enrolled in art class. Given a ciné camera to work with, he stripped the emulsion off a film and painted it himself, projecting the results while musicians played his scores (Walley, 1972, p. 29). It was this kind of disregard for convention—and curiosity about material processes—that characterized his attitude towards sound recording.

Multitrack tape recording

Tape recording was a by-product of the exponential advance in technology achieved by the pressure of the second world war. In Europe, Pierre Schaeffer and Pierre Henry explored its artistic potential at the Radiodiffusion Studio in Paris. In America it was first seen as a convenient way of "doctoring" commercial recordings (early R & B is blighted with many crude overdubs[3]). Guitarist Les Paul pioneered the creative use of the multitrack tape machine, overdubbing at different speeds, building up impossibly brilliant bluegrass embellishments (bluegrass favoured virtuosic "quick picking" anyway). His jangling productions have a mechanical feel that is reminiscent of fair-ground steam-organs and spring-driven music-boxes. Singer Mary Ford's nostalgic, war-period crooning is so out-of-touch with Les Paul's gimmicky effects that the results are unconsciously surreal—but limited for all that.

In the early 60s Les Paul had an eight-track machine; his nearest competitor on the West Coast was Paul Buff, who had five. Buff learned electronics in the Marines with the express intention of setting up a recording studio on discharge. He housed his mixing console in an old 1940s dressing table and advertised himself as the Pal Recording Studio. After recording various novelties with Buff, Zappa used payment for scoring the music for a cowboy film (*Run Home Slow*, 1963) to buy up Buff's studio, which he renamed Studio Z.

---

3. For example, the electric harpsichord overdubbed on Johnny "Guitar" Watson's original tracks (*Hot Little Mama*, Big Town Records BT1002).

Zappa's first marriage broke up at this time and he moved into Studio Z, initiating what he described as "a life of obsessive overdubbage—non-stop, twelve hours a day" (Gray, 1985, p. 32). It is instructive to compare his efforts with those of Les Paul. There is the same fascination for multitracks recorded at different speeds (something also done by Hendrix and then Prince), but Zappa had something entirely foreign to Les Paul's country-pop perspective. For one thing, he recorded electric guitar R & B style, using amplification to distort the sound—not just ringing hillbilly clarity, but complex harmonics ("fuzz and growl") too. Zappa also applied his idiosyncratic notion of melody—phrases which copy the patterns of verbal expressions rather than those suggested by conventional notation. "Speed Freak Boogie" and "Toads of the Short Forest" (unreleased Studio Z recordings broadcast on Australian radio in 1975) also pushed multitrack capability beyond what might be played in real time. The chipmunk banality of speed-ups is now an element within a collage of sources, a technique designed to rush the attention into sudden suspensions and shocks.

Recording technology became much more sophisticated as the 60s proceeded. The number of tracks available multiplied. In 1972, Zappa used a 24-multitrack as a creative tool, making a virtual big band out of six pieces (*Waka/Jawaka*). Live versions of "Big Swifty" are much shorter than the recorded version, indicating that much of its seventeen minutes on *Waka/Jawaka* must have been the result of manipulating improvisations at the mixing desk. At this date Miles Davis and his producer Teo Macero were making albums by recording endless jams and making judicious edits, but Zappa's efforts were characteristically more zany and action-packed.

Multitracking was also crucial to the impact of the "rock" album *Sheik Yerbouti*. The inside of the gatefold sleeve showed Zappa's hands adjusting slides at the mixing desk. Earlier versions (broadcast but never officially released) have a realtime, "live" sound: by inserting layer upon layer of synthesized textures, Zappa created a decorative fraudulence. The net effect is like picking up a sandwich to find it is made of polystyrene. At the same date that punk was vilifying the stadium rock spectacle—"I'm So Cute" and "Tryin' To Grow A Chin" made references to punk—Zappa was collapsing it from within. On *Sheik Yerbouti*, songs like "Broken Hearts Are For Assholes" hurled obnoxious words at the audience. The very mix taunts the rock consumer, too.

Recording as sacrifice of innocence

Jacques Attali began his book *Noise* by pointing out music's origins in ritual sacrifice.

In the chapters that follow, music will be presented as originating in ritual murder, of which it is a simulacrum, a minor form of sacrifice heralding change. (Attali, 1977, p. 5)

Sacrifice serves to bind society together by creating a unique occasion whose importance everyone can acknowledge (our own calendar, for example, begins with the birth of the "sacrificial lamb", Jesus Christ). Zappa's first release—*Freak Out!*—placed a "sacrifice" at the record's heart. After this desecration, he implied, pop could never regain its innocence. The first part of "The Return Of The Son Of Monster Magnet" was titled "Ritual Dance Of The Child-Killer": Zappa was parodying the ritual of Stravinsky's *Sacre De Printemps*. The whole double album is heavily ironic and self-reflexive, encrusted with manifesti, polemics and quotations.

In the "sacrifice" of Suzy Creamcheese, Zappa was seeking a symbol for the power of recording: Zappa asks Suzy Creamcheese "What's got into you?" and the soundtrack erupts with siren, screams and banging drums. During the climax of the piece there are cries that sound like female orgasm. The founding crime of recording, in Zappa's view, is that it can make private moments public. The title "Return Of The Son Of Monster Magnet" points to the monstrous way a tape-machine's magnetic pick-up can reproduce events.

However, if the music had just been about a school-girl losing her virginity, it would have been as forgettable as the records of those other 60s anarcho-sexists, The Fugs. Actually, though claiming to document "what freaks sound like at one o'clock in the morning", the piece is stringent in its formal construction. The drums speed up, slow down, pan between metres. It incorporates sarcastic expostulations (Zappa saying "America's wonderful!") and a bleak section of sped-up voices that sound like bats in a derelict warehouse. The license to "freak out" the listener is an opportunity to experiment with recording techniques beyond the limits set by Les Paul's country pop. Zappa's sharp ear for rhythm allows him to cut together non-singer chants and maunderings into coherent music. The invocation of Creamcheese accompanied by clacking spoons is repeated at double speed. This compression makes the internal organisation of the notes more evident, while piano notes give the ending a classical formality. One merely has to compare the piece to the Beatles' disastrous attempt at free-form "weirdness" ("Revolution No. 9" on *Double White*) to recognise its musical coherence.

Still, formal logic does not remove the scandal of Creamcheese's heavy breathing. "Right There" (*You Can't Do That On Stage Anymore Vol. 5*) featured live broadcast at a Zappa concert of a "bed recording" by the band's saxophonist. The idea of recording as a desecration of the private, integral personality continually reoccurs in Zappa's music. For example, the theme that arrives in the last four minutes of "Big Swifty" on *Waka/Jawaka* is in fact a transcribed guitar solo of Zappa's arranged for overdubbed trumpets. This makes use of a fairly obvious benefit of recording: that of being able to slow down, repeat and transcribe an improvisation (as has been done for Charlie Parker by Super Sax and for John Coltrane by Andrew White). This was just the first of a series of scores Zappa derived from transcribing his improvisations. Recording becomes an analytical tool, something that can "freeze" spontaneity and generate musical instructions. Just as a recording of someone reaching orgasm does violence to their privacy, so overtracked trumpets playing someone else's solo begs questions of identity. You can recognise Zappa's wit in the way the "Big Swifty" theme sets up a "Batman" riff and then perverts it, but the fanfare trumpets give his personal, improvised line a pompous lilt.

On *The Grand Wazoo* (1972), Zappa developed a whole concept round the idea of fraudulent splendour. The music tells the story of Emperor Cleetus Awreetus-Awrightus and his war against Mediocrates of Pedestrium. It is as if the public presentation of the "personality" is inevitably corrupt and preposterous. In this, Zappa links to a long and venerable tradition of literary satire; what is new is that his satire enters right into the technology of sound reproduction and its ability to capture personality and reproduce it on a mass level.

Zappa returned to the scandal of recording's power to desecrate privacy with "The Torture Never Stops" on *Zoot Allures* (1976). A woman's orgasmic moans are surrounded with lyrics about dungeons and implementations of torture. It was in part a satirical reply to Donna Summer's disco hits, where she breathes sensually over mechanical rhythms produced by Giorgio Moroder, who derived his machine aesthetic from "Kraut Rock", itself greatly influenced by Stockhausen. References to pork, white fish and "pumping the gas every night" made dark hints about Nazi treatment of the Jews and the Teutonic propensity for order. On the same record, "Ms Pinky" made something utterly militaristic out of a disco beat. Formats copied from glam rock and disco mocked the restrictions of commercial music. Both sides of the record ended with songs about masturbation, satirizing Moroder's marketing of sex by a reminder of the loneliness of modern life.

"The Torture Never Stops" also works as a piece of abstract music. One can draw parallels between the woman's vocal extremities and the extended vocalese of Cathy Berberian singing Berio—or the indignities inflicted on an instrument by an avantgarde composer like Isang Yun. Though Susan McClary argues that the model of the sexual climax is a male-oriented tradition that postmodernism has abolished (Steve Reich's eventless music as an *imago* of a new sexuality) (McClary, 1991, p. 122), Zappa is more concerned to psychoanalyse musical processes than to pass judgments. Indeed, the way he reveals a sexual basis to musical development works rather like McClary's analysis of *Carmen*: Zappa is concerned to bring such structures to consciousness rather than using them to manipulate. "The Torture Never Stops" is an upsetting record, but that is its function and its achievement.

Zappa's commentary on private and public realms of sound was continued on *Sheik Yerbouti*, which placed arena rock frenzy between snippets of *musique concrète*. These snippets combined backstage discussions about sexual orientation with pointilistic, unstable effects that echoed Elliott Carter's *Double Concerto for Harpsichord and Piano with Two Chamber Orchestras* (1975). The album's lyrics revolved around castration-complex aggression, anality and sodomy with an unrelenting glee most critics found insupportable. For Zappa, sacrifice of sexual innocence was intimately bound-up with technical discovery and innovation.

Recording as documentary

Although Zappa achieved stretches of music that deserve abstract appreciation, he uses materials that most electronic composers would consider beneath them. If recording is taken seriously (something the orchestral world has been slow to do, wedded as it is to a more traditional mode of musical reproduction), it immediately suggests such a collage principle. One of the "pop songs" on *Freak Out!*, "Hungry Freaks, Daddy", referenced the riff of "(I Can't Get No) Satisfaction" by copying its timbre rather than its notes.[4] In the 90s, sampling was to make such practices widespread: already in the 60s Zappa presented a music in which every sound was surrounded by quote-marks. Where most pop production aims to rationalize the production of music—making it cheaper and more standardized—Zappa used technology to create something unheard-of.

Zappa's sidemen have frequently complained that he stole their ideas.

---

4. One that imitated the effect of a swing/R&B horn section, as pointed out by Dave Marsh (Marsh, 1989, p. 8).

In a Borgeslike hall-of-mirrors, Zappa even "stole" such complaints themselves. In his 1972 film *200 Motels,* a musician overdoses on drugs. "Quick," say the others (following Zappa's script), "we've got to get him back to normal before Zappa finds out and steals it and makes him do it in the movie!" When Zappa toured, tape-recorders ran on the bus, in the dressing rooms, in the street. Snippets from these tapes wind up on the records, which become a documentary collage of the process of making music.

Zappa relished the documentary aspect of recording, the way it can register the ambience of a specific place.

> What qualified as an "acceptable drum sound" on a 1950s recording seems laughable today. Since they didn't have digital echo then, the "flavor" and quantity of the reverberation used on a song were determined by the acoustics of the room in which the recording was made. The echo (or absence thereof) described the geography of an "imaginary landscape" in which a song would be "photographed" by the microphone. (Zappa, 1989, p. 157)

Paying attention to recorded sound liberated Zappa from the straitjacket of the academic score—the restricted notion of music as specification of pitches over regular bar lines. The example of Varèse encouraged Zappa to think of composition as the weighing of "blocks of sound", the manipulation of sounds from an external viewpoint. Zappa himself called his music "junk sculpture" (Steel, 1991, pp. 32–33). Instead of seeking to provide an alternative, transcendent sound world, Zappa makes music out of the banalities of modern existence.

For Hans Richter, the dadaists' use of everyday life was a major technological breakthrough. It also begged political questions.

> Technology, overcoming time and space, has brought all life on earth so close together that the most remote "facts", as much as those closest to hand, have become significant for each individual's life. Life has given rise to the secularisation of the divine. Everything that happens on earth has become more interesting and more significant than it ever was before. Our age demands the documented fact. (Richter, 1938, p. 42)

As well as anticipating Zappa's abhorrence for religion, Richter's utopian materialism—a vision of a world in which the detail of everyday life holds more interest than transcendent beauty—also anticipates Zappa's documentary impulse.

Recording freezes a moment of time. By including in his records documentation of chaos—on the bus, on stage, in the street—Zappa ingested bits of reality, with all its irreducible complications and contradictions. These provided a stimulus to his extremely orderly imagination, which sought to embroider thematics which can include these "external" moments in a coherent artwork, something personal. Jonathan Jones writes:

> Zappa's intention is to create a paranoid listener, who picks up with each new version some extra nuance, another hint. (Jones, 1994)

Zappa was himself a paranoid listener to his own work. He did not use recording to paint a picture which allows the audience to gaze unruffled at the object portrayed, but to dramatize recording's power to freeze and repeat.

On the other hand, Zappa had no qualms about releasing a "straight" recording if a live event was deemed significant enough in itself. The plain cover of *Fillmore East June 1971*—pencil scribbles on plain white—was designed to make the music appear raw and unfinished, like a bootleg (in 1971 these were almost always lo-fi audience recordings). The record was both a comment on rock hysteria and an example of it. Many admirers of the Mothers of Invention baulked at Zappa's willingness to emulate what he parodied.

> The later records, however, seem to sacrifice this tension [between the spheres of popular and of radical music] for a more obviously popular appeal (lengthy virtuoso guitar solos, and moments when parody comes so close to the thing parodied as to be almost indistinguishable from it). (Paddison, 1982, p. 215)

Production values on *Fillmore* were appropriately rockist, far from the speed-ups and fold-ins of "Monster Magnet". Pop songs, opera and abstract tunes were all performed with the same headlong rock *timbre*. The rumbustious dialogues between ex-Turtles Flo & Eddie were a celebration of the taboo-breaking *mores* of the counter culture, but also satire on the sexual frustration of the touring musician. As usual, Zappa is concerned to remind us of the actual people behind the music. However, breaking a guitar solo at the end of side one (and then having it continue on side two) also dramatized the album's material existence as a vinyl disk (the same technique was used on *Burnt Weeny Sandwich*, where Ian Underwood's delicate piano is split between the two sides).

Zappa has pointed out that *timbre* is more important than note-choice in determining genre: "Purple Haze" played on an accordion would not be rock, while Beethoven's *Fifth* played on a fuzz guitar definitely is. On *Fillmore*, "Little House I Used To Live In" is played as a burlesque romp, an introduction to Flo & Eddie's account of using a mudshark in the sex act; on *Burnt Weeny Sandwich* (1970) an acoustic, ambient recording made it sound like an *étude*. Zappa's presentation of the same tune in different modes asks questions about cultural value. Is a fuzz guitar really a "lower" form than a violin? Although today's postmodernists often claim to do this—piano sonatas dedicated to Jerry Lee Lewis, the Balanescu Quartet playing Kraftwerk at the Festival Hall, the use of amplification by the Kronos Quartet—it often seems more like an attempt to make high culture more palatable (less austere), than a real interrogation of our ideas of hierarchy. Much has been made of the "flattening out" of social meaning engendered by the equivalence of recorded sound (once anything has been made into a record or a compact disc, it indeed becomes comparable to anything else in that medium, whatever its social provenance). Zappa's "equivalence", though, is not a flattening-out, but a scandal: a dadaistic breach in formal etiquette.

Zappa's stress on recording as a document of a real situation was paramount in *Roxy & Elsewhere*, which featured virtuosic rendition of difficult scores. Tom-foolery among band members (suggestions that a bandmember smoke a high-school diploma stuffed with a gym sock) co-existed with scores which are an amalgam of Varèse, Dolphy, Nancarrow and the blues/funk of Johnny "Guitar" Watson and Etta James. Deriving both guitar licks and composed tunes from speech patterns, Zappa's music offers extreme rhythmic challenges. Here the difficulties are dramatized. The spotlight is put on a percussionist to "show what's she's capable of"; the saxophonist is warned, "here comes the drill!" The tightrope walked between such discipline and the improvised comedy is fraught with psychological tension.

"Be-Bop Tango (Of The Old Jazzmen's Church)" occupied side four. The theme is full of eccentric cross-rhythms and interpolated sections of fast runs, as if Zappa were making tucks and joins across time itself. Taking on board the bebop idea of an intimidatingly difficult tune that will exclude outsiders, it worked like an obstacle course. "Be-Bop Tango" in fact constituted a virtuosic solution to a musical problem faced by jazz rock in the 70s: how to integrate the sensuous (and saleable) impact of rock sonority with musicianly challenge. However, the fetishism of skill in fusion—the idea that John McLaughlin's velocity on guitar made him some kind of spiritual hero—is scorned by what follows, as Zappa invited audience members up on stage to attempt to dance to George Duke's bebop scatting. The incredible precision of the playing appears to disintegrate into the crowd-pleasing antics.

However, looked at in another way, the dance-event raises all sorts of issues. "Jazz is not dead, it just smells funny", Zappa quips. Having audience members come up on stage and attempt to dance to Duke's bebop "perversions" of the tune underlines the distance between jazz specialism and everyday life; in responding to the "little notes" they must perform grotesque physical jerks. Zappa asks up a woman called Brenda, and introduces her as a "professional harlot" who has been stripping for crewmen at Edwards Air Force base: "two hours of taking it off for the boys", he says, then adds, with a leer," . . . in the car". In 1956 Zappa's father moved the family to California in order to do weapons research at Edwards Air Force Base; in 1970 Zappa wrote a song about servicemen, fumbled sex and nationalism ("Would You Go All The Way?", *Chunga's Revenge*). Brenda's presence threads all these themes together.

Such observations require commitment to eking out what Zappa called "conceptual continuity", the embedding of cross-references to other records throughout his *oeuvre*. His dadaist achievement is to make us turn that attention onto everyday life. Like real life, the "audience participation" of "Be-Bop Tango" is not entirely under Zappa's control, yet Zappa gives us the paranoid idea that it might be. It is a powerful and suggestive model for the artistic use of documentary recording in *musique concrète*.

Zappa, Cage, Zen

Zappa's "acceptance" of chance and the incorporation of everyday life into his art parallels John Cage. Both found inspiration for such an in-mixing in Zen Buddhism. On *Roxy & Elsewhere*, Zappa said: "A true Zen saying—nothing is what I want" ("Dummy Up"). He had found Zen a useful antidote to Catholicism.

> I started reading about Zen which I found the most attractive of all the philosophical points of view at the time I was studying [comparative religion]. I thought, Now look, *this* makes sense. This is real. Why didn't somebody tell me about this before? (Occhiogrosso, 1987, p. 337)

David Revill sums up the Zen teaching Cage received from Daisetz Suzuki thus:

The world proceeds without our permission. It will be hot or cold, rain will fall, trees rustle in the wind. (Revill, 1992, p. 110)

The première of Cage's *4'33"* was an object lesson in this *haiku*-like pronouncement.[5]

Anyone who listened would have heard the wind in the trees, then rain blown onto the roof and, in due course, the baffled murmurs of other audience members. (Revill, 1992, p. 165)

(Though Revill notes the antagonism of the audience, a social fact that, unlike Zappa, Cage did not like to dwell on.) On the CD release of *Roxy & Elsewhere,* Zappa added a sleevenote:

Sometimes you can be surprised that "the Universe works whether or not we understand it".

Another Zen tenet. Words to "Wild Love" on *Sheik Yerbouti* implied that Zappa was familiar with Suzuki's argument. The "chaos" of the dance event in "Be-Bop Tango" is a blemish which opens up Zappa's artwork to the concepts of the avantgarde.

Such moments naturally left rock critics non-plussed. They generally responded with the charge of "self-indulgence". However, they rarely explored the paradox of this becoming the critical cliché for the most notorious workaholic in rock. According to Jacques Attali, music journalism is concerned

to give meaning to the object being sold, to make the consumer believe that there was use-value in it, to promote demand. (Attali, 1977, p. 42)

---

5. Just before his death in December 1993, Zappa "recorded" *4'33"*: Zappa maintained that you can record "silence", i.e., the ambience of any space, and there is a muffled thump—presumably an accident—which gives the idea of someone sitting at a piano. Gary Davis, editor, (1993) *A Chance Operation: The John Cage Tribute*, Koch International Classics 3-7238-2 Y6x2.

Such ideologues are understandably aghast at someone who hints that everyday life might actually be more interesting than buying records: a satirist who seeks to unmask the charade. Whereas in high art it is widely accepted that (at least since Marcel Duchamp, Pop Art and Fluxus) art and anti-art tend to work in close proximity, rock critics tend to seek substantive, unproblematic value in music.

Despite his parallel use of Zen, Zappa's satirical impulse made him very different from Cage. He took seriously Cage's assault on the boundaries between art and life, but accepted neither Cage's disinterest in selling records, nor his quietistic social message. His political impulse is closer to Dada as described by Walter Benjamin.

> Let us recall Dadaism. The revolutionary strength of Dadaism lay in testing art for its authenticity. Still lifes were compiled from tickets, rolls of yarn, and cigarette butts that were merged with painterly elements. The whole lot was put into a frame. And then it was shown to the public: Look, your picture frame breaks the bounds of time: the tiniest authentic fragment of everyday life tells more than painting does. Just like the bloody fingerprint of a murderer on a book tells more than the text. (Benjamin quoted by Pachnike and Honnef, 1991, p. 99)

Zappa's paranoid listener actively traces the chaotic "live" portions of his music for clues, a very different response to the "quiet mind" hoped for by John Cage. In the case of "Be-Bop Tango", Zappa's slice-of-life reveals stumbling ineptitude in the face of contemporary specialisations, whether musical, military or sexual. The ability of technology to preserve a tract of time makes us look more closely at the reality of American life. Zappa makes the Black Mountain School project of treating life as art critical and political, rather than accepting and aesthetic.

Looking at everyday life

Zappa often left in slips of the tongue and mistakes. Since his productions were meticulous in the extreme, this vaunting of flaws was highly motivated. In the introduction to "Muffin Man" on *Bongo Fury* there is a fluff: "I'm sorry, I'll try that again . . .". The "Central Scrutinizer" on *Joe's Garage* is forever tripping up on his narrative. Slips of the tongue are famous *loci* of the unconscious in the Freudian schema. By stressing these moments rather than editing them out, Zappa emphasizes the way recording makes human dishevelment public.

On *Uncle Meat,* the idea of Zappa's music as a complex, hermetic discourse was achieved by a "laboratory" sound and the inclusion of snatches of dialogue and music in evidently "unreal" multitrack mixes. By contrast, the sound on a live record like *Zappa In New York* was raw and brash and public, the Halloween crowd large and noisy. As with *Fillmore,* one might suspect that Zappa had suppressed his dadaistic stress on the way representation works. The sleeve consists of photographs of the band onstage, without the cryptic neo-dada collages Cal Schenkel supplied for earlier albums. However, there are little touches—a scatological dedication to an old bass player, Zappa being asked if he is interested in Stravinsky ("Titties & Beer" is in fact a reworking of *The Soldier's Tale*), the presence of a *Zoot Allures* enamel badge on a female musician's bottom (to mark the allure she might hold for the Illinois Enema Bandit, who is holding her from behind)—all of which encourage speculation from the paranoid listener. Although *Zappa In New York* is a document of a major event—attended by "27,500 deranged fanatics" according to the sleevenotes—Zappa provides clues for the "conceptual continuity" sleuth. In this way even the most public events are injected with private meanings. Documentary suddenly becomes surrealist collage: life and art swap places.

Treating musical material in a collage manner emphasizes its brute objectivity. It prevents us interpreting it as personal expression, bringing Zappa's music close to Cage, who described his aesthetic attitude thus:

> It had nothing to do with the desire for self-expression, but simply had to do with the organization of materials. I recognized that expression of two kinds, that arising from the personality of the composer and that arising from the nature and context of the materials, was inevitable, but I felt its emanation was stronger and more sensible when not consistently striven for, but simply allowed to arise naturally. (Cage, quoted in Pritchett, 1994, p. 17)

On *You Are What You Is,* "Doreen"—a hysterical, bended-knee, hand-on-heart, please-hear-my-plea love song—resurfaces as an out-of-tempo backing chorus in the next track ("Goblin Girl"), a ditty about oral sex. Complex, abstract music results from collaging inane songs (rather as the youthful Charles Ives experimented with playing hymn tunes to the wrong accompaniment). "Sinister Footwear" (on the same album) started life as an improvised guitar solo called "Persona Non Grata". Once transcribed,[6] Zappa's line was duplicated by another guitar, by marimba and embellished with tuned metal percussion. Improvisation is conventionally deemed a means of personal expression; by turning his line into a score, Zappa makes it something spatial and objective. The piece finishes with a dry, clacking piece of percussion; just as you think the track has finished, it rattles again, like some piece of sinister machinery. Zappa's note sequences fight standardization, taking absurdist intervals and rhythmic liberties; but this death rattle is also a reminder that all recorded sound is a lifeless, preordained stretch of time to which the listener is subjected.

On "Beat The Reaper" (*Civilization: Phaze III*), there is a persistent sound like rain guttering on a roof. The ear gets used to it and ceases to notice. However, when it cuts out towards the end, it is as if the shelter you have been in has vanished and you are in the open air: truly a surrealist coup. Zappa's music now appears to be thunder booming in the heavens; in fact it is random gunfire recorded in San Fernando Valley by Zappa at New Year in 1987. Zappa's special framing of documentary sound makes us look at reality with the attention we give art.

Records as inert objects

At the conclusion of *Lumpy Gravy*, the phrase "'Cos round things are ... are boring" is followed by an exhalation (perhaps someone blowing a smoke ring), and a trite circular melody. The words comment on the fact that the listener has been subjected to a record, a fixed and unchanging and repeatable experience.

> Fetishized as a commodity, music is illustrative of the evolution of our entire society: deritualize a social form, repress an activity of the body, specialize its practice, sell it as a spectacle, generalize its consumption, then see to it that it is stockpiled until it loses its meaning. Today, music heralds—regardless of what the property mode of capital will be—the establishment of a society of repetition in which nothing will ever happen any more. (Attali, 1977, p. 5)

---

6. Its bizarre complexity may be examined in Frank Zappa (1982), *The Frank Zappa Guitar Book*, pp. 206–212, Munchkin Music (distribution: Music Sales Ltd (UK and Eire), Music Sales Pty. Ltd (Australia), Hal Leonard Publishing Corporation (USA & Canada).

Zappa's "conceptual continuity" was an attempt to prevent meanings becoming fixed and rigid. The listener is continually making "discoveries" that alter a record's reception (eight years later the phrase "Round Things Are Boring" appeared written round a starmap on *One Size Fits All,* for example). Zappa's dissatisfaction with "product" and his satire on his own records as "boring" resembles the Fluxus movement and its attempts to outwit commodity-production in art.

Foregrounding human labour

On a pop record *musique concrète* effects sound more like satirical provocation than art music (Dada rather than Expressionism). *We're Only In It For The Money* (issued in tandem with *Lumpy Gravy)* foregrounded recording as the very substance of Zappa's art. After some stoned dialogue and electronic blurts, you can hear the "creepy whispering" of the sound engineer.

> One of these days I'm going to erase . . . whirl—whirl—whirl. Tomorrow I'm going to make all the Frank Zappa masters blank—empty—space. That's what they are now, blank—empty—space. I know he's sitting in there in the control room now, listening to everything I say, but I really don't care . . . hello, Frank Zappa!

Whilst *Freak Out!* had established some kind of sound and identity for the Mothers, *Money* continually goads the listener. On "Nasal Retentive Calliope Music" promises of heavy rock are dangled, only to vanish into mocking snorks. On "The Chrome Plated Megaphone Of Destiny", the pianist (a prize-winning interpreter of Mozart) plays Zappa's scores with incongruous sensitivity. In "Harry, You're A Beast", a climax of teen sexual ineptitude—"don't come in me"—is played backwards in order to "avoid censorship". Softcore psychedelia is ruined by someone shouting "flower power sucks!" Side one finishes with two separate monologues occurring simultaneously in each speaker. You can only work out the words by ignoring those in the opposite channel: instead of using stereo to give an illusion of depth, Zappa uses it to multiply confusion. Sped-up munchkin cries mock seriousness and the whisperer returns, wondering "what everyone else is whispering about". In a nod to the "mystery message" on *Sgt. Pepper,* side one ends with lines omitted from side two's "Mother People" ("Shut your fucking mouth about the length of my hair"), again played backwards. Retrogrades are a traditional technique in classical music; Zappa treats tape in a similar spirit of abstraction.

The famous cover for *Money* parodied Peter Blake's cover for *Sgt. Pepper*, making a lurid mess of his tidy montage. In dramatizing tape manipulation—speed-ups, overdubs, sudden splices, multitracks—Zappa expounded a completely different aesthetic from The Beatles. Where arranger George Martin expertly summoned up nostalgic references—the charleston of "When I'm Sixty Four", the steam-organ of "Mr. Kite", the symphonic orchestra of "Day In The Life"—Zappa piled on brute effect after effect. This bald presentation of technical materials links him to Dada: an impatience with the charade of representation.

In talking about the ethereal sound quality of New Age music, John Corbett traces its suppression of the playing body back to Manfred Eicher's production for ECM records.

> What set ECM apart was its use of several key production techniques: echo and compression. The combination of these, along with other studio methods, allows for the next step in the fetishization of autonomous sound—the elimination of the musician. (Corbett, 1994, p. 43)

Zappa's recordings persistently emphasize the people—musicians, engineers, even roadies—behind his music, attacking the way consumer culture mystifies production, presenting music as a gift from a higher realm. "Absolutely Free" on *Money*—a scabrous attack on flower power—mocks the way hippie listening erases the element of human labour that produced the sounds we hear. In "Mother People" there is a violent gouging sound as if the needle is being dragged across the record, followed by a section of some restful scored music from *Lumpy Gravy*. However, the way that we have arrived at these sounds forces us to see how they are merely other areas on the record surface. Zappa breaks the illusion that we are doing anything else than listening to a record. Imagination and creativity result from play with material processes, not by drifting off to some transcendent zone.

This play with technology corresponds to John Cage's description of what he gleaned from Marshall McLuhan.

> New art and music do not communicate an individual's conceptions in ordered structures, but they implement processes which are, as are our daily lives, opportunities for perception (observation and listening).

McLuhan emphasizes this shift from life done for us to life that we do for ourselves. (Cage quoted by Pritchett, 1994, p. 151)

What separates Zappa from Cage, though, is the violence of the perceptions engendered; a moral indignation that brings Zappa closer to Dada than to Cage's mystical quietism.

On *Uncle Meat* the intimate, crafted beauties of the overdubbed studio tracks occasionally break into live confusion, a contrast that brings home the distance between studio control and rock-concert hysteria. The upfront opinions of Suzy Creamcheese (Pamela Zarubica) on Zappa's "groupie status", and drummer Jimmy Carl Black's complaints about money seem at first merely part of a bizarre "freak" aesthetic: however, their presence is actually part of Zappa's documentary realism. Like Dada, this is a realism that will not accept any formal constraints in delivering its "picture". The subject matter keeps bursting the frame: collaged actuality rather than confected representation.

"The Air" includes words about recording. The idea of a special art which the authorities wish to extirpate resurfaced eleven years later on *Joe's Garage*. Such fears are reminiscent of drug paranoia, but Zappa is being concrete: he is concerned to inform the listener of the material provenance of the music.

The title track of *Sleep Dirt* is a close-miked acoustic duet between Zappa and another guitarist. The latter asks "at that tempo?" and Zappa grunts an affirmative. Zappa plays a shimmeringly evocative solo over his accompanist's ostinato, his left hand miked as closely as the right, bringing out extra squeaks and clicks. Although the elegiac tone is new for Zappa, the intimacy with which the two guitarists seem to tangle their strings is very physical. As if distrustful of evocation, "Sleep Dirt" finishes with a broken ending: "getting tired?" says Zappa; "no, my fingers got stuck" is the reply. Sleep dirt is a name for the mucous that collects beneath the eyelids during sleep, and the inclusion of the "slip of the hand" seems a deliberate effort to catch a glimpse of the unconscious. Just as the abrupt end of "Orange County Lumber Truck" on *Weasels* prevented the listener relaxing into the beat, foreknowledge of the piece's abrupt disintegration leads you to track each finger stroke with close attention. Although Zappa's playing is lyrical, he prevents the listener taking off into fantasy, emphasizing that this music is the product of human work—the very opposite of the cool impersonality Corbett notes in New Age production.

A sleevenote on *Money* points out that

> all the music on this album was composed, arranged and scientifically
> mutilated by Frank Zappa (with the exception of a little surf music).
> None of the sounds are generated electronically . . . they are the product
> of electronically altering the sounds of NORMAL instruments.

This was a point only likely to interest those embroiled in 60s debates
about the relative merits of *musique concrète* and "pure" electronics.
Although he was aware of Karlheinz Stockhausen's attempts to reach
an "absolute" music by building up harmonics from pure sine waves,
Zappa favoured a *collage* approach. He'd use scores to get musicians to
play what he wanted—especially where verbal directions did not
work—but he composed by weighing sonic actuality rather than by the
kind of score-based mathematical procedures that led serialists like
Stockhausen into thinking they could generate every musical parameter
from pure electronic sounds. Like Stockhausen in his "absolute" phase,
Pierre Boulez conceives of electronics as a method for the serialist composer to realise compositional extrapolations humans find impossible
to play[7]: for Boulez, the score is the artwork, not the master-tape.[8]
Involved from the beginning with recording studios, Zappa did not
have such a concept of the score as an end in itself. Like Joe Zawinul
of Weather Report, Zappa was acutely aware of the part studio ambience played in making records. "Chrome Plated Megaphone Of
Destiny" (*We're Only In It For The Money*), for example, featured
piano music written by Zappa: but the reverberant *sound* of the piano
is just as much the theme of the piece, as clanging piano-notes are alter-
nated with sped-up laughter.

---

7. "He [Boulez] sees these [experiences in the *musique concrète* studio] as offering the potential for the strict treatment of certain problems relating to the long-sought 'inclusive gram-
mar of sound' and (notably with regard to durations) for 'realizations' more perfect than
with human interpreters, rather than merely regard them as an amazing source of preposterous or unbelievably wonderful sounds" (Jameux, 1984, p. 45).
8. When questioned as to whether he considered the score or the master-tape to be the work
of art, Zappa answered, "the master-tape" (Watson, 1994, p. 545).

"Form," said Adorno, "is itself a sedimentation of content" (Adorno, 1970, p. 209). In the debates about the construction of electronic music—with the purists of modernism insisting on the pursuit of abstract sound patterns and the postmodernists welcoming "literary" and "referential" motifs—Zappa's position is unique. Although his piebald macaronic refuses the homogeneity necessary for non-referential art, he has no truck with those who claim that we can only re-arrange the pre-recorded sounds of the past (a claim that links postmodernism to neo-classicism[9]). Zappa is interested in *transmutation*. Formally, the urgency of his music is down to a fine rhythmic sensitivity that can hear an underlying pulse in external materials: but it is his grasp of the social meaning of his materials that makes the cuts and surprises so provocative.

Repetition as death

Zappa's hostility towards minimalism (he calls it "monochromonotony", Zappa, 1989, p. 189) could have been predicted from the satirical record *Ruben & the Jets* of 1969, which expertly adumbrated the perils of repetition. It was a "tribute" to the innocent rock 'n' roll of the 50s which bands like the Mothers of Invention had done so much to destroy. Where *Freak Out!* had twanged and hummed with the group-solidarity dissonance of electric guitars, and *Money* had subverted expectations with its continual splices, *Ruben* was so smooth it was unsettling. A sleevenote referred to the "cretin simplicity" of the music; this was emphasized by using the multitrack tape-machine in a manner that isolated different levels of the music. Thin and dry, the drum sound is disturbingly artificial—likewise the machine-like bass and the regular guitar. Zappa called *Ruben* his "neo-classical" album (after Stravinsky's adoption of traditional forms in the 1920s), but his adoption of the restrictions of the 50s is sinister rather than celebratory. At one point the phrase "there's no room to breathe in here" provides a pointer to the suffocating restrictions of the music (and by extension, the suffocating restrictions of 50s society too). *Ruben* emphasized the oppressive restrictions of the music by refusing any illusion of ambience, of a "real" recording space. The album concludes with "Stuff Up The Cracks", where the singer gasses himself. Far from

---

9. Adorno's polemic against neo-classicism and Stravinsky may now be read as an attack on postmodernist "poly-stylism" (Adorno, 1949).

being a symbol of progressive sexuality (McClary, 1991, p. 122), repetition is a symbol of social inertia.

"Straight" state-of-the-art recording

Zappa was quite capable of doing recordings that did not play games with the listener, and indeed some of his records have set "benchmarks" for production values of whole genres. After Frank Zappa disbanded the Mothers in late 1969, he recorded an album called *Hot Rats*, showcasing his ability to play guitar and arrange inventive charts. Although highly artificial—the CD release "replaced" many embellishments vinyl had not been able to cope with, indicating that this was not a "live" record so much as a multitrack montage that required compromises in translation to mass-consumption formats—*Hot Rats* has an organic impact that makes it a favourite Zappa album for non-Zappa fans. The clarity and precision of the recording set a standard for jazz-rock and fusion; in contrast to the anti-establishment quaintness of *Uncle Meat*, it created three-dimensional credibility for each instrument. Zappa's turn-about resembles Max Ernst's turn to oil-painting when he initiated his series of decalcomanias: the marginalised members of the avantgarde proving that they can outflank the mainstream.

Likewise, *Overnite Sensation* used the upfront garishness of contemporary soul and funk recordings, complete with touches like a "Superstition" clarinet sound and backing vocals by Tina Turner and the Ikettes. As with *Fillmore East June 1971,* many devotees complained about what was considered to be a turn to commercialism. Zappa introduced special "effects" that rubbished seriousness—a nasal "sniffing" sound from a scraper after the line "by where some bugs had made it red" on "Camarillo Brillo", for example—everything delivered with a gloating, provocative glee. The intricate complexities of the arrangements—truly bravura in both concept and execution—are not presented as "art" music, but as glossy irritants. Zappa's lyrics, spoken close up to the mike in the manner of TV commercials, reproduced the banality of advertising with references to dental floss, poodles and zircon-encrusted tweezers. Production is state-of-the-art (*Overnite Sensation* was originally issued in quadraphonic, the next-step-beyond-stereo that never caught on). Whereas fusion bands like the Mahavishnu Orchestra made "spiritual" claims for their virtuosic musicianship and crystalline production, Zappa offered a torrent of vulgarity. To outflank the "cosmic" fusioneers on their own technical territory was part of his dada-materialist critique.

Apostrophe (') was even better recorded. Here the special effects, and Zappa's avuncular narrative delivery, made the record sound like a cartoon sound track. A story about Nanook the Eskimo showed Zappa's awareness of Flaherty's film (whose documentary realism had inspired Hans Richter). Though the title track is live improvisation, the mannerist brilliance of the rest of the album exploits the increasing control new studio technology was giving to producers. Absurd lyrics—a diabolically complex piece of marimba playing is meant to portray the "evil fur trapper" on his way to "St. Alfonzo's Pancake Breakfast"—deflate the pretensions of contemporary "progressive rock". That he decided to lavish state-of-the-art production on songs at once so musically intricate and lyrically silly was a mark of his cynicism about the great significance being laid on mega-selling rock in the days before punk.

Multitrack mixing as a form of musique concrète

On the album *Burnt Weeny Sandwich,* the title theme is faded in over close-miked crunches and scrapes, making the full-tilt sound of the band playing in public merely another piece of time trapped on tape that can be brought up in the mix. Side two also shows Zappa using the mixing desk as a form of *musique concrète.* Sugarcane Harris was an electric violin player who used a "distorted" sound to emulate John Coltrane's famous "sheets of sound" (fabulously expressive harmonics). When Harris starts his solo, everything is engulfed in an avalanche of white-noise; the bass is given a new depth in response. Mixing with attention to Varèse's "blocks of sound", Zappa is less concerned to keep metrical order than to contrast the objective musical "weight" of the playing on the separate bands of the multitrack. In "Holiday in Berlin, Full Blown" the dull thunder of the bass guitar and the dead beat of the drums separate out from the melody in a manner that is distinctly surreal. Working with a regular touring band, making frequent live recordings and writing scores meant that Zappa could transcend the limitations faced by those concerned with only one such area. His compositions are mixed like electronic music.

"Eric Dolphy Memorial Barbecue" (*Weasels Ripped My Flesh*) is an intricately thorough-composed piece that emulates the humour and abstraction of Eric Dolphy's *Out To Lunch* (1964). Although bass and drums have the raw crunch of live playing, sped-up marimbas punctuate the longer notes of the tune with comedic pipping sounds. "Dwarf Nebula Processional March" suggests a Disneyesque "march of the gnomes", though it suddenly bursts into an outrageous motley of electronics—backwards sounds, streaming fragments, puttering distortions, munchkin cries—which screws itself up into a perfectly-timed couple of coughs before the punk aggression of "My Guitar Wants To Kill Your Mama". The presence of *musique concrète* amongst "regular" rock music points to how artificial is music realized on a mixing desk: an extravagant mid-section features the trumpet-emulating sped-up-clarinets of *Uncle Meat,* along with a preposterous section of romantic Latin guitar. The psychedelic rock-out of "The Orange County Lumber Truck" is suddenly cut off—we're laughed at, and the record ends with the title track, two minutes of excruciating feedback, recorded live in Birmingham, England. As Zappa says "Good night boys and girls", we can hear the audience shout for more.

Zappa's *musique concrète* foregrounds the technology of mixing, but not in order to diminish recording's documentary power. He is concerned to inform us that an audience could listen to the Mothers play the worst noise in the world for two minutes and then ask for more. The cravenness of the rock audience, the terroristic imposition of volume, the hurt engendered on subjectivity by the exalted position of the star, are all being commented on in "Weasels Ripped My Flesh". If Zappa lost the idea of recording as document—and decided to compose entirely with "unrecognizable", "abstract" sonorities—he would never be able to make such points.

The voice of the oppressed

Zappa's approach was pragmatic. When questioned about various methods of recombining multitracks, he pointed out that he does not seek to justify particular procedures, or work within their limits.

> I mean, basically, what you're looking for is a musical result that works, y'know, so . . . there's nothin' "pure" about me, and the tools that I use. I mean, I'm the guy that sticks "Louie Louie" in every fifteen minutes. (Simms, 1991, pp. 19–20)

This clashes with some key tenets of the post-war avantgarde. In the 1950s, serial techniques were prized because they generated new sound worlds beyond the intention of the composer. The score was a directive that could realize new music by specifying new procedures. The composer's "ear" was distrusted as leading back to tradition. Zappa was interested in new techniques, but insisted on the right to edit the results. When Pierre Boulez says he distrusts talk of "inspiration", he argues that at such times memory is just being turned on like a tap.

> When people say, I'm free to invent, I can use any language, I use the language which is appropriate to what I want to say, I say that what they are doing is just like tap-water, opening a tap of their memory, they think that's new, but it's not, it's just pure memory. If you want to be involved in the discovery of your own personality you have to be demanding of yourself than just to feel free—you never feel free unless you have a strong discipline before.[10]

Boulez is criticizing the ideology of a composer like Alfred Schnittke who claims simply to "hear" the music he wishes to achieve and then "transcribe" it. Both Cage and Boulez criticized the humanistic concept of the personality at ease in the symbolic system into which he or she has been born (as if musical expression is transparent and unmediated, and culture as "natural" as the air we breathe). To contradict such reactionary "commonsense", Boulez used the structuralist ideas available to a post-war Parisian intellectual, Cage the paradoxes of Zen Buddhism (themselves so often reminiscent of Dada). Conversely, attacks on the modern school pioneered by Cage and Boulez decry the "anti-humanism" of questioning traditional means of musical communication.[11]

Does Zappa's insistence on his own ear as final arbiter mean that he can do no more than "turn memory on like a tap", confined within the limits of Cage's bugbear, "personal taste"?[12] To answer this question, it is necessary to examine the social role of the musical genres under discussion. Cage and Boulez are modern classical composers, chafing at institutions designed to realize the music of the past. Romanticism's ideology of "personal expression" is experienced as a shackle; hence their interest in processes that go beyond the "control" of the expressive intentions of the composer.

---

10. Boulez, P. (1990) Talk at the Royal Festival Hall, 9 September 1990.
11. E.g., the attack on Richard Barrett and the New Complexity (Hewett, 1994, pp. 148–51).
12. Despite Cage's Zen rhetoric, there are indications that he *did* exercise his own taste: for example, abandoning works if, once he examined the outcome, he decided the questions he had answered with chance were "superficial" (Pritchett, 1994, p. 3).

Zappa operated in a different realm. Unlike Cage and Boulez, Zappa was not in a position to make a name for himself as composer pioneering new sounds; he brought master-tapes to market and hoped they would sell. To insist on art integrity on a pop record—which Zappa did by quoting Edgard Varèse's "The present-day composer refuses to die!" on his album sleeves—has a different resonance from perpetuating the myth of the expressive "genius" in classical music. All three are concerned to disrupt packaging clichés that threaten to box them in a corner (likewise jazz composer Anthony Braxton: see Radano, 1994). It is interesting to note that the record industry has managed to sell quantities of modern "classical" records in the 90s by promoting the image of the composer "mystic", a readily consumed entity with none of the prickly integrity of a Cage or Boulez.

Boulez often points out that progressive post-war composers wanted a new, international musical vocabulary because of the horrors nationalism had inflicted on the world. Likewise, Adorno saw folk music—and nationalist composers who used folk sources—as an example of the forced reconciliation between individual and community that characterised the totalitarian regimes of Hitler and Stalin. The revival of folk music in an industrialized society was artificial and ideological.

However, Adorno had good words to say about Bartók and Janacek, reasoning that the folk music of an oppressed, non-industrialized nation had an altogether different function from Nazi blood-and-soil propaganda (Adorno, 1949, p. 35, n. 5; also Paddison, 1993, pp. 37–38). Adorno's comments echo Lenin on the national question, arguing that national struggles need to be assessed according to whether they express the aspirations of an oppressed or colonizing nation (Lenin, 1913, pp. 17–51). Adorno here provides a better basis for understanding blues and jazz—the music of an oppressed people—than his blanket condemnation of the "regressive" hearing brought about by "jazz" on the radio (Adorno, 1938). Zappa's affinity for Black R&B came about because, as for a whole generation of American adolescents, it voiced his social alienation (aggravated, in Zappa's case, by a Sicilian/Greek background which meant he suffered from WASP racism). When Zappa trusts his ear as the final arbiter, it is because—unlike Cage and Boulez—he does not need a self-denying ordinance on his sensibility. For someone who declared a lack of interest in *any* tonal classical music at all (Zappa, 1963), the rigours of chance and serialism were not required to prevent a return to the past.

Though frequently portrayed as a prescriptive mandarin with a gloomy outlook, Adorno was actually much less enamoured of the system than many post-war serialists. He called for *emancipation* from twelve-tone techniques:

> the amalgamation and absorption of twelve-tone technique by free composition—by the assumption of its rules through the spontaneity of the critical ear. (Adorno, 1949, p. 115)

This is precisely where Zappa stands.

As pointed out above, Black music evolved through a dialectic of recording and improvisation. Although the way that musical problems are verbalised in classical composition furnishes many insights, it also divides composers into different schools specialising in various declared techniques. In Europe, electronic music and free improvisation are frequently hampered by ideologies and institutions which prevent the two sides communicating[13] (although excluded from the academy since the 1960s, free improvisation is still very much alive, as demonstrated by the survival of the record labels Incus in London and FMP in Berlin, and the worldwide network of free improvising clubs); electronic composers develop a horror of not being "in control", whilst free improvisors often have grave doubts about the validity of recording anything at all (or record in an uncreative "documentary" vein). Zappa meanwhile eschewed ideological commitment to any particular method, using a palette of technical means as wide-open as his musical sources.

Zappa and modern art

Zappa's refusal to accept a social niche for his music has delayed his reception by the musically literate. Coming from a counterculture that revolted against the privilege implied by "education" (reinforced by Zappa's standing in the long line of American self-taught, crackpot "inventors" like Charles Ives, Buckminster Fuller and Cage himself), Zappa's music does not "explain itself" politely, but instead supplies problems for reified thought, getting close to Adorno's definition of modern art in *Aesthetic Theory*.

---

13. Notable exceptions are: Conrad Boehmer, who uses free improvisors on *Apocalipsis cum figuris* (1984; available on *Acousmatrix*, BVHaast 9011); Richard Barrett, who both writes scores and improvises with an electronics group called Furt; Simon Fell, whose *Compilation* series adds in an experimental attitude towards the recording studio to an improvisation/composition dialectic.

Without the homeopathic ingestion of the poison itself—reification as the virtual negation of the living—the pretense of art to resist subsumption under "civilisation" would have remained a helpless pipe-dream. By absorbing into art, since the beginnings of the modern, objects alien to it that can never be fully transformed by its own internal formal laws, the mimetic pole of art yields to its counter-principle, and this all the way up to the emergence of montage. (Adorno, 1970, p. 193)

Following this line of thought allowed Adorno to grant that a satirist like Kurt Weill could work with "regressive" musical material and end up with something far removed from the collusive kitsch of neo-classicism. Similarly, Zappa's musical eclecticism should not just be racked alongside Schnittke as an example of polystylism.

In mirroring contemporary culture—from Sinatra to Varèse—as a giant scrap heap of disposable consumer trash, Zappa and the Mothers of Invention (in the earlier records at least) must certainly come close as any to meeting Adorno's requirements as outlined . . . on Weill. (Paddison, 1982, p. 215)

In taking Varèse as his guiding light, Zappa adopted the most radical and "abstract" composer of the twentieth century. In *Poème électronique* (1958) tape recordings of bells, woodblocks, sirens and a woman's sighs are contrasted with pure electronic signals in a constructivist drama of call and response, irruption and echo. A similar delight in formal shaping underlies all Zappa's music, but aligned with a sneer at the manner in which the sounds he uses are usually employed to manipulate the listener rather than as ends in themselves.

Rock versus classical

Zappa examined the relationship between rock and classical music in the "surrealist documentary" *200 Motels,* a film which placed the Royal Philharmonic Orchestra and members of the Mothers of Invention inside a vast concentration camp. From the beginning, with the title "Semi Fraudulent/Direct-from-Hollywood Overture", the status of composition is highly ambiguous. As in *Lumpy Gravy,* Zappa's scores appear to delineate processes internal to the musicians' thoughts. In contrast, the rock songs are chances for blatant extroversion. As with *Fillmore East, 200 Motels* is presented as a live event, like a 60s pop-art or Fluxus "happening". In later years, Zappa had the finance to do close-focus recording of both orchestras and rock bands, combining aspects of both into single works. Here, the two genres are compared by being filmed and recorded in the same physical space: musicians from both "camps" are being placed in an "experimental reorientation facility" (as Ringo Starr calls it in his introduction). In "Lucy's Seduction Of A Bored Violinist & Postlude", seductive "groupie" gestures are projected over a violinist sawing away at Zappa's portentous score, guying the repressed professionalism of the orchestral musician.

"A Nun Suit Painted On Some Old Boxes" is a definitive celebration of post–*Pierrot Lunaire* vocalese, though it is closer to the disorienting insanity of the Cabaret Voltaire than the expressionism of Boulez. It mocks conventional demands for "some old melodies", "4/4" time and an "aura" (precisely that which Walter Benjamin said was destroyed when art is reproduced). The segue from this to "Magic Fingers", a blistering rock number, is virtuosic, the final note from the soprano seeming to invite the guitar explosion that follows. Rock and classical music, the products of distinct social strata, may be combined to produce something stronger than either in isolation.

The Perfect Stranger appeared on the Angel classical label in 1984 and featured three of Zappa's compositions played by the Ensemble InterContemporain under the direction of Pierre Boulez. This was a coup for Zappa's attempts to be taken seriously as a composer. Zappa showed an ambivalence towards being accepted in the art world. His sleevenotes on *The Perfect Stranger* concluded: "All material contained herein is for entertainment purposes only, and should not be confused with any other form of artistic expression" (likewise his sarcastic emphasis on the word "fine" in his introduction to the Ensemble Modern concert on *The Yellow Shark*). Like any dadaist, Zappa is allergic to claims to art transcendence. A comedy of errors has characterised his relationship with the classical world (for the 1985 "While You Were Art" scandal see Zappa, 1989, p. 176, and Shrader, 1992), though the Ensemble Modern's *Yellow Shark* concerts and recordings were undoubtedly a triumph. The interest in Zappa's scores shown by progressive figures like pianist Joanna MacGregor, conductor Clark Rundell and the Meridian Ensemble indicates a bright future for Zappa as an orchestral composer.

Schizophrenia

Although this paper contends that Zappa's art constitutes a dadaist response to the manipulations of the mass media, for Zappa, living and working in Hollywood, isolated from artistic and political currents that could contribute solidarity, such refusal to collude in culture-industry myths could easily feel like schizophrenia: a radical dislocation from social reality. Since Zappa's musical method is to construct assemblages from materials that are externally available, lack of "inwardness" causes a powerful existential anxiety. "Andy" on *One Size Fits All* packs some of the force of Varèse's abstractions. Its lyrics concern Andy Devine, the cowboy actor, asking "Is there anything good inside of you?" The music evokes schizophrenia, the chilling idea that all reality is a façade as flimsy as the flats of a B-movie Western. On the same record "Sofa" parodies the pomp of romanticism (God sings to his sofa in German), not allowing transcendent high art to pose as an alternative to the junk heap either.

Musical abstraction and social strata

Weasels Ripped My Flesh was a bravura example of Zappa's skill with the razorblade, a collection of live musical events spliced together like *musique concrète*. "Didja Get Any Onya?" achieved some of the absurdist conjunctions of Varèse's *Poème électronique*: dense, hysterical passages abutted to unaccompanied vocal wails, low slurring sounds abraising regular beats, call and response, a sense of complexity raised by overlaying metres running in different time zones—in short, the whole liberated universe of post-war avantgarde music. But this abstraction is segued straight into Sugarcane Harris singing "Directly From My Heart To You" by Little Richard. Instruments that have been exploring free-form abstraction suddenly coalesce in rock-solid R&B. All this appears to be achieved in real time because the instrumental sound—amplification and recording—is identical. Continuity of the recording ambience allows us to hear R&B in an abstract manner, the bass as a mighty industrial machine, the violin like an expressive siren. An astute producer's ear allows Zappa to make connections between musics conventionally regarded as products of distinct social strata.

On "Prelude to the Afternoon of a Sexually Aroused Gas Mask" the falsettos are so strained and silly-sounding (the audience can be heard laughing in response), it is easy to miss what sophisticated harmonic layerings are being achieved. The sparseness of the music makes us aware of the audience and their sense of outrage, recalling Dada provocations at the Cabaret Voltaire. "Toads of the Short Forest" (a tune originally produced by overdubbing at Studio Z) realizes its metrical layerings here in real time. Blues and jazz grew out of a dialectic with the recording process—a player's personal sound and improvisations came to be prized because there was the technology to reproduce it (previous eras could only preserve the score, not the performance). Zappa's ricochet between studio experimentation and live reproduction is a high-pressure version of this dialectic.

Using the same engineer and studio as *One Size Fits All,* Johnny "Guitar" Watson (an R&B legend who guested on the album) recorded an album that has the same steely objectivity as "Andy", raising the bizarre idea that Varèse might find a correspondence in 70s funk. The introduction to "Love That Will Not Die" on *Funk Beyond The Call Of Duty,* an album Watson made in 1977, has woodblocks, chimes and sirens that could come straight from Varèse's *Hyperprism.* Like Mondrian's delighted response to the modernity of New York—his *Broadway Boogie-Woogie series*—Varèse's futurism is not in a different world from Black music: both are responses to the city, both celebrate the vital "primitivism" of the metropolis. The riveted precision of Watson's no-note-wasted arrangements have the same futurist refusal of "soul" that guided Varèse in constructing his music: an eroticism of the machine. The assumed divide between "high" and "low" culture of course make such any such comparison preposterous—especially given classical music's genteel image (an image Varèse cordially hated) and the assumed irrelevance of funk ("feet music") to philosophy ("head music"). Zappa's "Andy", by using state-of-the-art studio technology to realize abstract sound pictures, allows us to make observations about the sounds of modernity across such social (and corporal) boundaries.

Xenochrony

On *Zoot Allures* Zappa played most of the instruments himself. This gives a sense of closure which is quite claustrophobic, with no window on spontaneity or improvisation (rather like the repetitions of *Ruben*). However, just at the point where Zappa seemed to be asserting absolute control, he introduced a chance procedure, just as total serialism opened the door to chance as an alternative method of reaching similar-sounding results.

Called "re-synchronization" or "xenochrony", the procedure involved taking a track off a master and combining it with something entirely different. In "Friendly Little Finger" the guitar solo is happening in a different time-zone from its backing. In a way, this is merely a technical version of a practice common in jazz since Eric Dolphy and Ornette Coleman began disassociating the metres of the various players, opening up the strict bar-lines of bop; and already, because of the model of Varèse, Zappa often composed via contrasting *timbres* rather than using the horizontal/vertical concept of the traditional score. Still, xenochrony was new: he had to fight his own engineers to allow him to do it, and it resulted in some extraordinary music. "Rubber Shirt" on *Sheik Yerbouti,* ostensibly a bass/drum duet, had a complex provenance. The sleevenote ran:

> The bass part is extracted from a four track master which I had Patrick O'Hearn overdub on a medium tempo guitar solo track in 4/4. The notes chosen were more or less specified during the overdub session, and so it was not completely an improvised "bass solo". The bass track was peeled off the master and transferred to one track of another studio 24 track master for a slow song in 11/4. The result of this experimental re-synchronization is the piece you are listening to. All the sensitive, interesting interplay between the bass and drums never actually happened.

The spacious, delayed metrical scheme of xenochrony became a regular feature of Zappa's music—all but one of the guitar solos on *Joe's Garage* are presented in this way. Zappa would replicate the liberties of xenochrony in his live playing, taking off on extended sequences that played to other rhythms. On the album *Shut Up 'N Play Yer Guitar* Zappa is asked to "identify your last port of entry, space wanderer" ("Canarsie"). However, this was not like free jazz, which generates its own shapes in process; there was always a point where the musicians sought to resolve their metres—more or less successfully.

As in Cage, chance is a vehicle for objectivity. The epic guitar solo on *Sheik Yerbouti*'s "Yo Mama"—three separate solos conjoined and xenochronously laid over alien backing tracks, with tumultuous keyboard overdubs welding the outrageous events together—has the gigantic impersonality that characterizes the major works of the Darmstadt avantgarde.

Filth

From the point of view of recording, *Sleep Dirt* is one of Zappa's most intriguing records. Different recording ambiences are used for different instruments in the mix, indicating how bound to "realistic" representation is most recording of rock, jazz and classical music. "Filthy Habits" begins with a feedback whine on multitracked guitars, every note redolent of Zappa's touch (like any authentic blues or rock performer, his sound is instantly recognisable). A bass riff that seems to imply cavernous inevitability (but is in fact full of subtle variations) sweeps the music along with a flow like lava. A guitar "solo" (a curious entity when it is surrounded by guitar textures provided by Zappa himself) is sustained as an alternation between propulsive plucks and whining feedback. Zappa once said that his guitar sounded to him like a bouzouki; his modal note choices and microtonal variations here recall Transylvanian gypsy music, a combination of rock timbre (fuzz and feedback guitars) and Bartókian "barbarian" harmony. At the end of the solo, an electronic piano picks out the notes of the mode, making it sound like East European accordion music (these are then repeated in the other speaker, reminding the listener that this is all happening on the domestic stereo). Trills deep in the mix conjure up Bulgarian peasant dances.

The music is also utterly filthy-sounding. Although it gains salaciousness from association with the sonorities of "The Torture Never Stops", it also connects to a world music politics. This microtonal succulence is what the tempered system banished from western music as "uncivilised". Such timbral complexity is the opposite of the C-major brightness favoured by Steve Reich's minimalism, which paradoxically claims a closer connection to the "simplicities" of world music than the "élitism" of microtonal composition. Taking rock guitar out of its usual context, placing it in a harmonic context that recalls Bartók, Zappa places its textures in a critical relation to western tonality.

Close-miking

Zappa was alert to the special eroticism of close-miking. "Flam Bay" on *Sleep Dirt* begins with cocktail piano accompanied by double bass. The bass has been close-miked, giving every finger-click and abrasion an expressiveness that verges on parody. There is a parallel here with the close-up as theorized by Walter Benjamin.

> By close-ups of its subject-matter, by focusing on the hidden details of objects familiar to us, by investigating the everyday environment with the ingenious guidance of the lens, film not only gives new insights into the necessities which rule our lives; it also supplies us with immense, undreamed-of spaces for play! . . . Just as magnification does not simply clarify what would otherwise be unclear, but rather brings wholly new textural formations to light, so slow motion doesn't just record familiar gestures, but discovers in them the unknown . . . We already know in general the act of reaching for a lighter or a spoon, but we hardly know anything at all about what really goes between hand and metal, not to

mention how this may change depending on our state of mind. This is where the camera comes into its own, with its ability to go up or down, to interrupt or isolate, to slow down or speed up, to close-up or pan away. We discover the optic unconscious with the camera, just as we discover the unconscious of drives with psychoanalysis. (Benjamin, 1936a, pp. 161–62 [my translation]; 1936b, pp. 229–30)

Anyone who has watched advanced bass players like Fred Hopkins or Simon Fell will be aware of the eroticism involved with passionately innovative handling of an instrument as tall as a person. Zappa's recording brings out these qualities, focusing attention on the physical act of playing rather than abstractions of pitch and metre.

The swelling romanticism of "Flam Bay" reaches a peak only to tumble into pompous march music. Music's use as a glorification of gentility (cocktail) or power (electric guitar, fanfares) is guyed by showing that these two elements can be combined simultaneously, rather as Jeff Koons showed the harmlessness of hardcore pornography by exhibiting blowups of penetration shots next to gift-store effigies of poodles. By repeating the techniques of manipulation in self-immolating circumstances, advanced art seeks to break their spell.

Alienation and virtual reality

Zappa distinguished between the way 50s recordings "photographed" real ambient space and the touch-of-a-button ambience available to a digital mixer (Zappa, 1989, pp. 156–57). Zappa's three-volume *Joe's Garage* dealt with the alienation such virtual reality implies. Unlike other 60s rebels—Neil Young, the Grateful Dead, Bob Dylan—who felt that their recordings should emulate the feel of live music, an element of unmediated communication in an increasingly packaged industry, Zappa accepted the alienation of commercialism whilst commenting on it.

Joe's Garage was built up in the studio, beginning with tunes played on a Wurlitzer, an iconically trashy 60s electronic keyboard. All the guitar solos (apart from "Watermelon In Easter Hay") were xenochronous, creating a spacious, free-floating sonic universe. Posing as "the Central Scrutinizer" Zappa whispered an irritating between-tracks commentary down a plastic megaphone, full of bad jokes and slip-of-the-tongue. At one point he can hardly speak for mirth. Alongside this rubbishing cynicism, though, is incredible attention to minute detail; the spatial arrangement of the sounds is bravura, unique in either pop or classical electronics.

Embedded in "Wet T-Shirt Nite" (a typically ambivalent "satire" on moronic Americana) is a percussion section of quite bewildering complexity. The *finale* is an absurd piece of semi-improvised studio "self-indulgence" called "A Little Green Rosetta". Poised at the knife-edge between virtuosic brilliance and self-defeating degradation, *Joe's Garage* is simultaneously a rubbish heap and an imaginative universe (like James Joyce's *Finnegans Wake*, which mythologized itself as a midden heap picked over by a chicken/reader).

An aspirant rock musician, Joe is utterly "plucked" by the record industry and ends up dreaming "imaginary guitar solos". The modern studio's ability to create illusory ambience is put in overdrive, creating an aggressive insubstantiality. Distrusting the social consequences of scientific "progress"—the rationality that leads to musicians being reduced to "imaginary guitar solos" because canned music has stolen their jobs—invites paranoid, fantasist response. Zappa's use of modern studio techniques dramatizes their powers of fakery.

Musicians and machines

The Dada perversity of Zappa's method reached a climax with a live rendition of "Brown Shoes Don't Make It" (*Tinsel Town Rebellion*), a piece of music originally constructed via thousands of overdubs and splices. Zappa forces his musicians to internalize the jumpcuts of technology in real time. In this he echoes one of the central themes of the avantgarde: from the Futurists, who wished to "conquer the enmity that separates our human flesh from the metal of motors,"[14] to Cyberpunk implantation of technology in the human body.

Graphics on *Joe's Garage* portrayed the daydreams of people at work (a man disinfecting a toilet thinks of a salami; an x-ray operative thinks of plucking a tiny banjo). Wilhelm Reich, too, was concerned to decipher the latent eroticism of everyday life in industrial society.

> The train engine has eyes to see with and legs to run with, a mouth to consume with and discharge openings for slag, levers and other devices for making sounds. In this way the product of mechanistic technology becomes the extension of man himself. (Reich, 1933, p. 324)

---

14. F. T. Marinetti's *Technical Manifesto of Futurist Literature*, quoted in McMillan, 1976, p. 37.

Convinced that religion and fascism exploit such currents without bringing them to consciousness, Zappa seeks to show our libidinal investment in technology. Though delivered alongside vulgarities that means that few respectable musicologists will pay attention, Zappa's dialectic between technology and the body (a dialectic that includes classical score/musician confrontation but also the recording/improvisation process of Black music) provides a psychoanalysis that connects to both Wilhelm Reich and the Futurists.

Conclusion: Zappa and postmodernism

Zappa spent much of the last five years of his life editing together an immense thirteen-hour, twelve-disc series entitled *You Can't Do That On Stage Anymore*. It featured live recordings selected from his entire career. Overdubs were restricted to a single short track. Critics once associated with the London-based magazine *Musics* (e.g., Toop, 1992, p. 63) are frequently critical of "no overdubs" slogans on records, pointing out there is something spurious about claims to "authenticity" on recorded product. Once we're listening to a recording, who cares *how* it has been produced? Isn't this merely a sentimental notion, a pretence at lack of mediation? However, as with John Heartfield's photo-montages, it is precisely Frank Zappa's strong idea of recording as *documentary* that allows him to make social and political points. These moments actually happened: in the teeth of music-industry standardization, which prefers bands to mime to DAT tapes, these musicians played and improvised in front of an audience of tens of thousands. The actuality matters.

Zappa's achievement was to save the notion of a critical, resistant art at a time when such an idea has become deeply unfashionable.

> It becomes minimally obvious that the newer artists no longer "quote" the materials, the fragments and motifs, of a popular culture, as Flaubert began to do; they somehow incorporate them to the point where many of our older critical and evaluative categories (founded precisely on the radical differentiation of modernist and mass culture) no longer seem functional. (Jameson, 1991, p. 64)

Although Zappa's critique of modern America does not proceed from a transcendental, superior position, neither does his art exhibit the "mildness" Achille Bonito-Oliva notes in postmodernism's warm stream of referentless signifiers (Jameson, 1991, p. 175). As a boy, Zappa was fascinated by chemistry and explosives, and his musical alchemy is similarly scientific and eruptive. By respecting the social provenance of his materials (documentary recording, musicians, genres) he fashioned provocative grotesques that beg critical thought. His epic "Porn Wars" on *Meets The Mothers Of Prevention*—a cut-up of senatorial voices discussing censorship of rock records—demonstrates that obscenity is constructed in the mind of the listener, it is not something that can be etched onto plastic. As in Dada, Zappa's technical procedures always engage social issues.

Schooled in R&B production values and avantgarde composition, Zappa's collage aesthetic does not repress dissonance or seek to homogenize the elements he brings together. Refusing to subscribe to any particular ideology of musical production allowed him to experiment with sound in a way that did not subordinate it to ideas. This respect for musical material—equivalent to a respect for people—sounds out like a protest against the triteness of both classical minimalism and radio pop: a dadaist denunciation of standardization at whatever cultural level it may be found.

References

Adorno, T. (1938) On The Fetish Character In Music And The Regression Of Listening. Arato, A. & Gebhard, E. editors (1978) *The Essential Frankfurt School Reader* Oxford: Basil Blackwell

Adorno, T. (1949) *The Philosophy Of Modern Music* (translated by Mitchell, A. and Blomster, W., 1973) London: Sheed & Ward

Adorno, T. (1962) *Introduction To The Sociology Of Music* (translated by Ashton, E., 1976) New York: Seabury Press

Adorno, T. (1970) *Aesthetic Theory* (translated by Lenhardt, C., 1984) London: Routledge & Kegan Paul

Attali, J. (1977) *Noise* (translated by Massumi, B., 1985) Manchester: MUP

Benjamin, W. (1936a) Das Kunstwerk im Zetalter seiner technischen Reproduzierbarkeit [The Work of Art In The Age Of Its Technical Reproducibility]. *Illuminationen* (1977) Frankfurt: Suhrkamp

Benjamin, W. (1936b) The Work Of Art In The Age Of Mechanical Reproduction *Illuminations* (translated by Zohn, H., 1992) London: Fontana

Bloch, E. *et al* (1977) *Aesthetics & Politics* London: Verso

Bloom, M. (1980) Interview with the Composer Zappa *Trouser Press* February

Cardew, C. (1976) Wiggly Lines and Wobbly Music *Studio International* November-December 1976 reprinted in Battcock, G. (1978) editor *Breaking the Sound Barrier* New York: Dutton

Colbeck, J. (1987) *Zappa A Biography* London: Virgin

Corbett, J. (1994) Bleep This, Motherf*!#er *Extended Play: Sounding Off From John Cage To Dr. Funkenstein,* Durham/London: Duke University Press

Gray, M. (1985) *Mother! Is The Story Of Frank Zappa* London/New York: Proteus

Hewett, I. (1994) Fail Worse, Fail Better *The Musical Times* March

Jameson, F. (1991) *Postmodernism or, The Cultural Logic of Late Capitalism* London/New York: Verso

Jameux, D. (1984) *Pierre Boulez* (translated by Bradshaw, S., 1991) London: Faber & Faber

Jones, J. (1994) Plugged in or hung up? Or What's the Matter with Frank Zappa?, *Eonta,* Vol. 2, no. 2 (*Eonta* is published from 27 Alexandra Road Wimbledon London SW19 7JZ)

Lenin, V. Critical Remarks on the National Question (1913) *Prosveshcheniye,* Nos. 10, 11, 12, *Collected Works* (1951) Vol. 20

McClary, S. (1991) *Feminine Endings* Minnesota: MUP

McMillan, D. (1976) *Transition 1927–1938* New York: George Braziller

Marsh, D. (1989) *The Heart Of Rock & Soul: The 1001 Greatest Singles Ever Made* New York: Plume

Occhiogrosso, P. (1987) *Once A Catholic* Boston: Houghton Mifflin

Ouellette, F. (1973) *Edgard Varèse: A Musical Biography* London: Calder & Boyars

Pachnike, P., Honnef, K. editors (1991) *John Heartfield* New York: Harry N Abrams Inc.

Paddison, M. (1982) The Critique Criticised: Adorno and Popular Music *Popular Music 2 Theory & Method* Middleton, R., Horn, D. editors Cambridge: CUP

Paddison, M. (1993) *Adorno's Aesthetics Of Music* Cambridge: CUP

Penman, Ian (1978) Review of *Studio Tan NME* 30 September

Pritchett, J. (1994) *The Music Of John Cage* Cambridge: CUP

Radano, R. M. (1993) *New Musical Figuration: Anthony Braxton's Cultural Critique* Chicago: U of Chicago

Reich, W. (1933) *The Mass Psychology Of Fascism* (translated by Carfagno, V., 1970) Harmondsworth: Penguin

Revill, D. (1992) *The Roaring Silence: John Cage, A Life* London: Bloomsbury

Richter, H. (1938) *The Struggle For The Film: Towards A Socially Responsible Cinema* (translated by Brewster, B., 1986) Aldershot: Scolar Press

Shrader, B. (1992) Live/electro-acoustic music—a perspective from history and California. *Contemporary Music Review* Vol. 6, Part 1

Simms, D. (1991) He's A Human Being, He Has Emotions Just Like Us Part 2 (12 January 1991) *Society Pages,* No. 7, September 1991

Steel, G. (1991) The Father Of Invention *Listener* (New Zealand) 22 April

Toop, D. (1992) Review of Scott/Casswell's The Magnificence Of Stereo *The Wire* No. 105, November 1992

Walley, D. (1972) *No Commercial Potential* New York: Dutton.

Watson, B. (1994) *Frank Zappa: The Negative Dialectics of Poodle Play* London: Quartet

Zappa, F. (1963) Lecture at Mount St. Mary's College (unreleased)

Zappa, F. (1971) *International Times* No 115

Zappa, F. with Occhiogrosso, P. (1989) *The Real Frank Zappa Book* New York: Poseidon.

PART FIVE

Plastic People:

Politics and Culture

RECORD LABELING: HEARING BEFORE THE COMMITTEE ON COMMERCE, SCIENCE, AND TRANSPORTATION, UNITED STATES SENATE, NINETY-NINTH CONGRESS, FIRST SESSION, ON CONTENTS OF MUSIC AND THE LYRICS OF RECORDS, SEPTEMBER 19, 1985

It seems hard to believe in retrospect that someone of Zappa's reputation, let alone his appearance, would be invited to appear before a Senate committee purportedly investigating obscenity in popular songs' lyrics. It is harder to believe the responses of some of his interlocutors. It must have been a classic performance in a tradition of classic Zappa performances.

Statements of Frank Zappa, accompanied by Larry Stein, Counsel

MR. ZAPPA. My name is Frank Zappa. This is my attorney Larry Stein from Los Angeles.

The first thing I would like to do, because I know there is some foreign press involved here and they might not understand what the issue is about, one of the things the issue is about is the First Amendment to the Constitution, and it is short and I would like to read it so they will understand. It says:

Congress shall make no law respecting an establishment of religion or prohibiting the free exercise thereof, or abridging the freedom of speech or of the press, or the right of the people peaceably to assemble and to petition the government for a redress of grievances.

That is for reference.

These are my personal observations and opinions. I speak on behalf of no group or professional organization.

The PMRC proposal is an ill-conceived piece of nonsense which fails to deliver any real benefits to children, infringes the civil liberties of people who are not children, and promises to keep the courts busy for years dealing with the interpretational and enforcemental problems inherent in the proposal's design.

It is my understanding that in law First Amendment issues are decided with a preference for the least restrictive alternative. In this context, the PMRC demands are the equivalent of treating dandruff by decapitation.

No one has forced Mrs. Baker or Mrs. Albert Gore to bring Prince or Sheena Easton into their homes. Thanks to the Constitution, they are free to buy other forms of music for their children. Apparently, they insist on purchasing the works of contemporary recording artists in order to support a personal illusion of aerobic sophistication. Ladies, please be advised: The $8.98 purchase price does not entitle you to a kiss on the foot from the composer or performer in exchange for a spin on the family Victrola.

Taken as a whole, the complete list of PMRC demands reads like an instruction manual for some sinister kind of toilet training program to house-break all composers and performers because of the lyrics of a few. Ladies, how dare you?

The ladies' shame must be shared by the bosses at the major labels who, through the RIAA, chose to bargain away the rights of composers, performers, and retailers in order to pass H.R. 2911, The Blank Tape Tax, a private tax levied by an industry on consumers for the benefit of a select group within that industry.

Is this a consumer issue? You bet it is. The major record labels need to have H.R. 2911 whiz through a few committees before anybody smells a rat. One of them is chaired by Senator Strom Thurmond. Is it a coincidence that Mrs. Thurmond is affiliated with the PMRC?

I cannot say she is a member, because the PMRC has no members. Their secretary told me on the phone last Friday that the PMRC has no members, only founders. I asked how many other District of Columbia wives are nonmembers of an organization that raises money by mail, has a tax-exempt status, and seems intent on running the Constitution of the United States through the family paper-shredder. I asked her if it was a cult. Finally, she said she could not give me an answer and that she had to call their lawyer.

While the wife of the Secretary of the Treasury recites "Gonna drive my love inside you" and Senator Gore's wife talks about "bondage" and "oral sex at gunpoint" on the CBS Evening News, people in high places work on a tax bill that is so ridiculous, the only way to sneak it through is to keep the public's mind on something else: Porn rock.

Is the basic issue morality? Is it mental health? Is it an issue at all? The PMRC has created a lot of confusion with improper comparisons between song lyrics, videos, record packaging, radio broadcasting, and live performances. These are all different mediums and the people who work in them have the right to conduct their business without trade-restraining legislation, whipped up like an instant pudding by "The wives of Big Brother."

Is it proper that the husband of a PMRC nonmember/founder/person sits on any committee considering business pertaining to the blank tape tax or his wife's lobbying organization? Can any committee thus constituted find facts in a fair and unbiased manner? This committee has three that we know about: Senator Robert Danforth, Senator John Packwood, and Senator Albert Gore. For some reason, they seem to feel there is no conflict of interest involved.

Children in the vulnerable age bracket have a natural love for music. If as a parent you believe they should be exposed to something more uplifting than "Sugar Walls," support music appreciation programs in schools. Why have you not considered your child's need for consumer information? Music appreciation costs very little compared to sports expenditures. Your children have a right to know that something besides pop music exists.

It is unfortunate that the PMRC would rather dispense governmentally sanitized heavy metal music than something more uplifting. Is this an indication of PMRC's personal taste or just another manifestation of the low priority this administration has placed on education for the arts in America?

The answer, of course, is neither. You cannot distract people from thinking about an unfair tax by talking about music appreciation. For that you need sex, and lots of it.

The establishment of a rating system, voluntary or otherwise, opens the door to an endless parade of moral quality control programs based on things certain Christians do not like. What if the next bunch of Washington wives demands a large yellow "J" on all material written or performed by Jews, in order to save helpless children from exposure to concealed Zionist doctrine?

Record ratings are frequently compared to film ratings. Apart from the quantitative difference, there is another that is more important: People who act in films are hired to pretend. No matter how the film is rated, it will not hurt them personally.

Since many musicians write and perform their own material and stand by it as their art, whether you like it or not, an imposed rating will stigmatize them as individuals. How long before composers and performers are told to wear a festive little PMRC arm band with their scarlet letter on it?

Bad facts make bad law, and people who write bad laws are in my opinion more dangerous than songwriters who celebrate sexuality. Freedom of speech, freedom of religious thought, and the right to due process for composers, performers and retailers are imperiled if the PMRC and the major labels consummate this nasty bargain.

Are we expected to give up article 1 so the big guys can collect an extra dollar on every blank tape and 10 to 25 percent on tape recorders? What is going on here? Do we get to vote on this tax?

I think that this whole matter has gotten completely blown out of proportion, and I agree with Senator Exon that there is a very dubious reason for having this event. I also agree with Senator Exon that you should not be wasting time on stuff like this, because from the beginning I have sensed that it is somebody's hobby project.

Now, I have done a number of interviews on television. People keep saying, can you not take a few steps in their direction, can you not sympathize, can you not empathize? I do more than that at this point. I have got an idea for a way to stop all this stuff and a way to give parents what they really want, which is information, accurate information as to what is inside the album, without providing a stigma for the musicians who have played on the album or the people who sing it or the people who wrote it. And I think that if you listen carefully to this idea that it might just get by all of the constitutional problems and everything else.

As far as I am concerned, I have no objection to having all of the lyrics placed on the album routinely, all the time. But there is a little problem. Record companies do not own the right automatically to take these lyrics, because they are owned by a publishing company.

So, just as all the rest of the PMRC proposals would cost money, this would cost money too, because the record companies would need—they should not be forced to bear the cost, the extra expenditure to the publisher, to print those lyrics.

If you consider that the public needs to be warned about the contents of the records, what better way than to let them see exactly what the songs say? That way you do not have to put any kind of subjective rating on the record. You do not have to call it R, X, D/A, anything. You can read it for yourself.

But in order for it to work properly, the lyrics should be on a uniform kind of a sheet. Maybe even the Government could print those sheets. Maybe it should even be paid for by the Government, if the Government is interested in making sure that people have consumer information in this regard.

And you also have to realize that if a person buys the record and takes it out of the store, once it is out of the store you can't return it if you read the lyrics at home and decide that little Johnny is not supposed to have it.

I think that that should at least be considered, and the idea of imposing these ratings on live concerts, on the albums, asking record companies to reevaluate or drop or violate contracts that they already have with artists should be thrown out.

That is all I have to say.

THE CHAIRMAN. Thank you very much, Mr. Zappa. You understand that the previous witnesses were not asking for legislation. And I do not know, I cannot speak for Senator Hollings, but I think the prevailing view here is that nobody is asking for legislation.

The question is just focusing on what a lot of people perceive to be a problem, and you have indicated that you at least understand that there is another point of view. But there are people that think that parents should have some knowledge of what goes into their home.

MR. ZAPPA. All along my objection has been with the tactics used by these people in order to achieve the goal. I just think the tactics have been really bad, and the whole premise of their proposal—they were badly advised in terms of record business law, they were badly advised in terms of practicality, or they would have known that certain things do not work mechanically with what they suggest.

THE CHAIRMAN. Senator Gore.

SENATOR GORE. Thank you very much, Mr. Chairman.

I found your statement very interesting and, although I disagree with some of the statements that you make and have made on other occasions, I have been a fan of your music, believe it or not. I respect you as a true original and a tremendously talented musician.

Your suggestion of printing the lyrics on the album is a very interesting one. The PMRC at one point said they would propose either a rating or warning, or printing all the lyrics on the album. The record companies came back and said they did not want to do that.

I think a lot of people agree with your suggestion that one easy way to solve this problem for parents would be to put the actual words there, so that parents could see them. In fact, the National Association of Broadcasters made exactly the same request of the record companies.

I think your suggestion is an intriguing one and might really be a solution for the problem.

MR. ZAPPA. You have to understand that it does cost money, because you cannot expect publishers to automatically give up that right, which is a right for them. Somebody is going to have to reimburse the publishers, the record industry.

Without trying to mess up the album jacket art, it should be a sheet of paper that is slipped inside the shrink-wrap, so that when you take it out you can still have a complete album package. So there is going to be some extra cost for printing it.

But as long as people realize that for this kind of consumer safety you are going to spend some money and as long as you can find a way to pay for it, I think that would be the best way to let people know.

SENATOR GORE. I do not disagree with that at all. And the separate sheet would also solve the problem with cassettes as well, because you do not have the space for words on the cassette packs.

MR. ZAPPA. There would have to be a little accordion-fold.

SENATOR GORE. I have listened to you a number of times on this issue, and I guess the statement that I want to get from you is whether or not you feel this concern is legitimate.

You feel very strongly about your position, and I understand that. You are very articulate and forceful.

But occasionally you give the impression that you think parents are just silly to be concerned at all.

MR. ZAPPA. No; that is not an accurate impression.

SENATOR GORE. Well, please clarify it, then.

MR. ZAPPA. First of all, I think it is the parents' concern; it is not the Government's concern.

SENATOR GORE. The PMRC agrees with you on that.

MR. ZAPPA. Well, that does not come across in the way they have been speaking. The whole drift that I have gotten, based upon the media blitz that has attended the PMRC and its rise to infamy, is that they have a special plan, and it has smelled like legislation up until now.

There are too many things that look like hidden agendas involved with this. And I am a parent. I have got four children. Two of them are here. I want them to grow up in a country where they can think what they want to think, be what they want to be, and not what somebody's wife or somebody in Government makes them be.

I do not want to have that and I do not think you do either.

SENATOR GORE. OK. But now you are back on the issue of Government involvement. Let me say briefly on this point that the PMRC says repeatedly no legislation, no regulation, no Government action. It certainly sounded clear to me.

And as far as a hidden agenda, I do not see one, hear one, or know of one.

MR. ZAPPA. OK, let me tell you why I have drawn these conclusions. First of all, they may say, we are not interested in legislation. But there are others who do, and because of their project bad things have happened in this country in the industry.

I believe there is actually some liability. Look at this. You have a situation where, even if you go for the lyric printed thing in the record, because of the tendency among Americans to be copycats—one guy commits a murder, you get a copycat murder—now you've got copycat censors.

You get a very bad situation in San Antonio, TX, right now where they are trying to pass PMRC-type individual ratings and attach them to live concerts, with the mayor down there trying to make a national reputation by putting San Antonio on the map as the first city in the United States to have these regulations, against the suggestion of the city attorney, who says, I do not think this is constitutional.

But you know, there is this fervor to get in and do even more and even more.

And the other thing, the PMRC starts off talking about lyrics, but when they take it over into other realms they start talking about the videos. In fact, you misspoke yourself at the beginning in your introduction when you were talking about the music does this, the music does that. There is a distinct difference between those notes and chords and the baseline and the rhythm that support the words and the lyrics.

I do not know whether you really are talking about controlling the type of music.

THE CHAIRMAN. The lyrics.

MR. ZAPPA. So specifically we are talking about lyrics. It began with lyrics. But even looking at the PMRC fundraising letter, in the last paragraph at the bottom of the page it starts looking like it is branching into other areas, when it says: "We realize that this material has pervaded other aspects of society." And it is like what, you are going to fix it all for me?

SENATOR GORE. No. I think the PMRC's acknowledging some of the statements by some of their critics who say: Well, why single out the music industry?

Do I understand that you do believe that there is a legitimate concern here?

MR. ZAPPA. But the legitimate concern is a matter of taste for the individual parent and how much sexual information that parent wants to give their child, at what age, at what time, in what quantity, OK. And I think that, because there is a tendency in the United States to hide sex, which I think is an unhealthy thing to do, and many parents do not give their children good sexual education, in spite of the fact that little books for kids are available, and other parents demand that sexual education be taken out of school, it makes the child vulnerable, because if you do not have something rational to compare it to when you see or hear about something that is aberrated you do not perceive it as an aberration.

SENATOR GORE. OK, I have run out of time.

THE CHAIRMAN. Senator Gorton.

SENATOR GORTON. Mr. Zappa, I am astounded at the courtesy and soft-voiced nature of the comments of my friend, the Senator from Tennessee. I can only say that I found your statement to be boorish, incredibly and insensitively insulting to the people that were here previously; that you could manage to give the first amendment of the Constitution of the United States a bad name, if I felt that you had the slightest understanding of it, which I do not.

You do not have the slightest understanding of the difference between Government action and private action, and you have certainly destroyed any case you might otherwise have had with this Senator.

Thank you, Mr. Chairman.

MR. ZAPPA. Is this private action?

THE CHAIRMAN. Senator Exon.

SENATOR EXON. Mr. Chairman, thank you very much.

Mr. Zappa, let me say that I was surprised that Senator Gore knew and liked your music. I must confess that I have never heard any of your music, to my knowledge.

MR. ZAPPA. I would be more than happy to recite my lyrics to you.

SENATOR EXON. Can we forgo that?

SENATOR GORE. You have probably never heard of the Mothers of Invention.

SENATOR EXON. I have heard of Glen Miller and Mitch Miller. Did you ever perform with them?

MR. ZAPPA. As a matter of fact, I took music lessons in grade school from Mitch Miller's brother.

SENATOR EXON. That is the first sign of hope we have had in this hearing.

Let us try and get down to a fundamental question here that I would like to ask you, Mr. Zappa. Do you believe that parents have the right and the obligation to mold the psychological development of their children?

MR. ZAPPA. Yes, I think they have that right, and I also think they have that obligation.

SENATOR EXON. Do you see any extreme difficulty in carrying out those obligations for a parent by material falling into the hands of their children over which they have little or no control?

MR. ZAPPA. Well, one of the things that has been brought up before is talking about very young children getting access to the material that they have been showing here today. And what I have said to that in the past is a teenager may go into a record store unescorted with $8.98 in his pocket, but very young children do not.

If they go into a record store, the $8.98 is in mom or dad's pocket, and they can always say, Johnny, buy a book. They can say, Johnny, buy instrumental music; there is some nice classical music for you here; why do you not listen to that?

The parent can ask or guide the child in another direction, away from Sheena Easton, Prince, or whoever else you have been complaining about. There is always that possibility.

SENATOR EXON. As I understand it from your testimony—and once again, I want to emphasize that I see nothing wrong whatsoever, in fact, I salute the ladies for bringing this to the attention of the public as best they see fit. I think you could tell from my testimony that I tend to agree with them.

I want to be very careful that we do not overstep our bounds and try and—and I emphasize once again—tell somebody else what they should see. I am primarily worried about children.

It seems to me from your statement that you have no obligation—or no objection whatsoever to printing lyrics, if that would be legally possible, or from a standpoint of having the room to do that, on records or tapes. Is that not what you said?

MR. ZAPPA. I think it would be advisable for two reasons. One, it gives people one of the things that they have been asking for. It gives them that type of consumer protection because, if you can read the English language and you can see the lyrics on the back, you have no excuse for complaining if you take the record out of the store.

And also, I think that the record industry has been damaged and it has been given a very bad rap by this whole situation because it has been indicated, or people have attempted to indicate, that there is so much of this kind of material that people object to in the industry, that that is what the industry is.

It is not bad at all. Some of the albums that have been selected for abuse here are obscure. Some of them are already several years old. And I think that a lot of deep digging was done in order to come up with the song about anal vapors or whatever it was that they were talking about before.

SENATOR EXON. If I understand you, you would be in support of printing the lyrics, but you are adamantly opposed to any kind of a rating system?

MR. ZAPPA. I am opposed to the rating system because, as I said, if you put a rating on the record it goes directly to the character of the person who made the record, whereas if you rate a film, a guy who is in the film has been hired as an actor. He is pretending. You rate the film, whatever it is, it does not hurt him.

But whether you like what is on the record or not, the guy who made it, that is his art and to stigmatize him is unfair.

SENATOR EXON. Well, likewise, if you are primarily concerned about the artists, is it not true that for many many years, we have had ratings of movies with indications as to the sexual content of movies and that has been, as near as I can tell, a voluntary action on the part of the actors in the movies and the producers of the movies and the distributors?

That seems to have worked reasonably well. What is wrong with that?

MR. ZAPPA. Well, first of all, it replaced something that was far more restrictive, which was the Hayes Office. And as far as that being voluntary, there are people who wish they did not have to rate their films. They still object to rating their films, but the reason the ratings go on is because if they are not rated they will not get distributed or shown in theaters. So there is a little bit of pressure involved, but still there is no stigma.

SENATOR EXON. The Government does not require that. The point I am trying to make is—and while I think these hearings should not have been held if we are not considering legislation or regulations at this time, I emphasized earlier that they might follow.

I simply want to say to you that I suspect that, unless the industry "cleans up their act"—and I use that in quotes again—there is likely to be legislation. And it seems to me that it would not be too far removed from reality or too offensive to anyone if you could follow the general guidelines, right, wrong, or indifferent, that are now in place with regard to the movie industry.

MR. ZAPPA. Well, I would object to that. I think, first of all, I believe it was you who asked the question of Mrs. Gore whether there was any other indication on the album as to the contents. And I would say that a buzzsaw blade between a guy's legs on the album cover is a good indication that it is not for little Johnny.

SENATOR EXON. I do not believe I asked her that question, but the point you made is a good one, because if that should not go to little minds I think there should be at least some minimal activity or attempt on the part of the producers and distributors, and indeed possibly the performers, to see that that does not get to that little mind.

Mr. Chairman, thank you very much.

THE CHAIRMAN. Senator Hollings.

SENATOR HOLLINGS. Mr. Zappa, I apologize for coming back in late, but I am just hearing the latter part of it. I hear that you say that perhaps we could print the words, and I think that is a good suggestion, but it is unfair to have albums rated.

Now, it is not considered unfair in the movie industry, and I want you to elaborate. I do not want to belabor you, but why is it unfair? I mean, it is accurate, is it not?

MR. ZAPPA. Well, I do not know whether it is accurate, because sometimes they have trouble deciding how a film gets to be an X or an R or whatever. And you have two problems. One is the quantity of material, 325 films per year versus 25,000 4-minute songs per year, OK.

You also have a problem that an album is a compilation of different types of cuts. If one song on the album is sexually explicit and all the rest of it sounds like Pat Boone, what do you get on the album? How are you going to rate it?

There are little technical difficulties here, and also you have the problem of having somebody in the position of deciding what's good, what's bad, what's talking about the devil, what is too violent, and the rest of that stuff.

But the point I made before is that when you rate the album you are rating the individual, because he takes personal responsibility for the music; and in the movies, the actors who are performing in the movie, it does not hurt them.

SENATOR HOLLINGS. Well, very good. I think the actual printing of the content itself is perhaps even better than the rating. Let everyone else decide.

MR. ZAPPA. I think you should leave it up to the parents, because not all parents want to keep their children totally ignorant.

SENATOR HOLLINGS. Well, you and I would differ on what is ignorance and education, I can see that, but if it was there, they could see what they were buying and I think that is a step in the right direction.

As Senator Exon has pointed out, the primary movers in this particular regard are not looking for legislation or regulations, which is our function. To be perfectly candid with you, I would look for regulations or some kind of legislation, if it could be constitutionally accomplished, unless of course we have these initiatives from the industry itself.

I think your suggestion is a good one. If you print those words, that would go a long way toward satisfying everyone's objections.

MR. ZAPPA. All we have to do is find out how it is going to be paid for.

SENATOR HOLLINGS. Thank you, Mr. Chairman.

THE CHAIRMAN. Senator Hawkins.

SENATOR HAWKINS. Mr. Zappa, you say you have four children?

MR. ZAPPA. Yes, four children.

SENATOR HAWKINS. Have you ever purchased toys for those children?

MR. ZAPPA. No; my wife does.

SENATOR HAWKINS. Well, I might tell you that if you were to go in a toy store—which is very educational for fathers, by the way; it is not a maternal responsibility to buy toys for children—that you may look on the box and the box says, this is suitable for 5 to 7 years of age, or 8 to 15, or 15 and above, to give you some guidance for a toy for a child.

Do you object to that?

MR. ZAPPA. In a way I do, because that means that somebody in an office someplace is making a decision about how smart my child is.

SENATOR HAWKINS. I would be interested to see what toys your kids ever had.

MR. ZAPPA. Why would you be interested?

SENATOR HAWKINS. Just as a point of interest.

MR. ZAPPA. Well, come on over to the house. I will show them to you.

SENATOR HAWKINS. I might do that.

Do you make a profit from sales of rock records?

MR. ZAPPA. Yes.

SENATOR HAWKINS. So you do make a profit from the sales of rock records?

MR. ZAPPA. Yes.

SENATOR HAWKINS. Thank you. I think that statement tells the story to this committee. Thank you.

THE CHAIRMAN. Mr. Zappa, thank you very much for your testimony.

MR. ZAPPA. Thank you.

[The statement follows:]

Statement of Frank Zappa

These are my personal observations and opinions. They are addressed to the PMRC as well as this committee. I speak on behalf of no group or professional organization.

The PMRC proposal is an ill-conceived piece of nonsense which fails to deliver any real benefits to children, infringes the civil liberties of people who are not children, and promises to keep the courts busy for years, dealing with the interpretational and enforcemental problems inherent in the proposal's design.

It is my understanding that, in law, First Amendment issues are decided with a preference for the least restrictive alternative. In this context, the PMRC's demands are the equivalent of treating dandruff by decapitation.

No one has forced Mrs. Baker or Mrs. Gore to bring Prince or Sheena Easton into their homes. Thanks to the Constitution, they are free to buy other forms of music for their children. Apparently they insist on purchasing the works of contemporary recording artists in order to support a personal illusion of aerobic sophistication. Ladies, please be advised: the $8.98 purchase price does not entitle you to a kiss on the foot from the composer or performer in exchange for a spin on the family Victrola. Taken as a whole, the complete list of PMRC demands reads like an instruction manual for some sinister kind of "toilet training program" to house-break all composers and performers because of the lyrics of a few. Ladies, how dare you?

The ladies' shame must be shared by the bosses at the major labels who, through the RIAA, chose to bargain away the rights of composers, performers, and retailers in order to pass H.R. 2911. The Blank Tape Tax: A private tax, levied by an industry on consumers, for the benefit of a select group within that industry. Is this a "consumer issue"? You bet it is. PMRC spokesperson, Kandy Stroud, announced to millions of fascinated viewers on last Friday's ABC Nightline debate that Senator Gore, a man she described as "a friend of the music industry," is co-sponsor of something she referred to as "anti-piracy legislation". Is this the same tax bill with a nicer name?

The major record labels need to have H.R. 2911 whiz through a few committees before anybody smells a rat. One of them is chaired by Senator J. Strom Thurmond. Is it a coincidence that Mrs. Thurmond is affiliated with the PMRC? I can't say she's a member, because the PMRC has no members. Their secretary told me on the phone last Friday that the PMRC has no members . . . only founders. I asked how many other D.C. wives are non-members of an organization that raises money by mail, has a tax-exempt status, and seems intent on running the Constitution of the United States through the family paper-shredder. I asked her if it was a cult. Finally, she said she couldn't give me an answer and that she had to call their lawyer.

While the wife of the Secretary of the Treasury recites "Gonna drive my love inside you . . .", and Senator Gore's wife talks about "Bondage!" and "oral sex at gunpoint" on the CBS Evening News, people in high places work on a tax bill that is so ridiculous, the only way to sneak it through is to keep the public's mind on something else: "Porn Rock."

The PMRC practices a curious double standard with these fervent recitations. Thanks to them, helpless young children all over America get to hear about oral sex at gunpoint on network TV several nights a week. Is there a secret FCC dispensation here? What sort of end justifies THESE means? PTA parents should keep an eye on these ladies if that's their idea of "good taste."

Is the basic issue morality? Is it mental health? Is it an issue at all? The PMRC has created a lot of confusion with improper comparisons between song lyrics, videos, record packaging, radio broadcasting, and live performances. These are all different mediums, and the people who work in them have a right to conduct their business without trade-restraining legislation, whipped up like an instant pudding by The Wives of Big Brother.

Is it proper that the husband of PMRC non-member/founder/person sits on any committee considering business pertaining to the Blank Tape Tax or his wife's lobbying organization? Can any committee thus constituted "find facts" in a fair and unbiased manner? This committee has three. A minor conflict of interest?

The PMRC promotes their program as a harmless type of consumer information service providing "guidelines" which will assist baffled parents in the determination of the "suitability" of records listened to by "very young children." The methods they propose have several unfortunate side effects, not the least of which is the reduction of all American Music, recorded and live to the intellectual level of a Saturday morning cartoon show.

Teen-agers with $8.98 in their pocket might go into a record store alone, but "very young children" do not. Usually there is a parent in attendance. The $8.98 is in the parent's pocket. The parent can always suggest that the $8.98 be spent on a book.

If the parent is afraid to let the child read a book, perhaps the $8.98 can be spent on a recording of instrumental music. Why not bring jazz or classical music into your home instead of Blackie Lawless or Madonna? Great music with no words at all is available to anyone with sense enough to look beyond this week's platinum-selling fashion plate.

Children in the "vulnerable" age bracket have a natural love for music. If, as a parent, you believe they should be exposed to something more uplifting than sugar walls, support Music Appreciation programs in schools. Why haven't you considered your child's need for consumer information? Music Appreciation costs very little compared to sports expenditures. Your children have a right to know that something besides pop music exists.

It is unfortunate that the PMRC would rather dispense governmentally sanitized Heavy Metal Music, than something more "uplifting." Is this an indication of PMRC's personal taste, or just another manifestation of the low priority this administration has placed on education for the Arts in America? The answer, of course, is neither. You can't distract people from thinking about an unfair tax by talking about Music Appreciation. For that you need sex . . . and lots of it.

Because of the subjective nature of the PMRC ratings, it is impossible to guarantee that some sort of "despised concept" won't sneak through, tucked away in new slang or the overstressed pronunciation of an otherwise innocent word. If the goal here is total verbal moral safety, there is only one way to achieve it: watch no TV, read no books, see no movies, listen to only instrumental music, or buy no music at all.

The establishment of a rating system, voluntary or otherwise, opens the door to an endless parade of Moral Quality Control Programs based on "Things Certain Christians Don't Like." What if the next bunch of Washington Wives demands a large yellow "J" on all material written or performed by Jews, in order to save helpless children from exposure to "concealed Zionist doctrine"?

Record ratings are frequently compared to film ratings. Apart from the quantitative difference, there is another that is more important: People who act in films are hired to "pretend." No matter how the film is rated, it won't hurt them personally. Since many musicians write and perform their own material and stand by it as their art (whether you like it or not), an imposed rating will stigmatize them as individuals. How long before composers and performers are told to wear a festive little PMRC arm band with their Scarlet Letter on it?

The PMRC rating system restrains trade in one specific musical field: Rock. No ratings have been requested for Comedy records or Country

Music. Is there anyone in the PMRC who can differentiate infallibly between Rock and Country Music? Artists in both fields cross stylistic lines. Some artists include comedy material. If an album is part Rock, part Country, part Comedy, what sort of label would it get? Shouldn't the ladies be warning everyone that inside those Country albums with the American Flags, the big trucks, and the atomic pompadours there lurks a fascinating variety of songs about sex, violence, alcohol, and the devil, recorded in a way that lets you hear every word, sung for you by people who have been to prison and are proud of it.

If enacted, the PMRC program would have the effect of protectionist legislation for the Country Music Industry, providing more security for cowboys than it does for children. One major retail outlet has already informed the Capitol Records sales staff that it would not purchase or display an album with any kind of sticker on it.

Another chain with outlets in shopping malls has been told by the landlord that if it racked "hard-rated albums" they would lose their lease. That opens up an awful lot of shelf space for somebody. Could it be that a certain Senatorial husband and wife team from Tennessee sees this as an "affirmative action program" to benefit the suffering multitudes in Nashville?

Is the PMRC attempting to save future generations from SEX ITSELF? The type, the amount, and the timing of sexual information given to a child should be determined by the parents, not by people who are involved in a tax scheme cover-up.

The PMRC has concocted a Mythical Beast, and compounds the chicanery by demanding "consumer guidelines" to keep it from inviting your children inside its sugar walls. Is the next step the adoption of a "PMRC National Legal Age For Comprehension of Vaginal Arousal"? Many people in this room would gladly support such legislation, but, before they start drafting their bill, I urge them to consider these facts.

(1) There is no conclusive scientific evidence to support the claim that exposure to any form of music will cause the listener to commit a crime or damn his soul to hell.

(2) Masturbation is not illegal. If it is not illegal to do it, why should it be illegal to sing about it?

(3) No medical evidence of hairy palms, warts, or blindness has been linked to masturbation or vaginal arousal, nor has it been proven that hearing references to either topic automatically turns the listener into a social liability.

(4) Enforcement of anti-masturbatory legislation could prove costly and time consuming.

(5) There is not enough prison space to hold all the children who do it.

The PMRC's proposal is most offensive in its "moral tone." It seeks to enforce a set of implied religious values on its victims. Iran has a religious government. Good for them. I like having the capitol of the United States in Washington, D.C., in spite of recent efforts to move it to Lynchburg, VA.

Fundamentalism is not a state religion. The PMRC's request for labels regarding sexually explicit lyrics, violence, drugs, alcohol, and especially occult content reads like a catalog of phenomena abhorrent to practitioners of that faith. How a person worships is a private matter, and should not be inflicted upon or exploited by others. Understanding the Fundamentalist leanings of this organization, I think it is fair to wonder if their rating system will eventually be extended to inform parents as to whether a musical group has homosexuals in it. Will the PMRC permit musical groups to exist, but only if gay members don't sing, and are not depicted on the album cover?

The PMRC has demanded that record companies "re-evaluate" the contracts of those groups who do things on stage that THEY find offensive. I remind the PMRC that groups are comprised of individuals. If one guy wiggles too much, does the whole band get an "X"? If the group gets dropped from the label as a result of this re-evaluation process, do the other guys in the group who weren't wiggling get to sue the guy who wiggled because he ruined their careers? Do the founders of this tax-exempt organization with no members plan to indemnify record companies for any losses incurred from unfavorably decided breach of contract suits, or is there a PMRC secret agent in the Justice Department?

Should individual musicians be rated? If so, who is qualified to determine if the guitar player is an "X", the vocalist is a "D/A" or the drummer is a "V". If the bass player (or his Senator) belongs to a religious group that dances around with poisonous snakes, does he get an "O"? What if he has an earring in one ear, wears an Italian Horn around his neck, sings about his astrological sign, practices yoga, reads the Quaballah, or owns a rosary? Will his "occult content" rating go into an old CoIntelPro computer, emerging later as a "fact," to determine if he qualifies for a home-owner loan? Will they tell you this is necessary to protect the folks next door from the possibility of "devil-worship" lyrics creeping through the wall?

What hazards await the unfortunate retailer who accidentally sells an "O" rated record to somebody's little Johnny? Nobody in Washington seemed to care when Christian Terrorists bombed abortion clinics in the name of Jesus. Will you care when the "friends of the wives of big brother" blow up the shopping mall?

The PMRC wants ratings to start as of the date of their enactment. That leaves the current crop of "objectionable material" untouched. What will be the status of recordings from that Golden Era to censorship? Do they become collector's items . . . or will another "fair and unbiased committee" order them destroyed in a public ceremony?

Bad facts make bad law, and people who write bad laws are, in my opinion, more dangerous than songwriters who celebrate sexuality. Freedom of Speech, Freedom of Religious Thought, and the Right to Due Process for composers, performers and retailers are imperiled if the PMRC and the major labels consummate this nasty bargain. Are we expected to give up Article One so the big guys can collect an extra dollar on every blank tape and 10 to 25% on tape recorders? What's going on here? Do WE get to vote on this tax? There's an awful lot of smoke pouring out of the legislative machinery used by the PMRC to inflate this issue. Try not to inhale it. Those responsible for the vandalism should pay for the damage by voluntarily rating themselves. If they refuse, perhaps the voters could assist in awarding the Congressional "X," the Congressional "D/A," the Congressional "V," and the Congressional "O." Just like the ladies say: these ratings are necessary to protect our children. I hope it's not too late to put them where they really belong.

BATYA FRIEDMAN AND STEVE LYONS
REVOLT AGAINST MEDIOCRITY (1986)

In the late 1980s, Zappa became a favored subject for political magazines, sometimes of the statist "left," at other times of the libertarian "right." He was less an ideologue than a commentator whose sharp remarks appealed to various persuasions. (In this sense, he is Oscar Wilde a century later.) The following conversation appeared in *The Progressive*, a Wisconsin monthly traditionally associated with midwestern progressivism. Later appreciations of Zappa appeared in *Liberty*. Even though he was a family man opposed to both drugs and drink, Zappa was never a favorite of conservatives.

Frank Zappa is a rock musician who seems to defy categorization. He writes symphonic music, deplores drug use, and champions individual rights. Last year, almost alone among musicians, he stood up against the Parents' Music Resource Center, a group of prominent Washington women who objected to the sexual content of popular music and demanded that records be rated just like movies. Opposing this attempt at censorship, he testified before a Senate committee and toured the country debating the issue on radio and television.

We talked with Zappa about art in America, the music industry, and his current work. The interview took place in his studio from 11:00 one night until sunrise the next morning.

Q: You have said that "art is dying in this country." What do you mean?

Zappa: *Much of the creative work I find interesting and amusing has no basis in economic reality. Most decisions about what gets produced and distributed are made strictly on a bottom-line basis. Nobody makes a move without talking to an accountant first. There will always be people who will take a chance, but their numbers are dwindling. Those who are crazy enough to spend money on some unusual object or event are an endangered species. The spirit of adventurousness at any level of American society has been pretty much legislated away.*

In the 1980s, with a repressive, Republican, Yuppie-oriented Administration installed and ready to perpetuate itself with Supreme Court appointments that will keep us in trouble for the next half century, the prognosis is not good for things which differ from the viewpoint of the conservative Right.

Q: Do you think anything can be done to reverse the trend?

Zappa: *Perhaps. I tend to view the whole thing as a conspiracy. It is no accident that the public schools in the United States are pure shit. It is no accident that masses of drugs are available and openly used at all levels of society. In a way, the real business of government is the business of controlling the labor force. Social pressure is placed on people to become a certain type of individual, and then rewards are heaped on people who conform to that stereotype.*

Take the pop-music business, for example. Look at the stereotypes held up by the media as examples of great accomplishment. You see guys who are making millions of dollars and selling millions of units. And because they are making and selling millions they are stamped with the seal of approval, and it is the millions which make their work qual-

ity. Yet anyone can look at what is being done and say, "Jesus, I can do that!"

You celebrate mediocrity, you get mediocrity. People who could have achieved more won't because they know that all they have to do is be "that," and they too can sell millions and make millions and have people love them because they're merely mediocre.

Few people who do anything excellent are ever heard of. You know why? Because excellence, pure excellence, terrifies the fuck out of Americans, who've been bred to appreciate the success of the mediocre. People don't wish to be reminded that lurking somewhere there are people who can do some shit you can't do. They can think a way you can't think; they can run a way you can't run; they can dance a way you can't dance. They are excellent. You aren't excellent. Most Americans aren't excellent, they're only okay. And so to keep them happy as a labor force, you say, "Let's take this mediocre chump and we say, 'He is terrific!'!" All the other mediocre chumps say, "Yeah, that's right and that gives me hope, because one day as mediocre and chumpish as I am, I can. . . ." It's smart labor relations. An MBA decision. That is the orientation of most entertainment, politics, and religion. So considering how firmly entrenched all that is right now, you think it's going to turn around? Not without a genetic mutation, it's not!

Q: What are the issues that the music of the 1980s can address?

Zappa: What can music address today? It can address anything that it wants to, but it will only address those topics that will sell. Musicians will not address topics that are controversial if they want to have a hit. So music will continue to address those things that really matter to people who buy records: boy-girl relationships, boy-boy relationships, boy-car relationships, girl-car relationships, boy-girl-food relationships perhaps. But safe. Every once in a while somebody will say WAR IS HELL or SAVE THE WHALES or something bland. But if you talk about pop music as a medium for expressing social attitudes, the medium expresses the social attitude perfectly by avoiding contact with things that are really there. That is the telling point about the society that is consuming the product. If society wanted to hear information of a specific nature in songs, about controversial topics, they would buy them. But they don't. You are talking about a record-buying audience which is interested in personal health and well-being, the ability to earn a living, the ability to stay young at all costs forever, and not much else.

Q: How about the role of music in society? For example, Kent Nagano, who conducted the Berkeley symphony, said, "A composer has a job to do within a culture. Which is not to say a composer should write what the public already wants to hear, but rather that the public is employing the composer to lead them, to show them a direction." What do you think of that?

Zappa: I don't think a composer has any function in society at all, especially in an industrial society, unless it is writing movie scores, advertising jingles, or stuff that is consumed in industry. I respect Kent; however, I think he takes a very optimistic and naive attitude toward what it takes to be a composer. If you walk down the street and ask anybody if a composer is of any use to any society, what kind of answer do you think you would get? I mean, nobody gives a shit. If you decide to become a composer, you seriously run the risk of becoming less than a human being. Who the fuck needs you? All the good music's already been written by people with wigs and stuff on.

Q: If the public doesn't need composers, do composers need a public? Milton Babbitt, an electronic music composer, has advocated the virtual exclusion of the general public from modern music concerts. What is your opinion on that?

Zappa: That's unnecessary, they're already excluded; they don't go. Have you been to a modern music concert? Plenty of room, isn't there? Come on, Milton, give yourself a break. I hope you're not going to spend money trying to exclude these people. What are you going to do, have it legislated in Congress like those assholes who wanted to make it a law that you couldn't put anything backwards on a phonograph record?

Q: What do you think art will be like in twenty years?

Zappa: I don't think anything that a reasonable person would describe as art is going to be around. Not here. I'm talking about art in terms of valued, beautiful stuff that is done not because of your ego but just because it is beautiful, just because it is the right thing to do. We will be told what is good and it will be mediocre. There's always the possibility that an anomaly will appear—some weird little twisted thing will happen and there will be somebody who's doing it. But who's going to know? In the dark ages there was art, but who knew?

Q: How do unknown music groups attract the attention of record companies?

Zappa: Today record companies don't even listen to your tape. They look at your publicity photo. They look at your hair. They look at your zippers. How gay do you look? And if you've got the look, then it really doesn't make a fucking bit of difference what's on the tape—they can always hire somebody to fix that. And they don't expect you to be around for twenty years. The business is not interested in developing artists. They want that fast buck because they realize that next week there's going to be another hairdo and another zipper. And they realize that the people are not listening, they're dancing, or they're driving, or something else. The business is more geared toward expendability today. That's because merchandising is so tied to "visuals" now.

Q: How is music selected to be heard on pop radio? Is it determined by the taste of the listener or does the public listen to whatever the industry feeds it?

Zappa: A little of both. Radio is consumed like wallpaper is consumed. You don't concentrate on the radio, you turn it on while you're working, you turn it on while you're driving. It's not like the old days when families sat around and looked at it. So the stations are formatted to provide a certain texture and ambience that will be consumed by people who view themselves in a certain way. Are you a Yuppie? Well, you're going to listen to a certain texture because that reinforces the viewpoint you have of yourself and the viewpoint you want to project to other people of who and what you are. It's the same thing as what you leave on your coffee table for people to discover when they come to your apartment. It's not a musical medium, it's an advertising medium. If you have a nation of people who refuse to face reality about themselves, about the rest of the world, about anything, they want reinforcement for the fantasy that they're living in. And these consulting services that format the station know that. Market research will show you that. Obviously you want to deliver to the public things that will reinforce that. A station loses money when somebody turns it off the air. So as long as your station sounds like the kind of swill that the Yuppie needs to consume, you got it.

Q: How does a record become a hit?

Zappa: It's simple. It's called "payola." You pay somebody to play your record. Hits are okay. I think they're wonderful for people who want them. They're wonderful for people who like to listen to them. But then, hits shouldn't be the sum total of music history. Let's face it, Mozart had hits. Beethoven had hits. Did you ever look in Grove's Dictionary of Music and Musicians? *There are thousands of names of people who wrote music throughout history, yet we haven't heard one line they ever wrote. That doesn't mean it is bad music; it just means they didn't have hits. In the old days, if the king didn't like you or the church didn't like you or whatever, you didn't have a hit. As a matter of fact you might even be dead. So now you can have a hit if you are willing to pay. So who's the new king? Who's the new church?*

Q: As you compose, are you primarily guided by how you want the music to affect a listener's spiritual, emotional, intellectual, or physical state, or by the musical structure—melody, harmony, and rhythm?

Zappa: None of the above. It's more like, how did it turn out? Does it work? And if it works you don't even have to know why it works. It either works or it doesn't work. It's like drawing a picture. Maybe there are too many fingers on one hand, and a foot is too short over there. Or you could apply it to a recipe; maybe you've got too much salt over here. Or you could apply it to the design of a building. Did you forget to put in a toilet, or are there enough windows on the second floor?

Q: Those are examples of pragmatic considerations as opposed to aesthetic considerations.

Zappa: I don't know how to explain it. I just do it. It's not based on any academic regulations. If you take a blank piece of paper and pencil and just start sketching, it doesn't necessarily have to be a house and a tree and a cow. It could be just some kind of a scribble but sometimes those scribbles work and they are the right thing for that blank piece of space and you can enjoy them. Or you can say, "That's not a house, that's not a cow, that's not a tree, and so I don't like it; it's just a scribble." It depends on what your viewpoint is.

Q: Is your view truly as subjective as you are painting it to be? So, if I look at an image and it appeals to me, then all I can say is that it works for me and I can't say any more about it.

Zappa: What else do you have the right to say? If you go beyond that, you become a critic. Who needs those fuckers?

Q: Other people might say that there's something universal, some sort of consensus on what works and what doesn't.

Zappa: People are free to agree. If you want to join a committee and feel the warmth and reassurance that other people's opinions will provide to reinforce your own, then go for it. I happen to not care for that. It's not something that I aspire to, nor do I want to live my life in accordance with that ideal. In fact, I despise it. But it's okay for other people. There's no reason why I should inflict my point of view on somebody who really enjoys being part of a group consensus.

Q: What about the relative merit of various human pursuits? For example, do you consider jogging or playing ice hockey to be of equal value to, say, creating art, on some cosmic scale?

Zappa: No.

Q: Why? What's the scale?

Zappa: What is it that survives from an ancient civilization that characterizes that civilization? What do you find? Not their jogging! The music doesn't survive, but things that are related to art do. The beautiful things that the societies do is what survives. Let's look into the future. Let's look at the remnants of the American society.

Q: Wait a second, ugly things survive too.

Zappa: Yep. That's what will survive the American society!

Q: You seem to admire the raw emotional energy of some music, yet you have little tolerance for emotional love songs.

Zappa: It's quite a challenge to reach somebody emotionally without using words that have literal connections. To perform expressively on an instrument, I have respect for that. To get to the level of performance where you are no longer thinking about operating a piece of machinery and can just project something emotional through the machinery, that is worthy of respect. Writing a song about why somebody left you, that's stupid.

The performers and composers don't necessarily believe in what they're saying or what they're doing, but they know that if you write a song about love, it's got a 3,000 percent better chance of going on the radio than if you write a song about celery. It's a buy and sell. And so the value system builds up from that. What I think of as the emotional content of music is probably a lot different than what you think of. Since I write music I know what the techniques are. If I wanted to write something that would make you weep, I could do it. There's ways to do it. It's a cheap shot.

Q: Would you say it's sentimental?

Zappa: It's not just sentimental. There are certain harmonic climates that you can build. There are certain notes of a scale that you can play within a harmonic climate to "wreak pathos," and it's very predictable. The average guy doesn't know how predictable or easy it is to do that stuff; if you just look at it scientifically, you can do it. For example, you've got the key; it's A minor, right? And you're going to play a lot of Bs in the key of A minor and that's going to give you that little twinge. Well, that music played on an accordion is not the same as the exact same notes and the same melody played and the same rhythm played on six bagpipes. It's a different story. So the timbre is involved, too. And the amplitude is involved. And if that A-minor chord is very quiet and the Bs are just smoothly put in there, that's one attitude. If it's being played by a high-school marching band and it's being jammed in your face, it's sad all right, but it's not that kind of sad!

In different cultures there are also different norms for how certain sound combinations are perceived. That's why if you listen to Chinese classical music, everything sounds like it's being played on a kazoo and it's thin and weird, but to a Chinese person it's lush. I don't know why a person would think that the tone quality of Chinese classical music was really a warming sensation. The Chinese are different though. They've got 7,000 years behind them. Maybe after 7,000 years we're going to think that stuff sounds pretty good, too.

Q: Any plans for more of your own rock-'n'-roll?

Zappa: You know, I'm so involved with the Synclavier [a computer-based synthesizer] and what it can do and being able to hear compositions played exactly, that I'm not even interested in writing any other kind of music. I don't get a charge out of even thinking about it. I'm really interested in music and I always have been. Now that I'm in the stage where I can have the seemingly most impossible things performed exactly right, that's worth devoting some time to.

Q: You have a very prolific output. Do you have any special methodologies for getting things done?

Zappa: Just keep working, a little sleep, a lot of work. That's probably one of the best-kept secrets in America. I think there are a lot of people afraid to work that way because they are afraid somebody will say they are workaholics. It's not as bad as having somebody call you a "communist," but if you are in a jogging suit, you don't want to have that label attached to you.

Q: What do you see as your greatest accomplishment and your greatest failure?

Zappa: I would say that my entire life has been one massive failure. Because I don't have the tools or wherewithal to accomplish what I want to accomplish. If you have an idea and you want that idea to be done a certain way and you can't do it, what do you have? You have failure. I live with failure every day because I can't do the things that I really want to do. I can do some other stuff. I can do whatever my budget will allow me to do. Unfortunately, I have these ideas that are just too fucking expensive. In realistic terms, you're looking at a genuine daily failure syndrome. I have no fantasies about what the odds are that I'll be able to do what I want to do. It's not going to happen. Once you realize what your limitations are and realize that even if you "achieve" something it doesn't make a fucking bit of difference anyway, then you can be "okay." I enjoy sitting down here [in the studio] all by myself typing on the Synclavier. I can do twelve hours and love it. And I know that ultimately it doesn't mean a fucking thing that I did it. It's useless. That's okay; it makes me feel good.

Q: It seems that for most people that kind of isolation would lead to loneliness.

Zappa: Try to imagine what the opposite of loneliness is. Think of it. Everyone in the world loves you? What is that? Realize that you're in isolation. Live it! Enjoy it! Just be glad that there aren't a bunch of people who want to use up your time. Because along with all the love and admiration that's going to come from the people that would keep you from being lonely, there is the emotional freight you have to bear from people who are wasting your time, and you can't get that back. So when you're lonely and you're all by yourself, guess what you have? You have all of your own time. That's a pretty good fucking deal. Something you couldn't buy any place else. And every time you're out being sociable and having other people be "nice" to you so that you don't feel "lonely," they're wasting your time. What are you getting for it? Because after they're done being nice to you, then they want something from you. And they've already taken your time!

Loneliness, once you've come to deal with it so that it is not an uncomfortable sensation, so it doesn't feel like drowning or something, is not a bad deal. It's a good deal. It's the next best thing to solitude. I'm not talking solitary confinement. Solitude. If you're sensitive to loneliness, you're going to be in trouble, because then the loneliness turns into something really painful, a horrible depression and then you die. One way or another, you just die. So who needs that shit?

BOB GUCCIONE, JR.
SIGNS OF THE TIMES (1991)

This interview, done with the publisher of the monthly magazine *Spin*, became the platform for Zappa to announce his interest in running for president. In turn, that became the occasion for the libertarian bimonthly, *Liberty*, to consider the validity of his candidacy. A contributing editor to that magazine, Brian Doherty, runs Cherry Smash Records in Los Angeles.

The image of Frank Zappa as a mad scientist has, like a stubborn vine, so entwined itself through the garden of rock'n'roll mythology that its origin is completely indiscernible. But when I meet him in the dark living room that appears to be the center of the Zappa universe, he is dressed in a T-shirt and beach pants, and his long gray-streaked hair and moustache accentuate the intensity of his eyes and he looks more like a wizard in exile.

His most famous song is "Don't Eat the Yellow Snow," released back when the '70s still had credibility, and the most familiar Zappa record isn't even his, it's his daughter Moon Unit's "Valley Girl," which he collaborated on. Yet a generation that not only didn't grow up on his music but were mostly not even born when he first became popular has accepted his place of prominence. Like an ambassador, he means something, stands for something strong and resolute, but this generation is not really sure how and exactly why.

In his 25-year career as a recording artist, he has released 50 records: As of this writing, which is to say this morning—I can't vouch that he won't issue something later today. He has created almost every type of music from rock'n'roll to classical. Hardly a staple on MTV, the image of a conservatively suited Zappa testifying before the Senate at the infamous "Porn Rock" hearings in 1985 is his thumbprint on video culture: a soundbite from a sound banquet.

He speaks in a deep voice and with intellectual precision articulates his world view, which is dark, passionate, and finally optimistic.

Spin: Is education really out of reach now in this country? Are we twenty years away, a whole generation away, from repairing education in this country?

Zappa: No, we're further than that. Because in a way, I would agree with George Bush in that education in America needs to be reinvented, but certainly not in the way he would imagine it. Because the biggest problem we're facing right now is that education needs to be imparted to a postliterate generation. People who have no feeling whatsoever for a book or any data on a printed page, which should be worrisome to anyone who publishes a magazine.

Spin: It is.

Zappa: And if you have to teach people basic things that they will need in order to function normally, forget about achieving greatness, or even competing with Japan and Germany. Just to function, how are you going to do it if people can't read, refuse to read, and are so adapted to receiving data from optical and audio sources. I think you have to meet them halfway and install equipment into classrooms that are going to be able to deliver data into the language that the kids already understand. Costs money. And when you've got a state like California, with such a *huge educational system willing to take up the twelve billion dollar deficit out of the schools, it also tells you something about the parents that would allow that to happen. Because obviously the parents don't give a fuck, 'cause they didn't enjoy school that much themselves. And giving the choice between paying more taxes and just hoping that it gets better and letting the "education President" take care of it, I mean, everybody is sticking their head in the sand.*

Spin: Do you think somewhere along the line, it serves the powers that be, the pervading government for the last ten years, to have education dilapidate to where people don't think enough to really challenge?

Zappa: No question. I don't think it's any accident that the educational system in America has been brought to its current state. Because only a totally uneducated mass of people will be baffled by balloons. And yellow ribbons and little flags and buzz words and guys saying "new world order" and shit like that, I mean, only a person who has been dissuaded from any kind of critical thinking and doesn't know geography, doesn't know the English language—I mean if you can't speak English, then this stuff works on you.

One of the things that was taken out of the curriculum was civics. Civics was a class that used to be required before you could graduate from high school. You were taught what was in the U.S. Constitution. And after all the student rebellions in the '60s, civics was banished from the student curriculum and was replaced by something called social studies. Here we live in a country that has a fabulous constitution and all these guarantees, a contract between the citizens and the government— nobody knows what's in it. It's one of the best kept secrets. And so, if you don't know what your rights are, how can you stand up for them? And furthermore, if you don't know what is in that document, how can you care if someone is shredding it?

Spin: What was your reaction after the Gulf War, and the jingoism and the euphoria that followed?

Zappa: Well, I had a very bad reaction to the war in general because it was such an incredibly stupid idea to do it. All you got to do is look at what's happening in Iraq this week, and see whether it was a good idea to send a half a million guys over there to blow shit up. It's a bad idea. So I look at it as the utter failure of diplomacy, the utter failure, embarrassing failure of the U.N. to stand up for any of the original principles that it was supposedly constructed to uphold. It was well worded into putting a rubber stamp on the war, because George Bush decides that there ought to be something called the new world order. I did an interview with a German television station not long ago, and the guy said: "'New world order,' doesn't he know that Hitler said that? That is a Hitler line."

Spin: What's your theory of why America didn't finish off the war, why we left Saddam in power?

Zappa: *First of all, there's no guarantee you can get him. The other thing is, on* Crossfire *last night, Stephen Solarz was arguing that we should start the war again and go in there and not just get rid of Saddam Hussein, but root out every aspect of the Baathist Party in Iraq. Tell me, what the fuck kind of tweezers are you going to need to do that? If you kill Saddam Hussein the Baathist Party—it's just like trying to get the Communist party out of Russia. At every level. There's Baathist Party guys running everything. Plus five different forms of secret police. How are you going to do that?*

The thing is, there's nothing more threatening to those bogus monarchs down there than democracy. If the Kurds and the Shiites succeed in toppling Hussein's government and they go for a democratic parliament and the rest of that stuff, if that trickles southward then it endangers the Kuwait [Emir] and the whole Saudi royal family. They don't want democracy anywhere near that peninsula. And also from the U.S. national interest point of view it's probably easier for our business guys to deal with one corrupt monarch or another then to deal with some unruly democratic parliament. It's easier to pay off one guy and the rest of his relatives.

Spin: I think in many ways the reaction to this war was an attempt not only to exorcise the Vietnam syndrome, but also to distract attention from how screwed up we were in the '80s.

Zappa: *The only way you can feel good about the '80s is if you can't feel anything at all. In a ten-year period, twelve percent of the homeless are Vietnam vets with nowhere to go, maybe thirty percent were dumped out of mental institutions when Reagan closed them in the early part of the '80s, and the rest of the people were families that got* dispossessed during Reagan's depression during '82–'83, when his economics first took its toll, and other people are making a zillion dollars in the stock market by selling junk bonds and renting puffed air to each other.

So to feel good about the '80s, I think you would have to be mutated away from the human condition quite a bit, because if you look at the '80s, there was nothing that swell about it. Fortunately for us the music of that period leaves an accurate record of how empty that whole era was.

Spin: Do you think much music came out of the '80s that was valid, as music or as social criticism?

Zappa: Well, I kept doing it. I'm sure there were a few people in America who did it, but you never heard it, because the bulk of what you heard is what you saw. The beginning of the '80s gave us MTV, and music changed and switched from an audio to a video medium.

Spin: For better or worse?

Zappa: For worse, because I believe that the way music is to be consumed is through your ears, and it shouldn't be too important whether the person performing it looks like a model.

The record companies thought it was the greatest thing that ever happened to them because it was a way for them to get cheap commercials. And so the tail started wagging the dog. The record companies stopped signing groups that could play in favor of groups that looked good in pictures because they figured we could always get a producer to sing their songs and do their stuff for them, and that happened plenty of times. So you get a bunch of models to make the video and forget about the music. So that part of that worked. A young audience who never experienced any music to speak of started watching MTV the same way they watched Saturday morning cartoons. And it caught on. There was no competition. Before MTV if you wanted to have a hit record, there were probably 10,000 stations in America where you could break something regionally and have it spread. Now there is one MTV with a short playlist, and because of that the record companies put their own balls into the bear trap and sprung it on themselves, now they can't make a move without calling MTV and getting permission, they call up in advance to say we are getting ready to make a video, we are going to have such and such pictures in it, what do you think, and MTV is a total censorship organization and it has all the major record companies at its mercy.

I started getting really weary of MTV when they started inventing rock'n'wrestling, where we're seeing videos of Hulk Hogan urging kids to take their vitamins, urging kids to grow up big and strong like him, and be an American. It really was on the level of a Saturday morning cartoon.

Spin: What do you think about the crossover of rap? I don't mean Vanilla Ice, because that's just a cartoon character thing too, but the crossover of heavy black rap, and style and fashion, taken on by whites.

Zappa: I don't find anything strange or wrong with that.

Spin: No, I don't either. But how do you explain it?

Zappa: Well, there's a corollary when those black groups were singing about their girlfriends in the '50s. Because not everyone that bought those records was a black teenager in Manual Arts High School. And there were white suburban teenagers who were going, "I know a girl with that same name." It was their tune for their life. If the music speaks to you then I don't think it makes a difference what the race or orientation is. Besides, today, rage is rage. Rage is a commodity. And the unfortunate aspect is that I know there's white suburban rage, but there is no voice for it.

I believe they do have things that they are pissed off about, but I don't think they've found a vehicle to express it, because if the white suburban kid decides to do rap, then he's not using his voice, he's just shouting through somebody else's rented megaphone. And it's not too unique or original, and at one point, if you do that, it's like you're copying off someone else's commercial gimmick. And it takes away from the authenticity of whatever else you have to say.

Spin: You've gotten involved in doing business in Czechoslovakia. What has failed in Eastern Europe?

Zappa: The United States government.

Spin: What do you mean by that?

Zappa: Because after all these years of saying "We'd love to be rid of Communism," and then we built up these weapons to destroy Communism, and this huge army, it rots before your very eyes, and you've got this opportunity to go in and spread democracy, which all the Presidents have talked about. "This is democracy, it's good, everyone should have it, our way is the best," and all it would have taken is a couple of bucks, and some advisers to say, "Here's how a free-market system works" and a little friendly help. And that just wasn't there.

Spin: What was your background? Your father worked in a nerve gas company?

Zappa: Well it wasn't nerve gas, it was mustard gas.

Spin: Is it true he volunteered to be an experiment?

Zappa: That was a way during the war you could earn extra money, you could be a human guinea pig for these things called pap tests. They wouldn't tell you what it was, they would put stuff on your skin and then cover it up with a big bandage. So he'd have these big bandages on his arm, and sometimes come home with two or three on his arms, and they'd itch and burn, and he'd suffer with these things, but they'd be thirty dollars more a week. And I don't know what they put on it.

Spin: What was it like growing up in that environment—how aware of that were you?

Zappa: I thought I understood it pretty well at five or six years old. It was about killing people. My father worked at a place that manufactured stuff to kill people.

Spin: And how did that affect you? Looking back now, forty-five years later, how did it affect you?

Zappa: That was WWII. There was a reason for going out and doing these things. Everybody has a different outlook. And the other thing was that he was a Sicilian, and it was not a good idea to be of a Sicilian or Italian extraction at that point in American history; he had to try extra hard to be patriotic, I think.

Spin: How does that affect you today?

Zappa: It gives me some kind of perspective of how long we've been doing these things. At least forty to forty-five years.

Spin: What did you think of punk?

Zappa: Well I liked the attitude of punk, I didn't necessarily like it from a musical standpoint; it is anti-musical. The whole idea was we're gonna play shitty and fast and so what? The so what part I always like. But anybody who's against music I don't like. I don't like people who smash instruments. I don't like the abuse of things that could produce beautiful results.

Spin: Did you find any punk musically good? What about the Clash?

Zappa: One of my favorite punk records was "Gidget Goes to Hell" by the Suburban Lawns—I thought that was good.

Spin: Did you ever make any punk records?

Zappa: Oh sure, yeah.

Spin: You made punk records?

Zappa: Not whole records, but some punk tunes: "I'm So Cute" on the Sheik Yerbouti *album.*

Spin: What do you think about the sexism in heavy metal, and in Andrew Dice Clay routines, and in rap? How do you relate that to the criticism against you in the past, the way you allegedly depicted women in your songs?

Zappa: I don't think there's anything wrong with depicting women the way I depict them. I think I depict them in a rather accurate way. Because women are not perfect. But the bulk of my songs are about men and the stupid things that men do. And they never complain. So, is it because the men are so inferior—which then proves the women's point, that they're so fucking stupid they don't know what to do, or they're too lazy to complain—or is it because the women think they really should get special treatment and they should be treated with kid gloves, like Israel sort of? You could never say anything bad about Israel or people would say you're anti-Semitic. If you happen to say that Israel behaves like Nazi Germany toward the Palestinians, which happens to look like quite a fact when you see a videotape of what's actually going on, people go, "Oh, you're anti-Semitic." You know, it's not true. The same way, if you say, "Women do this thing that's stupid or that thing that's stupid," you should say it. It's a journalistic medium as well as a musical medium.

Spin: What's the thing you've been most criticized for, in sexist terms?

Zappa: "Jewish Princess" [from Sheik Yerbouti]. *The criticism came from an organized entity, the Anti-Defamation League of B'nai Brith. As if to say there was no such thing as a Jewish Princess. Like I invented this? They asked me to apologize. I said no. I told them I wouldn't. And they managed to get PR for their organization for a year out of me. And actually it helped me. The Sheik Yerbouti album turned out to be the best-selling album I ever had.*

Spin: Do you think the outcome of the censorship movement can ultimately be meaningful?

Zappa: Let me point out something about democracy. Does anybody remember how Hitler took over Germany? He was voted in. People said, Yeah, he's got the right message for us. Now when you have democracy, there's always the possibility that the guy who could turn out to be the biggest menace to the planet could just get voted in. And the place where it's most likely to happen is here, because of the media saturation, the illiteracy rate of the population, the social desperation of the population. Hitler came to power because things weren't so good.

All we have to do is look at the early days of the Reagan administration and see how these factors converged. First of all, he owed a big favor to all the fundamentalist Christians and the television evangelists who helped him one way or another get elected. Forget about the October Surprise, he also had the help of these other groups. Then there was that depression. Americans like to believe in miracles, they like to believe in magic and when they consume religion it's not on philosophical level, it's on a miraculous level. Jesus can do things for you. It's about goods, it's about the transference of goods and services from the cloud to your living room. You're broke, you lost your job in the early days of the Reagan administration and instead of watching Madonna on TV you're seeing these guys teaching prosperity theology. If you send your money, you gotta prove to Jesus that you really care, and he'll reward you tenfold. It's like buying a lottery ticket.

It's always the freeflow of information which is the major threat to the American way of life. To right-wing guys, there's nothing more dangerous than free access to information. And you know what that stems from? It stems from the beginning of Christian theology, when Adam and Eve were in the garden, how did we get into trouble? It wasn't because it was an apple, it was the fruit of the tree of knowledge, so the essence of Christianity is, nobody gets to be smarter than God and access to knowledge and ownership of knowledge damns you. Knowledge itself is the work of the devil. We must not have knowledge and what leads to knowledge? Information. Nip it right there, nip it in the bud.

Spin: What would it take to puncture the apathy of the average American, especially with elections coming up? Campaigns for that election will start in less than a year.

Zappa: *I don't think you're going to puncture it in one swell foop. It doesn't puncture that easily. I'll tell you, I'm considering running for President in the next election.*

Spin: Really?

Zappa: *Yeah. I've called two political consultants in Washington and we're just gonna do a little feasibility study to see what it would take. The idea is to run as a nonpartisan candidate and urge other people around the country to not only run but resign from the Democratic and the Republican parties because the Democrats stand for nothing except "I wish I was a Republican" and the Republicans stand for raw, unbridled evil and greed and ignorance smothered in balloons and ribbons. So that's really not much of a choice and it's nauseating to watch Democrats make speeches because they all wish they were Republicans.*

Spin: What do you think your chances'll be?

Zappa: Not good, but a chance is a chance.

Spin: You're very serious about this? You're not just making a statement?

Zappa: If I did it I would do a real run. The problems about doing it are that in order to do a credible run you have to be on the ballot in every state. That's about a million dollars in legal fees and organization and bullshit just to get on the ballot. That's before you even buy an ad.

The theory that I have is this: Instead of going out and running the same way the other guys do for one thing I got no primary that I have to compete in, I don't have to go to Iowa, I don't have to go to New Hampshire, I don't have to join the greased pig race, I don't have to do any of that stuff. All I have to do is say, I'm gonna volunteer to run, I'm willing to do this. I'm willing to give up music for four years. I like this country enough that I'll give up something that I love for four years to do this job that nobody is doing right here.

George Bush, what has he really done here? He brought the troops home. He never should have sent the fucking troops there! And we read his lips, and now this education President thing. That's going to turn into a fiasco.

One of the interesting things about my platform is I want to do away with income tax.

Spin: How would you do that?

Zappa: Income tax should be done away with anyway because when it was established it was an emergency tax and was supposed to have an end to it. Just like the toll booths on the highway. Income tax is a racket. The one thing the income tax does to everybody who pays it is it pisses you off because you earned that money and now the government is taking it away from you. If you gotta pay a tax, pay a tax when you buy something, not because you worked.

What this really gives you access to, in terms of tax recoupment, is the underground economy because when a guy is making a covert buck the goal is to spend the covert buck and at the point where you spent the covert buck you are now being able to tax every one of these guys who has laundered the cash. They gotta buy a yacht someday, a house, they're gonna buy something.

Spin: You're going to drive all of that Colombian drug money into foreign countries, like Canada.

Zappa: Let them do away with the income tax. The other thing is you would save a great deal of money on the personnel of the IRS itself. You still have to have somebody do administrative sales tax. I think you could do it with five percent of the labor force you have in the IRS. Naturally it would take an act of God to do away with state income taxes.

Spin: Fantastic idea. Not easy. Lots of problems.

Zappa: Well, here's the other thing, think about this. Suppose I told you, from tomorrow on, you pay no income tax, no federal income tax. You'd be happy. You'd suddenly realize that you had another couple thousand bucks in your pocket. And it doesn't go in the bank. You'd go out and spend it. And there'd be a spike in the economy that would just go boom! The Dow went to 3,004.42—what do you think happens the day after they know that there's going to be no more income tax?

What I would propose to do, is have a five-year plan where the sales tax would be at twelve to fourteen percent on certain products. I'd try to exempt necessary foodstuffs, because that's where the poor get hurt. And I don't think that many Colombian drug dealers are buying that many cartons of milk and eggs and stuff. And so you're really not going to cripple the nation's economy by exempting that sort of thing. So for five years you keep that sales tax a little higher just to deal with the deficit. And at the point where the deficit is done away with, then you bring the sales tax down again to a maintenance level. I think you can run a pretty good economy that way.

Spin: Have you discussed this with economists?

Zappa: I discussed it with my accountant who used to work for the IRS in Washington, D.C. He was head of collections for the Baltimore –Washington, D.C., area. He loves it.

The idea is that this is a zero balloon campaign. You want balloons then blow your own balloons. And the goal is to run the cheapest campaign in political history. I can sit at home and do talk shows all over the country on radio and answer questions directly to people who might want to vote. And it would cost what? Nothing. I don't believe that you really have to spend fifty million dollars or apply for matching funds from the federal government and then be forced to abide by all those rules in order to do it. Because if you're a nonpartisan candidate then what the fuck?

Spin: Do you think you'd be appealing to mass America even with that platform?

Zappa: There's only one way to find out. I mean, if I lose, then so what?

Spin: Do you think you'd make a difference if you won?

Zappa: Oh yeah. How could I make things any worse than what they already are?

Spin: The least that could happen is that a lot of consciousnesses could be raised.

Zappa: Well, here's the least that could happen. You know what the other guys are going to say before they say it. And television is an entertainment medium. Now, you don't know what I'm going to say. Now you're in the middle of an election year and it's real dull. Do you think they would send someone over to talk to me every once in a while just to liven things up a bit?

I'm not going to debate these guys. As far as I'm concerned, they don't exist. Why should I sit there and talk over their bullshit? These guys want to sit there and riddle you with statistics. And what do you know? You're watching a debate at home and you're like, "Oh yeah. He knew a lot of numbers." Total horseshit.

Spin: How do you define yourself as a musician? I was listening to on the way over here, *The Best Band You Never Saw.* I heard part Spike Jones, part Kurt Weill, part Mahavishnu Orchestra—many things.

Zappa: The thing I do is build things. And I have to participate in their manifestation. That's why I had to become a band leader and a guitar player. I would have been happy to just write it and turn it over to someone else. But they don't play it if you give it to them. I learned that when I first started to compose it.

Spin: Are you also a satirist?

Zappa: Yes. I'm a composer-slash-sociologist.

Spin: My last question comes from a 23-year-old waitress in Malibu: Are you happy?

Zappa: Today, yes. Tomorrow, I don't know. Yesterday, so-so. I go day by day. If you're looking for an average, maybe not. Because you can convince yourself that you're happy because of where you live and what you own, but if you watch TV and watch the news, it's hard to convince yourself that you're happy because of what's going on. I spend most of my free time watching the news. I'm addicted to it. If I'm not watching the news broadcasts then I'm watching the raw footage on C-Span. And it pisses me off.

BRIAN DOHERTY
ZAPPA FOR PRESIDENT? (1991)

Rock-classical composer/guitarist/smartass Frank Zappa—whose name had been bandied about as a potential Libertarian candidate in '88—has officially announced his intention to run for president in '92, but as an independent. I've heard that matchmakers within the Libertarian Party are trying to hook up with him, but with the convention only a month and a half away, the arrangement seems unlikely to be consummated. Besides, Zappa is too iconoclastic to want to be saddled with any party identification. He announced his intentions in an interview in the July issue of the rock culture magazine *Spin*. Libertarians of my acquaintance were impressed, particularly by his suggestion to abolish the income tax.

Zappa first came to the (non-rock world) public eye as a star witness against Tipper Gore's record labeling initiative in the mid-'80s. Hey— strong on civil liberties *and* economic freedoms! The very definition of a proper libertarian, right?

Well, I think it more than possible that Zappa is a libertarian by inclination. At least his broaching of the idea of the abolition of the income tax shows he's not just another idiot liberal showbiz loser. Could you imagine Ed Asner saying something like "the only thing the income tax does to everybody who pays it is it pisses you off because you earned that money and now the government is taking it away from you"?

Zappa also seems to understand that there are good *practical* arguments for gutting the income tax: he cheers the enormous economic boom that would result from an income tax abolition.

But on other issues he seems slightly soft in the head. He makes reference to "Reagan's depression during '82–'83, when his economics first took its toll." What could he mean by this? What policy unique to Reagan created this? This sounds like typical thoughtless left-liberal rhetoric about the "decade of greed," usually based on the widespread (and untrue) assumption that Reagan was a vicious slasher of social spending.

Zappa responds to the hopeless mess of the state education system with lame, vague prescriptions to "meet [children] halfway and install equipment into classrooms that are going to be able to deliver data into the language that kids already understand." In rap, I suppose? No, Zappa is merely pulling on the tired old McLuhan "post-literate" string here.

But he still has a positive side. He stands up to sensitivity pressure groups—he resisted a request to apologize for his song "Jewish Princess" by the Anti-Defamation League of the B'nai B'rith. He is also leery of democracy and very sincerely pro-free expression. He refuses to debate other candidates when he runs, just because he thinks they're all hopelessly full of shit. But of course.

Is this whole question anything more than a fanciful exercise in badinage? Would it really make any strategic sense for the Libertarian Party to pursue the candidacy of a long-hair modern classical/jazz/pop-rock composer? Especially one whose music is as alternately silly, scatological, overly mannered, and ill-conceived as Zappa's?

Well, why not? As I see it, what you want to do with a party like the LP—that is, one with no hope of winning a national election—is gain media attention for your organization and ideas, however possible.

Zappa would certainly deliver on press attention. He points this out as one of the pluses of his candidacy. "You know what the other guys are going to say before they say it. And television is an entertainment medium. Now, you don't know what I'm going to say. Now you're in the middle of an election year and it's real dull. Do you think they would send someone over to talk to me every once in a while just to liven things up a bit?"

He has a point. But, of course, he'd just be a laughing-stock—right? Could be. Just consider his hair, his past, hell, even his *views*. But perhaps his persona may help people think about heresies like abolishing the income tax—if only for a minute. And once that thought is in people's heads, who knows?

I am dubious about the combination of pop and politics on aesthetic grounds. Pop artists are generally idiot-savants utterly ignorant of politics (and everything else), and political thinking usually casts a pall of hypocritical solemnity over music—as over an extended family at the funeral of a universally hated patriarch—that is death to the pop aesthetic.

But on political grounds the marriage is fine with me. Anything to get attention, as the fisherman said to the salmon swimming upstream. We libertarian salmon ought to welcome a Zappa candidacy, LP related or not.

PART SIX

Don't Eat the Yellow Snow:

Life and Legacies

I ENTER THE AGE OF ABSURDITY (1988)

In this charming memoir, two of the twentieth century's most eccentric musical visionaries meet and share the stage together for one performance. What is missing from Slonimsky's memoir of working with Zappa is the former's connection to the Zappa hero Edgard Varèse. In short, Slonimsky conducted the premiere of Varèse's percussive masterpiece, *Ionisation* (1931); the latter was also the best man at the former's wedding a year later. Working with Slonimsky was the closest Zappa would ever get to working with the great Varèse.

One late Saturday evening in the spring of 1981, I received a telephone call. "Nicolas Slonimsky?" (correctly pronounced) the caller inquired. "This is Frank Zappa. I never realized you were in Los Angeles, and I want so much to get in touch with you about your book of scales." I was startled. Frank Zappa was the last person who, to my mind, could be interested in my theoretico-musical inventions. His name was familiar to me from a promotional record jacket showing him seated on the john with his denuded left thigh in view, and a legend in large letters: PHI KRAPPA ZAPPA.

We arranged to meet on the following Monday at 2.30 in the afternoon, and, at the appointed time on the appointed day, his assistant knocked at my door. I stepped out of my apartment and beheld something that looked like a space shuttle—a black Mercedes taking up almost half a block of Wilshire Boulevard. I could not refrain from asking the driver how much such a machine cost. "Sixty," he replied.

It took us nearly an hour to get to Zappa's place in the hills of Hollywood. Zappa met me at the door. He looked like a leading man in the movies—tall, slender, sporting a slight Italian moustache. For starters, I asked him the origin of his last name; he replied it meant "the plough" in Italian.

Zappa's wife came in, an ample, young woman, and served coffee and tea. Zappa told me he did not drink alcoholic beverages; contrary to the legendary habits of most rock-and-roll musicians, he never partook of drugs. But he smoked cigarettes incessantly, tobacco being his only, and quite venial, sin. Zappa led me to his studio, which housed a huge Bösendorfer piano. I asked him how much he paid for this keyboard monster. "Seventy," he replied.

Zappa declared himself an admirer of Varèse and said he had been composing orchestral works according to Varèse's principles of composition, with unrelated themes following in free succession. To substantiate this claim, he brought out three scores, in manuscript and each measuring 13 x 20 inches, beautifully copied and handsomely bound. Indeed, the configurations of notes and contrapuntal combinations looked remarkably Varèsian. Yet he never went to a music school, and had learned the technique of composition from the study of actual editions. He had had a contract with an orchestra in Holland to play one of his works, but they had demanded a piece from his recording royalties on top of the regular fee. "I offered them a quarter," Zappa said, "if they would put up a quarter." It took me some time to figure out that the fractions he used were those in millions of dollars.

Zappa's teenage daughter flitted in, introduced by Mrs. Zappa as Moon Unit. She did not seem to be embarrassed by this esoteric appellation. A year or two later she became a celebrity in her own right by making a record with her father's band in which she carried on a telephone conversation in a California language known as Valley Girl Talk. The Valley in question was the San Fernando, nestled north of Los Angeles and populated by a gaggle of young boys and girls, but mostly girls, who seemed to exude a special *joie de vivre*. Most of their lingo was incomprehensible to common terrestrials. Everything they liked was not just "great," but "tubular" (a term derived from surfing), and something extra good was "mega" or "awesome." They would say "fer sher" when signifying assent, and express their aversion with such locutions as "gag me with a spoon." "I mean, like, *totally,*" and "gross me out!" About that time, I acquired a cat, black and white and plenty mischievous, which I christened Grody to the Max, i.e., Gross to the Maximum.

Zappa invited me to try out his Bösendorfer. I sat down at the keyboard and played the coronation scene from *Boris Godunov* which required deep bass sounds. Zappa was impressed by these Russian harmonies. He asked me to play some of my own compositions, and I launched into the last piece in my *Minitudes,* based on an interplay of mutually exclusive triads and covering the entire piano keyboard. "Why don't you play this piece at my next concert?" Zappa asked. "When will that be?" I inquired. "Tomorrow. We can rehearse in the afternoon." I was somewhat taken aback at the sudden offer, but after all, I had nothing to lose. So I decided to take my chance as a soloist at a rock concert.

The next day I arrived at the large Coliseum in Santa Monica where Zappa's concert was to take place. A huge, towering man led me to Zappa's room. "Mr. Zappa is expecting you," he said, satisfied with my identity. He was Zappa's bodyguard, hired after Zappa had been attacked during a concert by a besotted admirer and hurt his back.

On the stage I sat at the electric piano and played my piece. For better effect, I added sixteen bars to the coda, ending in repeated alternation of C major and F-sharp major chords in the highest treble and lowest bass registers. Zappa dictated to his players the principal tonalities of my piece, and they picked up the modulations with extraordinary assurance. I had never played the electric piano before, but I adjusted to it without much trouble.

The hall began to fill rapidly. Zappa's bodyguard gave me ear plugs, for, when Zappa's band went into action, the decibels were extremely high. Zappa sang and danced while conducting, with a professional verve that astounded me. A soprano soloist came out and sang a ballad about being a hooker, using a variety of obscenities. Then came my turn. Balancing a cigarette between his lips, Zappa introduced me to the audience as "our national treasure." I pulled out the ear plugs, and sat down at the electric piano. With demoniac energy Zappa launched us into my piece. To my surprise I sensed a growing consanguinity with my youthful audience as I played. My fortissimo ending brought out screams and whistles the like of which I had never imagined possible. Dancing Zappa, wild audience, and befuddled me—I felt like an intruder in a mad scene from *Alice in Wonderland.* I had entered my Age of Absurdity.

ABNORMAL LIFE (1990)

This brief puff appeared in *TV Guide* in 1990, just as the Zappa family was becoming famous in toto.

Wouldn't you know it, even the way the Zappa sitcom got started was totally weird. A couple of summers back, Moon Unit Zappa and her brother Dweezil were in New York for a few days doing their MTV vee-jay thing when the gossip page of the *New York Post* ran an item saying the zany Zappa kids were developing a TV series. The item had absolutely no basis in fact, but the minute they got back to their home town, Hollywood, their phone started ringing. Suddenly everybody wanted to talk to the Zappas about developing a series around them and their highly unconventional upbringing.

"It was the emperor's new clothes, totally," admits Moon. Fast forward through countless Hollywood pitch meetings and endless reformulations until finally their sitcom with its ironic title, *Normal Life,* has made its debut on CBS, starring the Zappas as a lovably offbeat brother and sister, Cindy Williams as their unusually tolerant mother and Max Gail as their equally understanding father. In true Hollywood fashion, the concept has changed so radically from its original idea that the sitcom broadcast into living rooms throughout America actually has very little to do with the real Zappa family.

"It's vastly different," concedes Dweezil.

No question, the real Zappas would be difficult to portray under any circumstances. Their father, Frank Zappa, the brilliantly eccentric mastermind of the '60s rock group Mothers of Invention, has in recent years been politically outspoken on a number of fronts, including voter registration, abortion and his opposition to the possible creation of a rating guide for rock-music lyrics. Moon Unit, now 22, was just 14 when she recorded "Valley Girl" with her father and became an overnight national phenomenon. Dweezil, 20, is a rock musician, with a hit single and two albums already to his credit.

But what really made the Zappas different was the freewheeling, very '60s spirit in which the children, including younger siblings Ahmet and Diva, now 15 and 10, were raised. Both Moon and Dweezil were permitted—even encouraged—by their parents to drop out of school at age 15, which they did. (Both have earned equivalency diplomas.) As teenagers, if they wanted to experiment with drugs, alcohol or cigarettes, they were allowed to as long as they did it at home. They were even allowed to have friends of the opposite sex sleep over. As Dweezil explains it, "We were allowed to do anything and be anything and say anything."

And yet all of this freedom resulted in their utter lack of interest in normal teenage rebellious behavior because, as Dweezil points out, "there was nothing to rebel against." They claim they never did get around to trying drugs. "Our friends took them, and they were idiots," says Moon. Dweezil still lives at home and claims to be a homebody who rarely ventures out. "In real life we're real boring," he contends. "We don't like to do anything that's even remotely considered hip or fun or cool." Moon officially moved out of the house a couple of years ago only, she says, "because I knew I'd never get a boyfriend if I stayed." But she still spends most of her time at her parents' home. In other words, their parents are their best friends, and life at home is so great, why leave?

Clearly, this is too much for mainstream America to handle. Yet when the Zappas sat down with Bernie Brillstein, the executive producer of *ALF* and *It's Garry Shandling's Show,* they all agreed on a concept that was heavily inspired by the Zappa family. It would be a different kind of family from any television had seen before, a family fueled by anarchy but firmly bound by love. The kids would call their parents by their first names and be allowed to skateboard through the living room. There'd be lots of rock music blaring through the house.

"People in the business thought I was crazy when I was going to do this show," admits Brillstein, "but every hit I've had has been a little to the left." Still, when the pilot episode was shown to a test audience, it bombed. CBS, plagued by plummeting ratings and struggling to find new viewers by reaching a younger, hipper audience, still wanted to go with the show, but in a milder form that wouldn't scare viewers away. Brillstein then began the process of diluting the show to its latest incarnation, which viewers are now seeing—minus many of the radical details. The kids, for example, no longer call their parents by their first names, nor do they skateboard through the living room.

"I think this is a mainstream home now," Brillstein says. "I don't think this is a radical show. I think sometimes television is behind the time in portraying what people are really like. What we're trying to do is show that the house from *Father Knows Best* to today has undergone a huge change. I think television has to take a quantum leap towards the '90s.

Maybe if this catches on, we can do much closer to the original concept next year."

But if the dismal reviews are any indication, *Life* might not last that long. For all the advance hype, the show's watering-down process appears to have turned it into just another predictable sitcom. For instance, one episode has the Zappas' kid brother standing up to the school bully. Another has Moon Unit and her girlfriend dating the same boy.

The Zappa kids say they are only mildly disappointed by the changes and express a kind of philosophical balance. "They want to sell hamburgers. They don't want to scare people right away," acknowledges Moon. Still, they're proud of the battles they fought and won to keep in certain details of verisimilitude. The wall in the kitchen—just like in their own home—is covered with scrawlings of telephone numbers and other family graffiti. Dweezil was allowed to keep the earring he wears and to decorate his set bedroom with his own rock-music posters.

Moon, meanwhile, persuaded the producers to let her character have a crush on a real-life rock star she really is crazy about: Michael Penn. And she and Dweezil admit to subversively slipping in ironic little gestures when they were forced to acquiesce to things they weren't thrilled about.

"The audience will definitely be able to tell what is ours and what they made us do," says Moon. The Zappas say that much of the time on the set they were howling at their insiders' view of how TV works. "Network executives operate from a manual of television phrases," says Dweezil. "Words with certain syllables are supposed to be funny. There's a scientific approach to comedy. They were hysterical to us, yet frustrating beyond belief." Says Moon: "Anthropologically, I found it fascinating."

If nothing else, the Zappa kids, always self-learners anyway, figure they got a terrific Hollywood education out of the whole experience. "It may not be the show that we discussed originally, but it's a good show," says Dweezil. "We got what we now consider a formal college education in show business, and we graduated with honors."

DAVID SHEFF
PLAYBOY INTERVIEW (1993)

One of Zappa's last interviews.

I

You once said that your job is "extrapolating everything to its most absurd extreme." Does that still hold true?

It's one of my jobs. I guess it must have been my main job that day. But yes, I like carrying things to their most ridiculous extreme because out there on the fringe is where my type of entertainment lies.

Is it frustrating that more people don't get it?

The crux of the biscuit is: If it entertains you, fine. Enjoy it. If it doesn't, then blow it out your ass. I do it to amuse myself. If I like it, I release it. If somebody else likes it, that's a bonus.

How important is it to offend people?

You mean, do I wake up and say, "I think I'll go out and offend somebody today"? I don't do that. I don't write lyrics much anymore, but I offend people just as much with the music itself. I put chords together that I like, but many people want rhythms that they can march to or dance to; they get tangled up trying to tap their foot to my songs. Some people don't like that, which is OK with me.

You certainly offended people with the Phi Zappa Krappa poster.

Probably. But so what?

And some of your antics from the Mothers of Invention days, like the famed gross-out contest.

There never was a gross-out contest. That was a rumor. Somebody's imagination ran wild. Chemically bonded imagination. The rumor was that I went so far as to eat shit onstage. There were people who were terribly disappointed that I never ate shit onstage. But no, there never was anything even resembling a gross-out contest.

Another rumor was that you peed on an audience.

I never had my dick out onstage and neither did anybody else in the band. We did have a stuffed giraffe rigged with a hose and an industrial-strength whipped cream dispenser. Under it we had a cherry bomb. That's how we celebrated the Fourth of July in 1967. Somebody waved the flag, lit the cherry bomb. It blew the ass out of the giraffe.

Another guy reached behind the giraffe and pushed the button and had this thing shitting whipped cream all over the stage. That amused people for some reason.

So it was simply contained outrageousness?

Stagecraft.

To entertain or just to alleviate boredom?

There was a third factor, too. There's an art statement in whipped cream shooting out the ass of a giraffe, isn't there? We were carrying on the forgotten tradition of dada stagecraft. The more absurd, the better I liked it.

II

You tried to book Czechoslovakia's president Václav Havel as a guest, right?

I knew a guy who had been a rock-and-roll musician who, after the revolution, was a ranking member of the Czech parliament. I asked him whether or not he could arrange for me to meet Havel so that I could interview him about the country's economy for FNN. I met with Havel and found that the minute I started talking with him about economics, he turned me over to his advisors; he didn't know anything about it. We didn't do the interview, but it was great meeting with him.

Why Havel?

I happen to think that the Velvet Revolution was a little bit of a miracle. Since he was kind of the focal point of the whole thing, I thought he'd be a nice guy to talk with. He was. In the middle of everything, he mentioned that Dan Quayle was coming to visit. I expressed my condolences. I told him I was sorry that he was going to be forced to have a conversation with anyone that stupid. It eventually must have gotten back to the U.S. embassy. Instead of sending Quayle, Jim Baker—who was on his way to Moscow—rerouted his trip and went to Prague.

But hasn't your cancer affected the mood of the music?

*No, I haven't started writing sad music. Time is the thing. Time is every-
thing. How to spend time. We all want something to do with our
minds. The choices are a major human preoccupation. The people who
find the easiest solutions, like beer and football, might be happier if they
had just a little dimension to their lives. But most people, once they
achieve a certain level of gratification for time disposal, don't go beyond
it. They already know how good they're going to feel when a football
game comes on, and they have their beer. They don't want to know
beyond that. They build a life around it.*

    *It's been the same for me since I got cancer as it was before. I have
to look way beyond the football game and the can of beer. Once I've
gone out there and dabbled on that fringe, I feel as if I may as well
bring some artifacts back, in case anybody else is interested. That's what
I do. I come back and go, "Here it is. This is what happened after the
football game."*

TOM ISENBERG
FRANK ZAPPA, 1940–1993 (1994)

Tom Isenberg hosts a libertarian talk show in Seattle, Washington.

"Politically, I consider myself to be a (don't laugh) Practical Conservative.
I want a smaller, less intrusive government, and lower taxes. What? You
too?" Thus begins Chapter 17 of *The Real Frank Zappa Book,* the 1989
autobiography of the late rock star, social critic, classical composer, sometimes political activist, guitar virtuoso, entrepreneur, and all-around
Renaissance iconoclast.

    Zappa came to fame as the genius behind the Mothers of Invention, a
'60s rock group that satirized suburban squares and urban hippies alike
with songs like "Plastic People," "Rhymin' Man" (a.k.a. Jesse Jackson),
"Who Needs the Peace Corps," and "We're Only in It for the Money." Of
course, Zappa tweaked many conservative pretensions as well, on record
and off. He especially earned their ire during his 1986 congressional testimony against a proposed ratings system for records with "pornographic"
lyrics, as advocated by Tipper Gore's Parents' Music Resource Center.

Zappa argued that a ratings system was a violation of his constitutional rights, and that its focus on rock music was a protectionist strategy on behalf of the country music made in Mrs. Tipper Gore's home state of Tennessee. The man understood economic and civil liberties.

Indeed, Zappa was outspoken on many political issues. He was both an advocate of drug legalization and a staunch opponent of drug use. "All I require, if somebody is on my payroll, is that they don't use drugs and don't have any drugs in their possession at the time they are performing a service for me."

Zappa saw no conflict between music as art and music as a capitalist act. "I provide money for people to run their lives because they play notes that I write. It's a very simple relationship. My boss is the audience. They rely on me to hire the best musicians that I can find and to train them as well as I can in order to bring that music to an audience in the best condition possible for the money that they pay for the ticket."

In 1987, Zappa's organic libertarianism led to a brief brush with Libertarian Party politics. Robert Murphy, an LP activist, met with Zappa to propose that Zappa seek the Libertarian Party's presidential nomination. Zappa was interested, saying that if he did run, he would forsake the standard practice of campaign tours, relying instead on television. Alas, in the end he chose music videos over political ones.

Zappa died of cancer the same weekend the Clinton administration launched a new offensive against song lyrics—this time, against violent "gangsta rap." Therefore, a fitting epitaph might be one of his many quips from his debates with Tipper Gore: "If lyrics make people do things, how come we don't love each other?"

VÁCLAV HAVEL
REVOLUTIONARY (1993)

Poet, playwright, and president of Czechoslovakia, Havel tells of Zappa's importance to the democratic movement in his country.

Frank Zappa was one of the gods of the Czech underground during the nineteen-seventies and eighties. It was an era of complete isolation. Local rock musicians and audiences were hounded by the police, and for those who refused to be swept aside by persecution—who tried to remain true to a culture of their own—Western rock was far more than just a form of music. At that time, Frank Zappa hung somewhere high up in the heavens, a star as inaccessible as the many others whose influence was felt in the local scene, like the Velvet Underground and Captain Beefheart. I never dreamed that I might meet him one day, but shortly after the revolution, when I was already President, Zappa turned up in Prague. He arrived during a period still vibrant with revolutionary energy. He jammed with local musicians and paid me a visit in the Castle, and we went out drinking together. He was the first rock celebrity I had ever met, and, to my great delight, he was a normal human being, with whom I could carry on a normal conversation. He was eager to learn everything he could about the radical changes taking place in the countries of the former Soviet bloc. He was curious about what this sudden collapse of a bipolar world might bring. He wanted to know what we thought about the future position of the Soviet Union in world politics, and he probed us about the negative as well as the positive aspects of the "velvet" course we had set for ourselves.

What fascinated and excited him was the idea that the artist had a role to play in active politics. He gave serious thought to offering unofficial assistance to our country, in both cultural and economic spheres, and I learned later that he had discussed the matter in detail with several ministers. Perhaps his illness prevented him from taking on this kind of work, but his sincere concern for our country made a deep impression on me. So did his appearance with Michael Kocab and his band, Prague Select, at a gala concert in June of 1991 to celebrate the final departure of the Soviet troops from Czechoslovakia after an occupation of almost twenty-three years. He was seriously ill at the time, but he took part all the same. It was one of his last appearances as a rock musician.

I thought of Frank Zappa as a friend. Meeting him was like entering a different world from the one I live in as President. Whenever I feel like escaping from that world—in my mind, at least—I think of him.

(Translated, from the Czech, by Paul Wilson)

Selected Discography

This is basic, rather than definitive, as disks and tapes in forms were issued in various ways, both legitimate and illegitimate, over the past few decades. The number between brackets [#] notes if the number of disks, in the original release form, was greater than one. The number in parentheses is the date of release, as distinct from the dates in which the parts were composed or recorded. Other lists acknowledge slightly different years, which may or may not be correct. All of Zappa's recordings, except for *200 Motels* and his classical concert music, are now being made available on CD by Rykodisc in an agreement reached with the Zappa estate; the latest Rykodisc catalog number is given following each release.

Records

Freak Out! [2] (1966) 10501
Absolutely Free (1966) 10502
We're Only In It for the Money (1967) 10503
Lumpy Gravy (1967) 10504
Cruising with Ruben and the Jets (1967) 10505
Uncle Meat [2] (1968) 10506-07
Mothermania (Best of) (1969)
Hot Rats (1969) 10508
Burnt Weeny Sandwich (1969) 10509
Weasels Ripped My Flesh (1970) 10510
Chunga's Revenge (1970) 10511
Fillmore East (1971) 10512
200 Motels [2] (1971); out of print: was United Artists UA 50003
Just Another Band from L.A. (1972) 10515
Waka/Jawaka (1972) 10516

The Grand Wazoo (1972) 10517
Over-Nite Sensation (1973) 10518
Apostrophe (') (1974) 10519
Roxy & Elsewhere [2] (1974) 10520
One Size Fits All (1975) 10521
Bongo Fury (1976) 10522
Zoot Allures (1976) 10523
Zappa in New York [2] (1978) 10524-25
Studio Tan (1978) 10526
Sleep Dirt (1979) 10527
Sheik Yerbouti [2] (1979) 10528
Orchestral Favorites (1979) 10529
Joe's Garage, Act 1 (1979)
Joe's Garage, Acts 2 and 3 [2] (1979); the three original albums have
been issued on two Rykodisc CDs, 10530-31
Tinsel Town Rebellion [2] (1981) 10532
Shut Up 'N Play Yer Guitar [3] (1981) 10533-35
You Are What You Is [2] (1981) 10536
Ship Arriving Too Late to Save the Drowning Witch (1982) 10537
The Man from Utopia (1983) 10538
Baby Snakes (1983) 10539
The London Symphony Orchestra, Volume 1 (1983) 10540
The Perfect Stranger (1984)
Them or Us (1984) 10543
Thing-Fish [2] (1984) 10544-45
Francesco Zappa (1984)
The Old Masters Box One [7] (1985)
Frank Zappa Meets the Mothers of Prevention (1985) 10547
Does Humor Belong in Music? (1986) 10548
The Old Masters Box Two [9] (1986)
Jazz from Hell (1986) 10549
London Symphony Orchestra, Volume II (1987) 10541
The Old Masters Box Three [9] (1987)
Guitar [2] (1988) 10550-51
You Can't Do That on Stage Anymore Volume 1 [2] (1988) 10561-62
You Can't Do That on Stage Anymore Volume 2 [2] (1988) 10563-64
Broadway the Hard Way (1988) 10552
You Can't Do That on Stage Anymore Volume 3 [2] (1989) 10565-66
The Best Band You Never Heard in Your Life [2] (1991) 10553-54
You Can't Do That on Stage Anymore Volume 4 [2] (1991) 10567-68

Make a Jazz Noise Here [2] (1991) 10555-56
Beat the Boots [10] (1991), which includes bootleg tapes made as As An Am Zappa (1981), The Ark: Mothers of Invention (1968), Freaks & MotherfU*%@# (1970), Unmitigated Audacity (1974), Anyway the Wind Blows [2] (1979), 'Tis the Season to Be Jelly (1967), Saarbrucken 1979 [2] (1978), Piquantique (1973); Foo-Eee 8-70907
Beat the Boots #2 [8], which includes Disconnected Synapses (1970), Tengo Na Minchia Tanta (1971), Electric Aunt Jemima (1968), At the Circus (1978/70), Swiss Cheese/Fire! [2] (1971), Our Man in Nirvana (1968), Conceptual Continuity (1977); Foo-Eee 8-70372
You Can't Do That on Stage Anymore Volume 5 [2] (1992) 10569-70
You Can't Do That on Stage Anymore Volume 6 [2] (1992) 10571-72
Playground Psychotics [2] (1992) 10557-58
Ahead of Their Time (1993) 10559
The Yellow Shark (1993) 10560
Civilization: Phaze III [2] (1994)
Strictly Commercial: The Best of Frank Zappa (1995)
The Lost Episodes (1996)

Ben Watson recommends that "those who have difficulty obtaining material" should write Bark fo-Swill, P. O. Box 5418, N. Hollywood, CA USA 91616, fax: 1-818-761-9888; tel: 1-818-PUMPKIN (786-7546) or G&S Music, 7 Ullswaher Rd., Leverstock Green, Hemel Hempstead, Herts. HP3 8RD, England.

Films

200 Motels (1971), produced by Frank Zappa, who also composed music performed by the Royal Philharmonic and the guitar ensemble led by John Williams
Baby Snakes (1979)
Does Humor Belong in Music? (1984)
Dub Room Special, combines interviews, 1974 KCET footage, and 1981 MTV footage
Video from Hell (1986)
The True Story of 200 Motels (1989)
Uncle Meat (1989)
The Amazing Mr. Bickford (1992)
Yellow Shark (1993)
Zappa's Universe (1993)

Except for 200 Motels and Yellow Shark, all of the above videos were released by Barking Pumpkin–Honker Video.

Selected Bibliography

Bassoli, Massimo. *Zappa (é più duro di tuo Marito)*. Milan, Italy: Gammalibri, 1982.

Chevalier, Dominique. *Viva! Zappa*. Paris: Calmann-Levy, 1985. English ed., New York: St. Martin's, 1986. (This book also includes documentation to 1985 of Zappa's appearances in films and videotapes made by others, 45 rpm singles, unproduced musical comedies, "albums never released," his contributions to albums made by others, stage and orchestral appearances without his group, and so on.)

Dister, Alain. *Frank Zappa et les Mothers of Invention*. Paris: Albin Michelo, 1975.

Gray, Michael. *Mother! The Frank Zappa Story*. Revised and updated ed. London: Plexus, 1994.

Gweder, Urban. *Alla Zappa*. Adliswill, Switzerland: Buckerkarawane, 1976.

Kaiser, Rolf Ulrich. *Zapzapzappa*. Koln, Germany: Kinder der Geburtagpresse, 1969.

———. *Frank Zappa*. Holland: Hoorn, 1969.

Miles. *Frank Zappa—A Visual Documentary*. London: Omnibus Press, 1993. (This book includes an extended chronology and track-by-track discographies.)

Walley, David. *No Commercial Potential*. New York: Outerbridge & Lazard, 1972. Second ed., New York: E.P. Dutton, 1980. Third ed., New York: Da Capo, 1996.

Watson, Ben. *Frank Zappa: The Negative Dialectics of Poodle Play*. London: Quartet Books, 1993. New York: St. Martin's, 1995.

Weissner, Carl, and Frank Zappa. *Plastic People Songbuch/Corrected Copy.* Frankfurt, Germany: 2001, 1977.

Zappa, Frank. *The Real Frank Zappa Book*, with Peter Occhigrosso. New York: Poseidon, 1989.

Web sites

Frank Zappa's numerous fans have constructed a plethora of sites on the World Wide Web, some good, some kinky, some amusing, some boring. Two of the better fan pages (as of this writing) are Patrick Stockton's Zappa Page (www.willamette.edu/~pstockto/zappa.html) and the Frank Zappa Tribute Page (www.cs.tufts.edu/~stratton/zappa/zappa.html). Both have links to other sites.

The official site of the Zappa estate is the Real Frank Zappa Home Page at http://www.zappa.com. This has links for Zappa's children, his various recordings, and Rykodisc (although various attempts to contact Ryko at their web site of late sent this user's machine crashing; perhaps a temporary glitch.)

A Zappa "Quote of the Day," along with a file of quotes from previous days, is available at www.fwi.uva.nl/~heederik/zappa/quote. I had hoped to include some of Zappa's wonderful aphorisms, but was unable to clear permission from his estate. This unofficial (and, I suspect, outlaw) Web site should satisfy those with an appetite for Zappa's pungent wit.

A very complete discography, listing songs and personnel but not release numbers, is maintained at gopher://wiretap.spies.com/00/Library/Music/Disc/zappa.dis.

For those who want to chat or ask questions, check the Usenet site (alt.fan.frank-zappa) and FAQ at Zappa, Frank.

Chronology

1940	Born Frank Vincent Zappa on December 21, in Baltimore, Maryland, the eldest son, to Sicilian-Italian parents.
1951	Moves with family to first of several California residences.
1953	Takes up the drums before his family moves south to Pomona, California.
1954	Influence of both the avant-garde music of Edgard Varèse and black rhythm and blues. Earns first professional pay with a group called the Ramblers.
1955	For his fifteenth birthday, his parents pay for a long-distance phone call to Varèse in New York.
1956	Now with his family in Lancaster, California, on the edge of the Mojave Desert, Zappa meets in high school Don Van Vliet (b. January 15, 1941), who later records under the name Captain Beefheart both as a solo artist and with various Zappa groups. Together the teenagers form and join performance groups with various names.
1958	Graduating from Antelope Valley Joint Union High School, Zappa enrolls at the neighborhood Antelope Valley Junior College.
1959	Leaving home, he moves to Hollywood and marries Kay Sherman, whom he divorces a few years later. Hired to score a Western, *Run Home Slow,* but the project is postponed due to lack of funding.
1961	Zappa writes the sound track for the film *The World's Greatest Sinner,* which continues to have a cult reputation. His music demonstrates the precocious forms of his subsequent musical signature.

1962–63　First concert performance of Zappa's classical music at Mount St. Mary's College.

1963　Meets singer Ray Collins in a bar. Performs his "bicycle concerto" on Steve Allen's TV show. Forms short-lived band The Soots with Van Vliet on vocals; band makes demos for Dot Records. Payment finally arrives for his work on *Run Home Slow*; with the proceeds, Zappa purchases and renovates in Cucamonga, California (a town that a repeated Jack Benny routine made famous), Studio Z, which had specially designed five-track recording equipment.

1964　Arrested for producing and selling a pseudo-pornographic audiotape, he serves a ten-day sentence that incidentally exempts him from the Vietnam draft. Moving to Los Angeles, he joins the Soul Giants, replacing their original guitarist; the group features vocalist Ray Collins, drummer Jimmy Carl Black, and bassist Roy Estrada, all who remain with him for most of the decade. The band takes the name "Mothers" or "Muthers."

1965　Signing a management contract with Herb Cohen, he begins a more lucrative career. Meets Pamela Zarubica, and the two soon move in together.

1966　MGM record producer Tom Wilson signs the Mothers of Invention, as the group is now called, to a contract with MGM's jazz-centered Verve label. Their debut double-album, *Freak Out,* becomes the model of a 1960s underground classic. Zappa meets Gail Sloatman (b. January 1, 1945), whom he marries a year later; she becomes the mother of their four children and his most loyal business partner. The group opens for Lenny Bruce at San Francisco's Fillmore auditorium. Thanksgiving–New Year's Day, the group is in residency at New York's Ballroom Farm.

1967　Beginning on Easter, the group initiates an extended residency at the Garrick Theater in Greenwich Village. In September, backed by a 15-piece orchestra, the Mothers make their United Kingdom debut at Royal Albert Hall.

1968　In April, the group performs on the Grammy Awards show, annoying industry leaders. In June, Zappa returned to L.A.; Tom Mix's old house, The Log Cabin, becomes the center of the Mothers' activity.

1969　Zappa purchases a home off Mulholland Drive where he lives for the rest of his life. In partnership with his manager Cohen,

Zappa launches Bizarre and Straight Records, which will later produce not only Captain Beefheart but Alice Cooper. Lectures at the New School for Social Research on the topic of "Pigs, Ponies, and Rock & Roll."

1970   Performs at "Contempo 70," a Los Angeles new music festival organized by Zubin Mehta, premiering "200 Motels," a piece for rock group and orchestra. Forms new Mothers with ex-Turtles Howard Kaylan and Mark Volman, aka Flo and Eddie.

1971   Films *200 Motels*. In December, at a London concert, Zappa is pushed off the stage and into the orchestra pit by a deranged spectator, leaving Zappa in recuperation for most of the following year.

1972   John Lennon and Yoko Ono release *Sometime in New York*, featuring a jam session with Zappa recorded at the Fillmore the previous year. In September, Zappa premiered a new, 19-piece band at the Hollywood Bowl, which was cut down to 10 pieces for touring.

1973   Now producing for another new moniker, DiscReet, Zappa releases *Over-Nite Sensation*, which, at a half-million sales, earns him his first gold disk.

1974   "Don't Eat the Yellow Snow" becomes an underground hit; the album on which it appeared, *Apostrophe(')*, becomes Zappa's first gold album.

1975   Zappa loses his lawsuit with the Royal Albert Hall, which had canceled a performance of "200 Motels" back in 1971. He conducts a 37-piece orchestra in his symphonic compositions at Royce Hall, UCLA.

1976   Last performance as the Mothers of Invention; henceforth, he featured his own name. In an out-of-court settlement, the ever-litigious Zappa regains ownership of the Verve mastertapes, in addition to reimbursement for unpaid royalties. Appears on "Saturday Night Live."

1977   Zappa settles with manager Cohen and label Warner Brothers after several years of litigation to gain full control of his early albums.

1979   Zappa releases "Jewish Princess," which is greeted by protests from prominent Jewish organizations. Releases first part of an opera, *Joe's Garage*, with the offensive "Catholic Girls" as an answer to "Jewish Princess." In December, releases the animated music movie *Baby Snakes*.

1980	Builds a home studio, "The Utility Muffin Research Kitchen."
1981	Hosts and sponsors an Edgard Varèse tribute in New York City. Launches Barking Pumpkin label (for retail) and Barfko/Swill (for mail order).
1982	Scores his biggest hit with "Valley Girl," featuring his elder daughter, Moon Unit, speaking in the modish dialect and idioms of suburban Los Angeles teenagers. Three people are killed in a fight between Italian police and the audience at a Zappa concert in Palermo, Sicily.
1983	Performs and records with the London Symphony Orchestra. Conducts his modernist favorites Edgard Varèse and Anton Webern with the San Francisco Music Players at the city's War Memorial Opera House.
1984	The French classical music mogul Pierre Boulez records Zappa's *The Perfect Stranger* in the same year that Zappa delivers the keynote speech at the Nineteenth Annual Conference of the American Society of University Composers. Premiere performance on Synclavier of the works of Francesco Zappa, eighteenth-century Italian composer and possible ancestor. *Thing-Fish* premiered.
1985	Barfko-Swill releases a seven-album boxed set containing remixed versions of the first five Verve albums plus other previously unreleased material from the 1960s; Zappa horrifies his old fans by rerecording rhythm tracks and otherwise changing the original tapes. Zappa testifies before the Senate Commerce, Technology, and Transportation Committee, denouncing proposed censorship of records. He later sends out press packs and does many media interviews based on his testimony.
1986	Initial contract with Rykodisc, which remains the principal source of his recorded music. Synclavier album, *Jazz from Hell,* released.
1987	Founds video company, Honker.
1988	His last world tour ends prematurely because of disagreements among the performers. *Jazz from Hell* wins Zappa his first and only Grammy award. Rykodisc begins the retrospective *You Can't Do That On Stage Anymore* series.
1989	During trips to Moscow to arrange for licensing his records there, Zappa became interested in other kinds of licensing, establishing a company called Why Not? Zappa publishes his autobiography.
1990	Welcomed by the Czech president, Václav Havel, Zappa becomes an overseas emissary for trade, tourism, and cultural

matters for the reborn republic. He hosts a talk-show on the cable-only Financial News Network.

1991   On the Foo-Eee label, Zappa releases eight CDs collectively titled *Beat the Boots,* which clean up and remix bootleg releases that had circulated for years. Contemplates running for president. In June he joins Prague musicians to celebrate the departure of Soviet troops from Czechoslovakia. Contracted to compose music for the Ensemble Modern, a German classical group, for the following year's Frankfurt Festival. During a four-night New York City tribute in November, *Zappa's Universe,* his two eldest children announce that their father is battling prostate cancer.

1992   Illness forces him to leave peremptorily a Frankfurt (Germany) festival featuring his work, *The Yellow Shark,* and returns home.

1993   Records tribute album/video honoring Varèse (not yet released). On December 4, four months after the release of an essentially classical CD, Zappa dies.

Note: The most complete chronology of Zappa's concerts appears in *Frank Zappa—A Visual Documentary* (1993) by [Barry] Miles.

Permissions

Bill Milkowski, "Frank Zappa: Orchestral Maneuvers," reprinted from *Modern Recording Technology* (August 1994) by permission of the author.

Stephen Paul Miller, "Performing Quotations: Frank Zappa in *Freak Out*," reprinted by permission of the author. Copyright ©1997 by Stephen Paul Miller.

"Playboy Interview: Frank Zappa," *Playboy* magazine (April 1993). Copyright ©1993 by Playboy. All rights reserved. Used with permission.

Steve Rosen, "Frank Zappa: Guitarist," reprinted from *The Guitar Player Book* (Grove, 1983) by permission of the publisher. Copyright ©1978 by GPI Publications.

William Ruhlmann, "Frank Zappa: The Present Day Composer," reprinted, slightly revised, from *Goldmine* (December 9, 1994), by permission of the author.

Nicolas Slonimsky, "I Enter the Age of Absurdity," excerpted from *Perfect Pitch* (1988) by permission of Elektra Yourcke. Entry from *Baker's Biographical Dictionary of Musicians* (1984) by permission of Schirmer Books.

David Walley, "We're Only in It for the Money," excerpted from *No Commercial Potential* (1972) by permission of the author.

Elaine Warren, "Abnormal Life," reprinted from *TV Guide* (April 14–20, 1990) by permission of the publisher. Copyright ©1990 by News America Publications, Inc. (*TV Guide* Magazine).

Ben Watson, "In Respect of Rubbish," reprinted from *Society Pages* #11 (July 1982), by permission of the author, who supplied camera-ready artwork. "Frank Zappa on Disc," with Mike Fish, from *The Wire* #91 (September 1991), by permission of the authors. "Frank Zappa as Dadaist," reprinted from *Contemporary Music Review*, XV/1 (1996), pp. 104–32, by permission of the publisher. All copyright ©1997 by Ben Watson.

Every effort has been made to identify the sources of publication of these essays and make full acknowledgments of their use. If any error or omission has occurred, it will be rectified in future editions, provided the appropriate notification is submitted in writing to the publisher or editor (P.O. Box 444, Prince St. Sta., New York, NY USA 10012-0008).

Index

About the Editors

Richard Kostelanetz has written and edited many books about contemporary music, including *John Cage (ex)plain(ed)*, *Fillmore East*, *Recollections of Rock Theatre*, *The Portable Baker's Biographical Dictionary of Musicians*, *The B.B. King Companion*, and *Writings on Glass*.

John Rocco specializes in James Joyce and popular culture, and teaches in the City University system. He was assistant editor for *AnOther E. E. Cummings* and editor of *The Doors Companion*.